D1496383

Building Bridges

Building Bridges

The Negotiation of
Paradox in Psychoanalysis

❦

Stuart A. Pizer

THE ANALYTIC PRESS

1998   Hillsdale, NJ   London

Published by The Analytic Press, Inc.
101 West Street, Hillsdale, NJ 07642

Library of Congress Cataloging-in-Publication Data

Pizer, Stuart A.
  Building bridges: The negotiation of paradox in psychoanalysis /
Stuart A. Pizer.
        p.   cm.
  Includes bibliographic references and index.
  ISBN 0-88163-170-1
  1. Psychoanalysis. 2. Negotiation. 3 Paradox.   4. Object relations
      (Psychoanalysis)   I. Title
  RC506.P57   1998
  616.89'17—dc21

                                                              98-19362
                                                              CIP

Printed in the United State of America
10 9 8 7 6 5 4 3 2 1

--- & ---

Not only
For Barbara
but
With Barbara

Contents

*"For the most part, we are unaware that
our existence is being carried out in the midst
of a life process of active organizing
mechanisms at a spectrum of levels that
are constantly harmonizing disparities."*

— Louis Sander, 1983, p. 337

*"One feature of the mature ego is the better
capacity to tolerate and even, on occasion,
to appreciate unresolved paradox. This
implies a more successful mastery of primitive
anxieties, and an inner feeling of wholeness
which will not be so threatened by the sense
of division inherent in a paradox."*

— Ivri Kumin, 1978, p. 482

*"I learned to make my mind large, as
the universe is large, so that there is
room for paradoxes."*

— Maxine Hong Kingston, 1976, p. 29

Preface

When Freud (1915a) described transference love as both real and unreal, he was reporting the paradoxical quality of analytic reality without articulating or acknowledging a concept of paradox. Modell (1991) suggests that Freud was *avoiding* an explicitly paradoxical understanding of the analytic relationship and process because he was seeking to establish the scientific validity of psychoanalysis within a positivist cultural *Zeitgeist*. We already know that Freud was contending with his fear that the world would shun or dismiss his sexually based theory out of shock and moral repugnance. But what if his daring reports of unconscious mental phenomena and the healing practices that accessed and modified them were based in a theory, a technique, and a treatment relationship that also abounded in paradox? Certainly, then, the world could be expected to flee from his ideas in confusion and perplexity. Even now, in the postmodern age of relativism, constructivism, and commonplace uncertainty, psychoanalytic ideas tend to be framed in terms of dichotomies, polarities, and complementary entities: active–passive, masculine–feminine, rational–emotional, "good" object–"bad" object, reality–fantasy, drive–relational, and so on. Psychoanalytic discourse has its language-framing conventions, and the origin of analytic thinking in *conflict* theory continues to shape our thought. Traditions aside, however, we must recognize another basic factor: it is bedevilingly difficult for the mind to handle paradox.

In the chapters that follow, I explore how we negotiate paradox: in psychoanalysis, in development and in living. Originally having conceived this book as a study of *negotiation* at the heart of therapeutic action in the analytic relationship, I came to recognize increasingly that my project entailed a study of *paradox*, of the reciprocally contradictory multiplicity that we are all challenged to bridge in managing our subjective and relational lives. Paradox requires—indeed, coerces—negotiation. Negotiation straddles paradox. Negotiation also addresses and mediates conflict. But conflict may (or may not) be resolved—through choice, action, power, or compromise. Paradox must be tolerated, through bridging and bearing the irresolvable (Winnicott, 1971c).

In 1984, when I began to consider the central place of a negotiation process in the therapeutic action of psychoanalysis, I could find no literature on the subject of negotiation in psychoanalysis. (With paradox not yet on my screen, I had not yet extended my search to Kumin, 1978, or Sander, 1983.) In the decade or so since, several psychoanalytic writers have converged on the phenomenon of negotiation, from a range of perspectives that frame the issue with their various conceptual and terminological emphases. Goldberg (1987) was the first author to address directly the negotiation of the analytic frame and relationship and to place the word negotiation in the title of a psychoanalytic article. Stern (1985) and Beebe and Lachmann (1992) brought from empirical infant studies a perspective on intersubjective attunement, misattunement, and repair in the mother–infant dyad and described these meaningful affective negotiations as a basis for the development of competent self- and mutual regulations. Harris (1992) applied developmental psycholinguistics to examine the potential space negotiated between child and caregiver in the establishment of verbal dialogue. Benjamin (1995), outlining the development of intersubjectivity, has built on contributions by Winnicott, Stern, and Hegel to describe the developmental attainment of mutual recognition as a quality of relating. Mitchell (1993) explicitly recognized the therapeutic value of interpersonal negotiations between analyst and patient as the patient's wishes and needs shape transference–countertransference dilemmas and the analyst's responses negotiate a viable and transformational entry into the patient's inner world.

Hoffman (1991, 1994) has advanced a social-constructivist view of the dialectic between the analyst's positional authority and the analyst's yielding to each patient's personal authority and needs

for spontaneous adjustments that, together, coconstruct transference–countertransference repetitions and changes. Bollas (1989)
has considered the therapeutic efficacy of a "dialectics of difference." Aron (1996) articulated a "relational-perspectivist" view—
gathering many contributions, including mine (Pizer, 1992)—as
he examined comprehensively the issues of mutuality and sym-
metry–asymmetry, and reciprocal intersubjective influences, in
the analytic "meeting of minds." Slavin and Kriegman (1992) have
addressed intergenerational conflict from an evolutionary-biological perspective and argued how each person negotiates a self, in
development and in treatment, through psychic adaptations that
mediate self-interests and mutual interests. Bromberg (1991, 1993,
1994, 1995, 1996) has developed the view of a self constituted by
multiple subselves that are structured by dissociations. In the clinical process, as conceived by Bromberg, the analyst negotiates
ways of being with, and being "used" by, each patient's multiple
subselves and empathically respecting the patient's resistance as
part of a dialectical process that manages the paradox of remaining the same while changing. As the reader will see, my own
understanding of negotiation has gained texture and clarity as I
have absorbed each of these contributions over time in parallel
with my own unfolding perspective.

While my appreciation for the elemental role of paradox has
formative Winnicottian roots, I have valued Modell's (1989, 1991)
and Loewald's (1974) recognition of the multiple and paradoxical
levels of experience intrinsic to the transference relationship. And
I find notable resonances in these Winnicott-inspired statements
by Sander and Kumin. Sander (1983) writes:

> The analyst is left with a fundamental paradox, that posed by the
> child's "sophisticated game of hide-and-seek in which *it is joy to be
> hidden but disaster not to be found*" (Winnicott, 1965, p. 186)....
> There is an unavoidable uncertainty that the analyst is left with and
> must endure, recognizing and permitting the patient's private and
> unfound center while facilitating the integrative process necessary
> for his initiation of new adaptive organization that springs from it and
> cannot be carried out without it. The recognizing and enduring of
> this confrontation with uncertainty, paradoxically, is the fruition of
> the analyst's knowledge and certainty, a facilitation of the matura-
> tional process within which the analyst's own development is ongo-
> ing [p. 345].

And Kumin (1978) writes:

In practice, ordinary healthy people even have the capacity to play
with paradox, or at least to transform anxiety over paradoxical opposition into a productive cultural contribution. We see signs of this in
certain forms of humor, art, literature and music. For instance, an
undefended paradox is at the core of each metaphor. I am not referring here to the artificial creation of the synthesis between two opposites, which is in fact nothing more than a compromise, and as such,
a defence formation. Synthesis, while acknowledging paradox, ultimately attempts to dispel paradox. . . . For the reasonably healthy
adult, however, there are anxious moments when, paradoxically,
knowledge seems far less certain yet reality seems more palpable. Yet
ultimately the experience of paradox can be ego enriching and consoling [pp. 482-483].

One person who uniquely grasped the enriching and consoling
potentials in paradox, as well as the central place of negotiation in
the rendering of relational and affective competence, was Paul
Russell. In 1988, when I shared with my analytic candidate group
my interest in writing about negotiation and paradox at the heart
of therapeutic action, fellow candidate Jane Grignetti said, "You
have to talk to Paul Russell!" How right Jane was.

I made an appointment with Dr. Russell, and he listened to my
presentation of nascent ideas about the role of paradox and negotiation in the treatment process. Large, quiet, receptive presence
that he was, Dr. Russell sat and smiled. When I finished, he said,
"This is cutting edge stuff," and he offered to supervise me on an
analytic control case. He also offered me his entire manuscript of
unpublished papers, assembled as a book-in-progress that awaited
preparation for publication, some day. Back at home, when I
looked through Russell's manuscript, I was astounded to discover
that he already had written (copiously and brilliantly) in papers
with such titles as "The Negotiation of Affect" and "The Role of
Paradox in the Repetition Compulsion" about the very issues I had
just presented to him. Although his modern Freudian perspective
approached the issues with a cluster of informing constructs different from my own more Winnicottian framework, we had converged on startlingly, and notably Loewaldian, common ground. I
pictured Paul Russell as he had sat with open hospitality to my
venturing of ideas and had given me no sign that might post a "Do
Not Trespass" notice on his very own territory. Thus began a

supervision that was also a mentorship and that became a loving friendship. Paul died on Valentine's Day, 1996. I have not, in my lifetime, encountered another man with such a giant mind and such a modest competitive ego.

The reader will find Paul Russell's ideas reflected throughout this book and, I hope, eventually will find Dr. Russell's writings directly in published form. In the course of writing this book, I shared the first four chapters with Paul, and he offered valuable and encouraging comments. Chapter 4 is the last that Paul read, in January of 1996, as his health declined. In Chapter 5, written soon after his death, I engage in a particularly extensive interplay with Paul Russell's ideas.

The outline of this book is as follows. In Chapter 1, building on a Winnicottian perspective, I introduce the concepts of paradox and negotiation and define therapeutic action and analytic neutrality in terms of optimizing the potential in potential space for ongoing negotiation. I illustrate these concepts with the case of "Donald." In Chapter 2, I continue the detailed presentation of Donald's treatment as a way of discussing specific modes of a relational technique that may serve the analyst in negotiating a therapeutic potential space. I emphasize play, metaphor, and use of the subjunctive mood. The reader will note that, although Donald's analysis reached termination years ago, I narrate the clinical moments in Chapters 1 and 2 from the time perspective in which I actually wrote these chapters during the treatment process, retaining the present tense.

Chapter 3 considers the contradictory and paradoxical nature of our "distributed" selves and, by use of three of my dreams, suggests how a therapeutic dialogue may negotiate creative ways of bridging the multiplicity of self. Chapter 4, the most densely theoretical, examines the person's ability to tolerate and straddle paradox within the self and in relationships. This chapter seeks to address a set of questions: How may the tolerance of paradox be a developmental achievement? Is the negotiation of paradox different from the negotiation of conflict? How does paradox challenge the mind? And what is the impact of trauma on the ability to tolerate and bridge paradox? I take up the problem of dissociation in the structuring of mind and explore the role of the caregiver, and the relative severity of paradox, in determining the difference between a "distributed" and a "dissociated" multiplicity. I also suggest how the analyst, in the clinical process, may foster a patient's developing competence at negotiating paradox.

Chapter 5 returns to a clinical focus, asking what it is like for the analyst to face "the nonnegotiable" in a patient and what it is like for the patient to face "the nonnegotiable" in an analyst. I also consider what may need to remain nonnegotiable in analysis, and I offer a model for understanding the delicate transition from hopelessness, through despair, toward hope in relationship as analyst and patient negotiate and renegotiate the paradoxes of transference-countertransference repetitions.

In Part II, Chapters 6 through 8 widen the lens on paradox and negotiation. Chapter 6 considers binary, categorical thinking about the individual or society as a resistance to, or collapse of, paradoxical thought and examines the particular case of dichotomized, or "tribalized," concepts of gender in the psychoanalytic literature. Contemporary, postmodern, and feminist critiques of psychoanalytic gender theory are understood as building new paradigms based on an appreciation of multiplicity, complexity, contradiction, and paradox, all of which require an openness to, and a facility for, negotiation. Chapter 7 looks at the evolutionary-biological view of psychoanalysis (Slavin and Kriegman, 1992) refracted through a lens that highlights the presence of paradox. In Chapter 8, a study of negotiation theory from disciplines outside of psychoanalysis—including law, diplomacy, and dispute resolution—is brought into the consulting room to query how the ideas and techniques from these fields of negotiation may help us understand when and how psychoanalytic technique may be consistent with the principles of good negotiation technique.

Finally, in an Epilogue, I return to the case of Donald, the therapeutic relationship with which this book begins, and illustrate the unfolding clinical process through which he and I negotiated the paradoxes of an analytic treatment toward completion and termination.

Acknowledgments

Looking back over the process, I am amazed at how much the writing of a book has been a negotiation between solitary creation and dialogical coconstruction. Personal imagination, authority, and authorship have combined essentially with interpersonal consumership, interdependence, and indebtedness. Because the early chapters of this book are based on presentations or previously published journal articles, I have benefited from the responses of discussants and audiences, friends, and colleagues in the unfolding conversations of our literature. This interactive exchange, over time, has provided me with corrections of my course, confirmations of my bearings, and discoveries of new channels to explore in this vehicle. Tossed between pride and humility, I have felt the excitement of introducing fresh ideas only to discover how similar ideas had already been introduced, or were being developed concurrently elsewhere. I have felt piqued when it seemed as if my ideas had been coopted by others without sufficient acknowledgment, only to discover—at times with shock—how much the textures of my own thinking have been unwittingly influenced by others.

Negotiation, including the negotiation of psychoanalytic concepts, as a living process, remains ongoing and ever incomplete. Challenged, on occasion, by the queries of colleagues responding to my ideas, I find myself in the paradoxical position of affirming the distinctions held and accentuated by my perspective while also somehow disagreeing with myself. Negotiating between confidence and doubt, I believe that these essays represent thought in progress and that, at some arbitrary point, a book must be released so that it can be used and interpreted by others.

Among the many people to whom I am deeply grateful, I give a special thanks to two: my grandfather, Nathan Spritz, provided my first instruction in negotiating from a personal perspective when he said, "If you don't like it, spit it out. If you like it, swallow it." And Ralph Engle offered me vital encouragement, saying, "The wheel needs to be reinvented again and again."

James Barron introduced me to Paul Stepansky and The Analytic Press and, in his generous and generative way, supported me to launch this writing project. At The Analytic Press, I have found a family of receptive, flexible, and resourceful folks who maintain a spirit that combines a welcoming warmth, a sensible clear-sightedness, and a needed patience. Paul Stepansky's mix of openness and firm judgment set the tone. Eleanor Starke Kobrin (Lenni) has a gift for filtering the mud from prose so that it becomes increasingly clear and flowing. Joan Riegel provides a responsive and collaborative stewardship. I consider myself fortunate to be an Analytic Press author.

Stephen A. Mitchell has been a great editor. He remains utterly true to the title of his own most recent book, *Influence and Autonomy in Psychoanalysis*. Chapter by chapter, over the years in which this book grew, Steve offered advice that almost always improved my manuscript while at the same time nudging and supporting me to own it more fully myself. Steve's ideas reflected his grasp of my ideas and, in a Loewaldian sense, his recognition of where my ideas were potentially heading. His suggestions and negotiations, in the best analytic spirit, combined clarification with nonintrusiveness. I thank Steve for sharing with me his rich knowledge, his reliable judgment, and his enthusiasm.

Lewis Aron, a friend and colleague before he became coeditor of the Relational Perspectives Books series, has read each of my chapters and offered the astute, prompt, critically incisive, and invaluable reactions of his own lively mind. Philip Bromberg, also as an act of friendship, has read most of this manuscript as chapters were written and has given me generously the benefits of his characteristically sensitive reading as well as his clinical wisdom, wit, and particular turn of mind. Lynne Layton not only read and critiqued my chapter on gender but also graciously shared with me portions of the manuscript of her own book.

Others have contributed significantly to this book by reading and commenting on various chapters and helping, over time, to add focus, detail, accuracy, and nuance to what I had written. I particularly thank Jessica Benjamin, Steven Cooper, Jeanne Flanagan, Jay Greenberg, Jane Grignetti, Andrea Massar, Arnold Modell, Thomas Ogden, Owen Renik, Susan Rosbrow-Reich, Malcolm Slavin, and Robert Weiss.

David Woodberry steadfastly and reassuringly helped to word process vast handwritten portions of my manuscript and, in so doing, joined me in discussions that sharpened my writing. At one point in our conversations, David declared, "If there's no such thing as paradox, I'd like to see it."

I owe Paul Russell a special debt of gratitude, as do so many of us in the analytic community around Boston. I have described in the preface the particular influences and inspirations that were Paul's gift to me.

Several patients have kindly and bravely consented to my writing about our work in this book. I am grateful to each of them for what they have taught me and what our shared experience has given me, and for their generosity in allowing something of themselves to be used by me in writing. To "Donald" I remain forever indebted for his willingness to permit so much of our therapeutic negotiations to become known to others, and I honor his explicit wish for others to benefit from his experience in analysis.

Finally, I thank Barbara, my wife and partner in work and play. Barbara's unique heart, mind, and soul housed me and my struggles throughout the writing of this book. Whether at home or at the beloved Landauer cottage on Nantucket, where we would turn a vacation into a writer's retreat, Barbara tolerated, contained, and transformed the intensities of a writer's moods. She managed the burdens of my absences as well as the sometimes greater burdens of my importuning presence. She served as intuitive Muse, tough-minded critic, and, at times, lovingly nonpossessive source of thoughts. I am blessed by Barbara's creative partnership in conception.

Part I

Paradox and Negotiation in Development and Analysis

1

The Negotiation of Paradox in the Analytic Process

A patient reports the following incident in the course of a "good-enough" analysis with a good analyst. He was lying on the couch, in the midst of whatever associations, when he was distracted by a smell as if someone were spraying trees in the neighborhood. He registered this impingement by saying, "I smell insecticide spray." From behind the couch, the analyst's voice replied, "It is neither insecticide nor spray. It is something burning." The patient shrugged internally and went on with whatever his associations had been. At the end of the session, when the patient walked out to the street, he saw a tank truck from a nursery service, such as might spray insecticide, parked in front of his analyst's house. He muttered, "Sonofabitch," not being certain at that moment whether he was referring to his analyst or himself. The patient began the following day's session with reference to this experience. A psychotherapist himself, the patient raised the issue of the analytic frame defined in terms of psychic reality and external reality as interpreted by analytic authority. He questioned his analyst's attitude of

1

certainty and his own attitude, as patient, of uncertainty. The patient further noted that whatever he had been implicitly communicating by saying, "I smell insecticide spray," whatever he had been seeking to bring into play—particularly with an analyst whom he knew to be an avid gardener—had been derailed by the analyst's peremptory response. At this point, the analyst affirmed, "This is the danger of too much certainty in the countertransference. I recognize that my remark served to close exploration rather than open it."

For me, this analytic moment illustrates the feeling of being up against a nonnegotiable stance on the part of one's analyst. Notably, the patient's protest had served to initiate a return to negotiation between them, as the analyst was able to recognize and acknowledge how he had ruptured analytic potential space. This chapter is about the process of negotiation as an intrinsic vehicle of the therapeutic action of psychoanalysis. I examine the nature of analytic negotiation and its relationship to paradox, with particular focus on the implicit place of this concept in the writings of Winnicott. I conclude with clinical material that illustrates the negotiation of paradox in the course of a treatment.

Negotiation is intrapsychic, interpersonal, and intersubjective, and it is vital to our biological existence.[1] Negotiation is intrapsychic in the sense that we must each mediate within ourselves the containment and expression of drive and affect, or inner contradiction and multiplicity, as well as the tension in living between engagement in the fresh potentials of the present moment and enmeshment in the conservative grip of repetition of our past experience; thus, negotiation is an ego function necessary for the internal management of paradoxical experience. Negotiation is interpersonal in the sense that we are always arranging with one another matters of desire, safety, anxiety, power, convenience, fairness, and so on. Negotiation is intersubjective in the sense that we constantly influence one another, consciously and unconsciously, from infancy onward in a myriad of ways, from minute

---

[1] Other writers (e.g., Racker, 1968; Sandler, 1976; Goldberg, 1987; Adler, 1989; Bollas, 1989; Mitchell, 1993; Modell, 1990; Russell, unpublished; Slavin and Kriegman, 1990, 1992; Bromberg, 1995) have converged on the issue of negotiation in the analytic process, either as an implicit factor in their thinking or an explicit term in their discourse.

adjustments to gross adaptations. So it is that we experience the fine choreography of infant and mother attaining, rupturing, and repairing states of attunement and affective communion (Stern, 1985; Beebe and Lachmann, 1992) or, in adulthood, the intersubjective exchange of the forces of projective identification by which we shape, and, in turn, are shaped by, our partners. In these ways, collusive relationships are forged around the negotiation of mutually invested defenses and repetitions, and therapeutic or mutually enhancing relationships are created and evolved through an ongoing negotiation that allows for self-expression, spontaneity, and self-realization in a context of safety, respect, and reciprocity.

I believe that, in the psychoanalytic process, the transference–countertransference tapestry is woven between analysand and analyst through a process of intersubjective negotiation. Much of what is essentially mutative in the analytic relationship is rendered through mutual adjustments that occur largely out of awareness in both parties. Only some of this process need ever become conscious to patient or analyst or be explicated through interpretation. The moments of explicit or implicit negotiation between analyst and patient may mark a discernible unit within the analytic process, as distinct from the analytic modes of historical narrative, reconstruction, interpretation, and reflection (although, as we shall see, even interpretation is a matter always subject to negotiation between both parties to the process).

The analyst, as he or she receives a patient's transference communications, is continually monitoring within himself or herself such questions as, What are you making of me? Can I accept this or that construction of me based on my own subjective sense of myself, my integrity, my commitment to the analytic framework as I see it, and my sense of our analytic mission? As a result, the analyst, whether making genetic or here-and-now interpretations (which, in themselves, have importance), is recurrently saying to the patient, "No, you can't make this of me. But you can make that of me." In turn, the patient receives the analyst's response with relief, gratitude, frustration, hurt, and the like and proceeds to generate further associations that seek to negotiate among past impressions, current experience, and future potential in this field of interplay between two subjectivities. Indeed, it may be the patient who, in response to an analyst's genetic or transference interpretation, declares, "No, you can't make this of me. But you can make that of me." In short, the very substance and nature of truth and reality—as embodied both in transference–countertransference constructions and in narrative reconstructions—are being negotiated toward consensus in the analytic dyad. The important therapeutic yield of these ongoing and recurrent negotiations goes beyond such products of negotiation as an accepted insight, a retrieved recollection, or a self-analytic reflection on the mind's defensive patterns. Essential as these analytic products surely are, I believe they are secondary to the therapeutic *action* of psychoanalysis, which is the engagement of two persons in a process of negotiation that, to borrow a phrase from Loewald (1960), is "an intervention designed to set ego development in motion."

I further believe that people looking back on their successful analyses commonly recall as particularly significant those moments in which their analyst seemed to step outside his or her accustomed position in a way that registered arrival at a deep recognition of the patient's essential being, an epiphanic state of rapport (perhaps marked by humor or sadness), or an affirmation of the personal caring that had spanned the vicissitudes of their relationship. While such moments may come as a surprise to the patient, they do not have the quality of coming from out of the blue or from out of some "left field" in the analyst's psyche, nor are they some whimsical bestowal or slip in analytic attitude. Rather, they have the quality of the analyst's yielding to some subtlety of being in the patient, some subtlety of their relatedness over time, which allows for a freshly discovered play in the analytic framework. These enactments by the analyst have been prepared for over time in the analytic partnership that has made them feasible, viable, and usable. Mitchell (1993) has made note of such analytic moments and attributed them to a negotiation between patient and analyst over the requisite countertransference response to the patient's relational needs, as differentiated from an enacted countertransference gratification of the patient's desires. As Mitchell observes,

> What may be most crucial is *neither* gratification nor frustration, but the process of negotiation itself, in which the analyst finds his own particular way to confirm and participate in the patient's subjective experience yet slowly, over time, establishes his own presence and perspective in a way that the patient can find enriching rather than demolishing [p. 196].

I would add that, while the process of negotiation does unfold "slowly, over time" and while moments of sublime, spontaneous rapport may be rare (and perhaps need not be frequent), the give-and-take of subjectivity, desire, stricture, and demand between patient and analyst is continual, recurrent, and always somehow new and incomplete. Out of this two-person process of negotiation, one may find emerging a patient's growing capacity to encompass wider experiential possibilities within his or her range of negotiable options in living, a growing trust and hope for participation in an increasingly negotiable interpersonal world, and a growing synthetic facility for bridging the inescapable paradoxes of human separateness and connection—in short, ego development set in motion by the analytic process.

Winnicott, that artful dodger of a psychoanalytic author, comfortably nestled in a British literary tradition that conveyed sense through nonsense, was profoundly sensitive to the elemental paradoxes that shape our being and our development (Phillips, 1988). Paradox requires negotiation, and Winnicott's theory is built on paradox.

Perhaps the most widely recognized statement of paradox in Winnicott's writings is in his paper on "Transitional Objects and Transitional Phenomena." As Winnicott (1951) wrote:

> We cannot ignore . . . an intermediate area of *experiencing*, to which inner reality and external life both contribute. It is an area that is not challenged, because no claim is made on its behalf except that it shall exist as a resting-place for the individual engaged in the perpetual human task of keeping inner and outer reality separate yet interrelated [p. 2].

Thus, out of need, the infant creates the mother's breast, which is there to be found. Later, the child makes of the first not-me possession, such as his Teddy or Blankie, a personal object imbued with life from the subjective world along with sentient qualities from the objective world. According to Winnicott, "The transitional object and the transitional phenomena start each human being off with what will always be important for them, i.e. a neutral area of experience which will not be challenged" (p. 12). Within the paradox of transitional space lies the potential for creative play. Within the preservation of paradox lies the necessity for an ongoing process of negotiation.

Probably the most profound spiritual paradox elucidated by Winnicott is the essential human need to communicate juxtaposed with the essential human need to remain incommunicado. On one hand, we need to experience our connection with objects in the external world in order to feel real. Winnicott recognized the terror to which we are subject if we feel threatened by submergence in the boundless ocean of our own subjectivity. Our psychic life requires both the limits encountered through our abutment with externality and the nourishment provided by other-than-me substance. Even to enjoy our solitude, we need to achieve the state of "ego-relatedness" that Winnicott (1958a) described as the product of the paradoxical experience in infancy of being alone in the presence of another. On the other hand, Winnicott grasped that, as the infant becomes increasingly competent, the mother who anticipates her baby's needs before her baby signals is no longer "good enough." What was once exquisitely empathic can become traumatically invasive, and the loss of inviolable privacy is an annihilation.

Winnicott (1958a) suggests that, when growth takes place under the best of circumstances, the child comes to possess "three lines of communication" (p. 188). The first is *"for ever silent"* and constitutes a nonnegotiable retreat to relaxation within the subjective world of the inviolable self. The second is *"explicit,* indirect and pleasurable" and consists of the capacity for language; and, as Stern (1985) has argued (following Vygotsky, 1962), the meaning of language is negotiated in each child–parent dyad. Thus, language equips the child, for life, with the competence to reveal while concealing, to portray an approximation of experience, to achieve consensual validation without utter exposure. Finally, Winnicott's third line of communication is that *"intermediate* form of communication that slides out of playing into cultural experience of every kind" (p. 188). This third area of communication, then, is the area of shared symbols, where the most intimate negotiations occur in the overlap between the subjective worlds of self and other, where two people may engage in the creative exchange of gestures, or squiggles,[2]

---

[2] "Squiggling" refers to the Squiggle Game used by Winnicott (1971b) in his therapeutic consultations with children. In the service of providing the child a sense of comfort and freedom, and the opportunity for a spontaneous or creative gesture that might crystallize the child's self-awareness, Winnicott employed this

and construct mutually useful metaphors. When Winnicott shifts the scene to the analytic process, he writes, "Here there is danger if the analyst interprets instead of waiting for the patient to creatively discover" (p. 189). Winnicott is referring to the crucial importance of the negotiation of meaning between analyst and patient, through linguistic approximations and with an attitude of joint creation and a sensitivity to mutual regulation.

As I see it, the process of psychoanalysis may be conceived as an exchange of "squiggles" between adults without pencil and paper. By such an exchange, mostly verbal, of marks and "remarks" offered in evocative and resonant sequence, analyst and patient become cocreators of a relational construction that represents and communicates a place of intersection of their separate experiences together over time. Neither the analyst's "squiggle"— be it interpretation, clarification, confrontation, empathic reflection, or self-disclosure—nor the patient's "squiggle"—be it historical narrative, transference impression, manifest dream, or other association—constitutes an X-ray rendering of "the self's core." Rather, analyst and patient, in their use of what Winnicott terms "explicit, indirect" communication—that is, language—become an intersubjective partnership for the collaborative creation of a shared culture of usable, and reusable, reverberative images. As analyst and patient come into play in the area of illusion, they create metaphorical renderings of the approximate meaning of their shared transference–countertransference experience (see Chapter 2 for further elaboration of the use of metaphor).

Human self-interest constitutes another basic paradox. We are not only consumers, but also providers. We realize our selves both through the care we receive and the care we give. This fundamental paradox of our nature is entailed in Winnicott's (1962a, 1963b) notion of the principal human drive: toward development. On one hand, it is easy for us to read Winnicott's theory of human development as a kind of infant advocacy theory. From this perspective, development seems to mean the development of a spontaneous self, the achievement of ego integration and psychosomatic unity, and

---

paper and pencil game. He would make a mark, a line or doodle, on the paper and ask the child to complete it. In turn, he would complete initial marks supplied by the child. Through this reciprocal exchange, representations of impulse, need, affect, or fantasy would take shape and come into focus.

the capacity to use environmental provision for internal robustness and a sense of subjective mastery over the external world. On the other hand, if we trace Winnicott's developmental schema from the phase of absolute dependence through relative dependence and toward independence, we may ask, What are the qualities of "independence"? In this manifestly baby-centered theory, which reminded the psychoanalytic field of the significance of the real facilitating environment in psychological development, we each grow to an adulthood in which we provide the facilitating environment for the next generation. Having once been babies, we now become mothers, fathers, or analysts. Our destiny, as we grow toward independence, is to develop the capacities whereby we may contribute back to the world, by our own adaptations, the holding environment for the nourishment of others. In a sense, reflecting the Kleinian roots in Winnicott's thinking, this generativity constitutes our reparation for our own earliest voracious feeding upon the world that held us in the bliss of our subjectivity. Although Winnicott describes the "primary maternal preoccupation" of the "good-enough" mother as a kind of temporary illness, this state is not based on maternal masochism or sentimentality. It is closer to primary creativity, the mother's illusion that she continues to create her baby while she is merged with it by "almost 100% adaptation" to its needs. The analyst, in moments of "primary analytic preoccupation," is fortunate to experience a similar joy at being found and used. But what of the human abhorrence of being found? If, as Winnicott has argued, to be found is to be violated, how do we willingly allow ourselves to be found by the infant or the analysand who needs to conjure us for personal usage?

How has the mother actually managed to survive as a separately existing center of need, affect, intensity, and will while adapting to her infant's moment-by-moment imperatives? The answer is implied in Winnicott's (1968) observation that, whereas the baby has not been a mother before—or even a baby—the mother has both been a baby and played at being a mother. Hence, the mother survives in her position as mother by having recourse to her survival as a baby, past, present, and future. Within herself, the mother must find ways of retaining access to her own ruthlessness through her dependence on the actual sustaining support of others; through memory, fantasy, and projection—including her fantasies of utterly creating her baby and utterly destroying her baby; and through her anticipation of her baby's development toward independence, as she has developed in her own course of time. The mother also knows, from her own experience as infant and child, that she is contributing both to her own survival and to her child's growth by imposing a disillusioning process as she introduces frustration where her needs and her baby's emerging tolerance intersect. Similarly, in analysis, the analyst has already been both a baby and a patient and has previously played at being an analyst. The analyst's survival of a patient's ruthlessness reflects the analyst's continued connection with his own inner ruthlessness.[3] The analyst, then, survives as an analyst by surviving as a patient, with his memories of patienthood; his projections of patienthood; his own fantasies of primary creativity and utter destructiveness toward his patient; and his anticipation of his patient's potential for development, including a firmer tolerance for the essential disillusioning process delivered through optimal frustrations (including interpretations). This very process within the analyst, surviving as a patient, constitutes the analyst's ongoing, self-analytic use of the countertransference and the opportunity to change and grow as a person while responsibly fulfilling his role to survive as analyst.

In the developmental process, as it approximately follows this course, the infant comes to recognize that its mother has endured its ruthless usage and has survived. The infant has been able to make of mother what it needed, and yet mother has been capable of remaining herself. This recognition allows for the emergence of love for the mother, a love that is not only libidinally based but also grounded in an identification with the mother of quiet moments of care and rapport. From this juncture in the child's development, the capacity for ruthlessness is joined by a capacity for concern for the object of ruthlessness that has survived destruction. Now the child is ready to become a full partner in the give-and-take of negotiation.

Ruthlessness, however, is never given up. Winnicott's theory is not one of conflict, renunciation, and compromise formation in

---

[3] Of course, this juncture is also where the analyst's or the mother's repetitions and actual destructiveness may predominate, introducing nonnegotiable elements that deform the relationship and its yield.

the classical sense. His theory is of paradox, the acceptance of paradox, and the negotiation of paradox. Herein lies another step toward answering our question of how the "good-enough" mother and the analyst have been equipped by their own development to remain unfound and unannihilated even as they are there to be found and used. Winnicott (1969) described what happens after the infant has destroyed the subjectively conceived object and faced its sturdiness—if, indeed, it has survived—and passed from relating to using:

> A new feature thus arrives in the theory of object-relating. The subject says to the object: "I destroyed you," and the object is there to receive the communication. From now on the subject says: "Hullo object!" "I destroyed you." "I love you." "You have value for me because of my destruction of you." "While I am loving you I am all the time destroying you in (unconscious) *fantasy*" [p. 90].

How profound are the implications of the last sentence! For, as Winnicott went on to say, "Here fantasy begins for the individual." I suggest that Winnicott here was deftly indicating the place of a dynamic unconscious in his theory. From this perspective, we may understand the unconscious to be the private repository of our most all-out, ruthless tendencies. It constitutes the taproot of our capacity to deconstruct the external world, to destroy the object as we find it, and to re-create it to suit our subjectivity. Clearly, we cannot afford to reveal to those near and dear to us that this full-tilt, ruthless potential underlies our every interaction. Hence, the core of the self remains hidden away, while we engage in interactions that accommodate the separate nature of the Other. As we have seen, these interactions are mediated by language, including metaphor, which is both explicit and indirect, and by play in the area of overlap between two subjectivities, wherein the ruthless potential in both parties may achieve a tolerable intersection. Thus, we negotiate with others, and the yield of this negotiation will not be based on compliance, reaction formation, or subjugation to the extent that we retain access to the ruthless base of our own subjective world while exercising our capacity for concern for the other. In this model, repression may be adaptive. It allows us to engage in negotiation while keeping alive within us what Winnicott called "a backcloth of unconscious destruction." A recognition of the adaptive function of repression, from the perspective of evolutionary biology, has been introduced into psychoanalytic thinking by the work of Slavin and Kriegman (1990; Slavin, 1990). In Winnicott's theory, repression is adaptive; it is dissociation that compromises psychological health by alienating our negotiations from their ruthless and creative taproots within the true self.

The passage from object relating to object "usage" is a crucial developmental attainment. From this juncture we may carry through life the capacity to poise at the threshold between ruthlessness and ruth, to straddle the paradox of our isolation and our connectedness, to retain our spontaneity while doing maternal or psychoanalytic work. In the psychoanalytic process, the analyst serves a dual holding function. On one hand, when indicated, the analyst adapts to the needs of the patient and thereby brings to the patient the experience and the hope of a negotiable world. On the other hand, the analyst tries his best to hold on, hold fast, and hold up, seeking to survive "the patient's destructive attacks," which Winnicott (1969) understood to be "the patient's attempt to place the analyst outside the area of omnipotent control, that is, out in the world" (p. 91). The analytic frame that the analyst maintains (for example, by interpreting rather than remaining enmeshed in projective identifications) represents the staunch durability of external reality; whereas the analyst's adaptations (for example, offering some personal information requested) present to the patient a world that is negotiable. And, in the intermediate area of intersection between the subjective worlds of analyst and patient, negotiation may be playful, creative, and mutually enlivening, and it may lead to ego development.

A word about analytic neutrality is relevant here. I have always liked Loewald's (1960) description of neutrality as "a love and respect for the individual and for individual development" (p. 229). I suggest, however, that neutrality may be defined as the analyst's responsibility to maintain the area of illusion for ongoing negotiation. The frame for the therapeutic action of analysis is provided by the continuing existence of paradox that requires negotiation between both parties. The negotiation of paradox is the transaction that articulates the potential in potential space at the intersection of transference and countertransference. From this perspective, analytic abstinence, interpretation, enactment, or disclosure may, at any given moment, preserve or violate potential space between analyst and patient. Silence, empathic observation, interpretation, metaphorical construction, evocative association, squiggling, laughter, and confrontation may all serve to maintain the area of illusion and are thus to be regarded as potential analytic responses within a stance of neutrality. Even some personal information about the analyst may, in some instances, open the field of association for the patient rather than truncate it.

The gauge of the analyst's neutrality is not whether he restricts his responses to interpretation, refrains from self-disclosure, or introduces his own personal imagery into the analytic discourse. The gauge of neutrality is whether a self-disclosure is the product of a jointly developed negotiation that exists between analyst and patient, that is evoked by the patient's need for something to go on, and that is used as a "personal object" for the patient's self-articulation; neutrality is violated to the extent that self-disclosure entails some personal information "bestowed" by the analyst out of his own urgency. Or the gauge of neutrality is whether the analyst's silence is a nonnegotiable stance imposing barrenness or lack of affect between analyst and patient; whether an enactment has violated or destroyed potential space by collapsing paradox with the intrusion of the analyst's all-too-concrete substance, which is neither created nor found, but inflicted; whether an interpretation, like a squiggle, manages to evoke, clarify, or connect while preserving paradox, and does not foreclose the patient's freedom of response and personal construction, within a range of what Modell (1990) calls the "multiple levels of reality" in the transference. The criterion for an analyst's neutrality thus becomes the maximizing of the creative potential in the negotiation of paradoxes preserved in the shared area of illusion, in the overlap of the play of two subjectivities. Greenberg (1986) was pointing in a similar direction when he stated the paradox that, unless the analyst is enough of a new object, the analysis does not begin; and, unless the analyst is enough of an old object, the analysis does not end.

A CASE REPORT

The following case report illustrates how both patient and therapist change as they find and use their points of intersection in the unfolding process of negotiation during the course of a treatment. Several years ago, a 26-year-old man—whom I will call Donald— came to me for therapy and said that he needed to learn how to conduct relationships and how to enrich his life. His manner was one of stolid and remote sobriety. He worked in a technical field and felt stunted in his career as well as in his personal life. He had virtually no friends outside of work acquaintances, except for a married couple whom he visited frequently. He stayed at their home to dog-sit, baby-sit, or tutor the wife in a technical subject. I sensed the vacancy of Donald's life when I called him at home and heard him say on his answering machine, "You have reached the home of 443-1413."

Donald presented me with a formative history of early loss, dis-ruption, parental unreliability, and relative poverty in inner-city Chicago. His father died before he was two. His mother, living next door to her own capricious mother, related to Donald on the basis of her own whims and needs in an invasive and controlling way. She did not permit him vigorous physical activity; bike riding was banned because of her inordinate worry about his congenital orthopedic problem. Donald retreated into science fiction. There was no family member with whom Donald could share his preco-cious intellectual interests. Donald did enjoy one stable and reli-able relationship with his maternal grandfather, a modest man who worked double shifts but, nevertheless, maintained a benign and consistent interest in Donald when he was at home. This grand-father's dying and death toward the end of Donald's college years delivered a serious blow. Donald had engaged in his first sexual relationship during the weeks his grandfather was dying. This rela-tionship ended abruptly with Donald's sense that the young woman had betrayed him and that he had betrayed his grandfather and his Catholic upbringing by dalliance with her. Since that time, he had not been open to another relationship.

We had our work cut out for us. Perhaps the first negotiation I faced with Donald was the question of whether or not we could undertake it together. I felt daunted by the challenge of working with him toward significant structural change, given the degree of his schizoid withdrawal. I noted how thoroughly he avoided eye contact and how, while speaking in his affectless manner, he held one arm extended over the back of the couch and drummed in an amazing, complex digital pattern. He seemed dissociated from me, from affect, and from his own fingers as they discharged energy in rapid precision tapping. I noticed another aspect of Donald that bore heavily on my choice of working with him: his body odor. I could not tolerate his smell, although, during our first weeks of meeting, I tried. The odor lingered in my office for a few more patient hours after he left. I questioned whether I could work with Donald under the distancing influence of my struggle to defend against his smell. So, with my heart in my mouth, I raised the issue with him. This issue forced on us a difficult and significant negotiation that would haunt the treatment to follow, as well as provide us with a central metaphor to which we could return in our explorations. When I asked Donald whether he used deodorant, he said he had never used one nor had he noticed his smell. No one had ever taught him about the use of deodorant. When he came to our next session, he had bathed carefully and had used a deodorant. He quite openly began by asking, "Is this OK?" Yes, the deodorant had worked. Donald adopted the use of deodorant, although sometimes he forgot, and in his rush to get to my office on a hot summer day, his smell would return. I reminded him a few times, and Donald began to keep a deodorant stick in his car for insurance and for extra use before his sessions.

With this response of Donald's, I chose to work with him. I felt moved by his earnestness and gentlemanly decency, I respected his intelligence and determination as valuable strengths, and I cared about the poignancy of his desire to surmount his meager early provisions.

The first several months of Donald's therapy focused on his family relationships: how, at an early age, he had walled himself in from his mother's intrusiveness and capriciousness while becoming the "fixer" in his chaotic household and how he still avoided going home for Christmas to face outrageous presents he had asked his mother not to buy with money she did not have (but would recurrently solicit from him) and her seven dogs roaming, unruly and ungroomed, throughout the house. I attempted linking interpretations aimed at connecting boundary issues with his mother and his current "triangle" with the married couple he frequently visited. We also talked about Donald's missing father and how hard it is to be a self-made man who lacks a paternal legacy.

For extended periods, the affective tone between us was largely formal, emotionless, arid. Donald avoided or broke eye contact.

He usually drummed on the couch in his mechanical finger patterns as he spoke. Sometimes, when my empathic response conveyed that I was moved by Donald's loneliness or low expectations, my affect-laden utterances had a visible effect on him. Donald withdrew. His eyes took on the glaze of dissociation. When I asked him what was happening, he would say, "I didn't hear your words" or "I went far away." I took this withdrawal to be a sign of Donald's intolerance for closeness or affective rapport. I thought about the hazards of a therapist's seeming to hover or crowd a schizoid patient. I adjusted myself accordingly, to give Donald room. I would not intrude more of my affect than he seemed to be able to assimilate. Rather than pursue him, I would wait nearby for signs that he was ready to approach me.

Concurrently, Donald asked me for more guidance. He requested that I recommend life activities, seminars, and so on that would augment his therapy. He asked for readings that would tell him what was wrong with him and how therapy would help. He wondered aloud if he should see another therapist, because we were not producing changes. He felt stuck.

I felt fluctuations of hope and pessimism and never settled into one or the other. Sometimes I would feel in conflict over my own optimism and accuse myself of projecting my own wishes for Donald—a false hope in the face of so much history of hurtful commission and omission. I refused to recommend readings. I feared that Donald would find in descriptions of the schizoid personality the pessimism of so many authors about treatment prospects. Since Donald often took things categorically, I worried that he would make extreme inferences from flat-out statements about prognosis. I also generally do not recommend readings in therapy. With Donald, I understood him to be asking for a kind of tutorial alternative to the treatment process. I was also resisting my own developing countertransference wish to take Donald in hand as a sponsor and guide, a fantasy reciprocal to his longing for a father. More personally implicated in my resistance was my memory of my own first analyst, who had offered me liberal advice on living, a kind of apprenticeship in the good life, in return for my admiration of his superiority. I knew, with benefit of hindsight, how superficially gratifying and relieving this analyst's guidance had been, and what a subversion and abandonment of true, structuralizing analytic work. Thus, I balked at the temptation to "educate" Donald in living and hoped for greater gain by preserving the intermediate area of therapeutic process.

Donald and I continued along in low gear until, unwittingly, we crossed a threshold in our relationship by a pivotal negotiation just prior to my second July vacation break. In the third week of June, Donald announced that he was uncertain whether he could make our final prevacation Friday appointment owing to a tentatively scheduled business trip. I asked him what flexibility he had in scheduling this trip. He explained that he was participating in a conference that involved several people and he did not see how he could initiate a request that might inconvenience several others. For my part, I was aware that our separations had their impact on Donald. He had told me after my first July vacation that he had felt abandoned and despairing. Knowing that the predictable structure of our relationship served an important framing function, I offered him the option of a back-up session on Saturday if he should, in fact, be out of town on Friday. I told Donald that, although Saturday was indeed July 1 and, in a formal sense, within the boundary of my vacation, I would still be in town and that I would rather see him on Saturday than leave us both uncertain whether or not we would have the opportunity to say good-bye.

In return, I asked if he might undertake to determine whether he had more say than he assumed over his part in the scheduling of the business conference. Donald came to his next session pleased and excited. He had spoken up at work and arranged to give his presentation on Wednesday and leave the conference on Thursday. We could keep our regular time on Friday. He was pleased to have taken this more active stance for himself and relieved not to impose on me and feel beholden to me for a July 1 meeting. Nevertheless, he reported having felt astonished that I had offered him the Saturday time during my vacation. He said he never before had experienced any arrangement in his world that accommodated to his needs or took his wants into account. I was saddened and moved by his feeling my gesture to be a kind of positive trauma, a jolting interruption of his assumptions about a nonnegotiable universe. My offer of the Saturday back-up appointment was not a self-conscious or calculated choice to bestow on Donald a "corrective emotional experience." Rather, it was a direct negotiation necessitated by our time constraints that happened to strike him with metaphorical significance.

While this moment between us felt potentially pivotal, it clearly did not pass a noticeable magic wand over our work. On my return from vacation, Donald continued to flounder in his efforts to find a way to feel that he was using our relationship. He expressed frustration over not knowing what to say, not knowing how therapy works. Once again, he asked me for readings. I asked him why he wanted to study the schematics before entering the process. Soon thereafter he became involved with a woman who seemed, from his descriptions, to have a very limited capacity for intimacy. Donald eventually broke up with her. He felt disappointed and, I think, somewhat embittered, as if to say, "So much for relationship."

Meanwhile, in my office, Donald and I oscillated between contactful and distanced moments. Donald continued to avert his gaze, and I reacted by reminding myself that I had to make an extra effort not to withdraw even while I so often felt deprived of engagement and affective rapport. At moments I resented his complex digital finger drumming. I felt like shouting, "Stop drumming and look at me when you speak!" I did not say this. I chose tact. At times I withdrew into my own reciprocal detachment. Donald initiated a new ritual. At the end of our meeting, as he walked to the door, he turned and looked back at me, and, as we held a moment's eye contact, he nodded. I found myself nodding reciprocally. Once begun, this ritual became our invariant pattern of leave-taking at the end of each session. I would wait for Donald to reach the doorway, he would turn, our eyes would meet and hold contact, and, usually with a smile and a nod, he would be out the door.

While this pattern of last-minute engagement took hold between us, Donald continued in our sessions to talk about his current life and his family history, with few moments of sustained contact between us. At one point, he informed me that he had discovered, on his own, Miller's (1981) *Prisoners of Childhood* and had found her book to be a revelation: here was a therapist who appeared to be a "sympathetic character." He asked me again to recommend further readings. I declined. Soon after, he reported that, since I would not recommend readings to instruct him in the use of psychotherapy, he had gone to the public library and begun to make his way alphabetically through the shelves on psychotherapy and psychoanalysis. He had read Arlow and Brenner, and his despair only increased. His reading confirmed his worst fears; he was expected somehow, on his own, to find the right things to say that would unlock my insightfulness so that I would finally grant him my interpretations. Meanwhile, I was expected to remain uninvolved, leaving him to work out for himself how to say the magic words that would yield my explanations and solutions to his life.

Hearing him, I relented on the issue of readings. I offered him some articles by Kohut and Tolpin on the development of the self through a psychoanalytic "dialogue." I lent him my copies to photocopy. I recommended that, at the library, he skip ahead and read some Winnicott. Donald[4] reported to me that his reading of Tolpin, Kohut, and Winnicott began to restore the hope he had first found in reading Miller. I am sure that my recommending and lending these readings contributed to that new hope. In his reading of these authors, Donald found people who seemed to understand him and his needs. Perhaps there were such people in this world. Perhaps he could find some similar experience with me. He began to see the potential for resuming the development of the self in a therapeutic interaction, even in the wake of massive, early childhood environmental failure. Months later, he explained to me that he had created out of Kohut, Miller, and Winnicott a transitional object that represented a benevolent and caring therapist. In his frustration over the limits of our closeness, he took steps toward me through this bridging metaphor of a therapeutic relationship. But would we truly follow this direction? From Donald's perspective, it was hard to see evidence that we had yet.

I returned from my next July vacation to face a new threshold in our therapy. Donald was angry and challenging (although he denied anger and said he was "upset"). He required to know whether I cared about him. Was my interest real? Was I merely practicing my technique with him? Is his participation real, or was

---

[4] As I write this narrative, a realization flashes on me. Why had I, over the past two days of sifting through my notes and synthesizing this clinical material, chosen for my patient the pseudonym of Donald? When I had thought of it, it had felt just right. But my only referents were Donald Trump, Donald Duck, and my next-door neighbor. Did I really want to use a name with those associations? Why does this name feel right? Now, in the text before my eyes, I see "Winnicott, Donald." The connection emerges out of repression. In writing this paper, I had created my own internal transitional object and metaphor. Neither Winnicott nor my patient nor myself alone, this narrative is my own negotiated amalgam.

he only mastering techniques of being with people? Was our relationship real?

In the first of these postvacation sessions in which Donald issued his ultimatum to our therapy, he embodied his challenge in what I felt was a particular way of conveying the paradoxes of our experience together. He delivered a metaphor between us. That is, while I sat and faced his anger and his disappointment and clearly heard his direct statement of his need to know from me that I cared, I felt myself unable to summon a caring feeling from within. Instead, I was recoiling. On this hot August day, he smelled again, and I felt put off. What could I offer at this moment? An insincere bromide? A refusal of his direct request for a sign of closeness? I chose to address explicitly the paradox before us and to ask if we could consider together its import. I told him that on a day in which he urgently asks for my caring response, he comes to me with his body odor unmodified. Yes, he says. He has just recently stopped using deodorant. I ask whether he connects the two. No, he does not. I venture for him to consider whether conflict and anger are expressed in his asking for closeness just when he discontinues his use of deodorant. Are you enacting your dread of the very closeness you so urgently request? Are you angrily saying, Show me a sign that you will struggle some on my behalf; care for me without my making it easy? None of these conjectures rang a bell for Donald, but he did immediately resume his use of deodorant.

In the months that ensued, our sessions were devoted repeatedly to shared reflections on our past years together. Donald often would begin a session with yet another question or protest about how our work had developed. At one point he told me he had never believed I understood what his life was like. He experienced too much disparity between us. He did not feel like a match for me. After all, he had no background of his own to bring to his part in a relationship. He had nothing to go on. He felt shame and did not expect that we could meet on common ground. He assumed it was up to him to do something different to make it better, but all he knew to do was to tell me more life history. He also had to worry about distancing me with his smell and probably in other ways as well. I reminded Donald that, in our early days, when I responded to his life story with affective warmth, he had signaled me that he went far away within himself where he could not hear me. He replied that, since he had felt that he could not match me, he had not known how to respond. He added, "I didn't mean stay away, but, help me." I replied, "Then my tact was not what you most needed." He returned, "And yet, there's a point there. I had nothing. And I couldn't take things in either. And there was nothing you could do."

Donald soon reported to me that he now began to hear me say some of the supportive and affirmative things about him and his work with me that he had missed all along. He also informed me that he could begin now to use my interpretations because he was becoming able to hear them as something other than a criticism. Soon thereafter, Donald said that he did not much need our ritual good-bye at the door anymore. He voiced his recognition of our unspoken ritual and said that he now saw it as a way to deal with his question of whether I held him in mind between sessions. He had been testing whether my connection with him lasted even up to the threshold of my office door or whether he would find a sign that I had already turned away from him. He also said that he would not like it if I ever tolerated his smell and hid from him that I did not feel good about being with him.

I came to recognize an unconscious, unacknowledged negotiation that had been transpiring between us over time, an essential paradox, perpetually unresolvable, which had contributed to the shaping of potential space between us. Donald was profoundly in need of a father. He needed to grieve the loss of his father and the loss of what Bollas (1989) would call a potential "future" that his father's living presence might have enabled him to elaborate for himself. I could not be his father, both because this role would be untrue and because Donald's grief had to be allowed without denial. Yet, in a way that was also utterly true, we both had to wait until Donald became, over time, like a son to whom, in my own countertransference, I could feel like a father. I could not recognize this paradox before I had overcome my own resistance to giving Donald the readings he requested. Several times Donald has said to me, "I will never receive the guidance I always wanted" or "I can't have the parenting I missed." Or, more within the idiom of transference, he would say, "I wish you could have told me what to say first. Couldn't you have spelled out what this process would be? I wish you had guided me and told me what to do." At one point, Donald said, "I know I need a father. And I look to you to replace him. And you can't." I responded with, "No. I can't. We both know I can't. And yet, we both know you have to find something here to go on."

With this paradox actively on my mind, I thought of my work with Donald as potentially a good treatment to use for clinical illustration in this chapter. I asked his permission, which he readily gave. He was pleased to think that his therapy might benefit others.

Soon afterward, Donald reported a dream (there had been just a few reported dreams thus far in his therapy). In his dream, he was with me in my office. We had a detailed conversation, which he does not remember. The central element of this dream is the feeling that we were connected and informal with each other—just the feeling he had wanted with me all along. He woke up feeling very good.

One therapeutic agenda that Donald now announced was his need to address his growing sense of anger toward his mother. He said he would have to bring either his anger or his mother into my office. He was mortified at the thought of being anything like her. He then recalled how he had been kept in his crib until he was five or six and how he would jump in the crib to break through the bottom. He recalled throwing his orthopedic device down the stairs, to be rid of it (his stepfather had whipped him and put him back in his crib). He remembered hitting his mother once and upsetting her more than once during his adolescence by telling her sadistically that she had never been a good mother. When I noted to him that he could reach her only in this sadomasochistic way, he said, "That's why I knew I had to move out as soon as I could. I was afraid of that. I was bigger than she." I suggested that he understandably needed to be able to protest in some form.

Interspersed with this material was Donald's redoubled protest toward me. Why had I so rigidly refused at first to recommend readings? Why had I not spoken more words of affirmation and encouragement? If I had doubted the prospects of a successful treatment, why did I not have the integrity to refer him on to someone else? Further, Donald protested, "Why didn't you understand the time I stopped using deodorant again? You called it anger. It was despair. I had tried everything here I knew how to try. I was about to give up. So I gave up on myself." I acknowledged here the convincing sense of Donald's own interpretation. I also felt rebuked and put to the test. In the face of Donald's disappointment and anger, I was on tenterhooks and expected him to quit this therapy abruptly. I responded to what questions I could and wondered if we would survive. I am reminded here of what Winnicott (1956) wrote. While the therapist's adaptations to the patient allow the patient to relax the "caretaker self" and permit a regression to dependence, the therapist's failures of adaptation offer occasion for the patient's protest. As I see it, protest, like the "antisocial gesture," is a sign both of anger and of hope—the hope for a negotiable environment that will heed the protest as a signal of distress. Protest in the transference is the patient's act in the present to renegotiate relational failures of the past that occurred prior to the ability to protest. The current protest is, to paraphrase Russell, both now and then. Paradoxically, the safety of therapy permits the risk of protesting the failures of the therapist. Donald asked me why he had to suffer so long in this therapy the feelings of disconnection, disappointment, abandonment, and helplessness. Why could I not help him avoid all this suffering by a more structured and instructional agenda? My understanding of this quandary, as I conveyed to him, was that our crucial work was to find our way out of this feeling together, which required that first we find ourselves in the feeling.

Donald expressed an interest in the subject of this chapter. I told him that, of course, he would have the opportunity to read it. I added that it was about negotiation in analysis and the Winnicottian paradoxes of ruthlessness and concern, isolation and connectedness. Donald responded that he had trouble with Winnicott's concept of ruthlessness. He said that if this perspective were applied to himself, he was afraid of developing an attitude of "What's in it for me?" He feared an internal pendulum swing by which he would become lazy and self-interested and abandon the one set of values he had ever internalized and embraced: the religious catechism teaching him to be good, sacrifice for others, put himself last, and "serve." He panicked that he might forget who he was and lose hold of the meaning of life. I explored this anxiety, which he was able to associate not only with his Catholic education but also with his fear of dying young as his father had ("You might die any day and face Judgment") and his fear of destructive impulses toward his mother. I asked Donald if he worried that my perspective might be a corrupting influence on him. He said that he did not regard my ideas or me as unsound, just unsuited to him. For him, "selfishness" and "self-assertiveness" were indigestible notions. He just did not understand how a child could or should be encouraged to be ruthless.

In that session, perhaps moved, in part, by a concern that I had imposed on Donald some half-developed theoretical ideas that seemed to him all-too Mephistophelian, I told him an anecdote about my own childhood. At age five or six, in the late 1940s, I had one major toy, a red tricycle. These tricycles were still hard to come by in the gradual postwar conversion to consumer goods. One summer evening, while my parents, my red tricycle, and I were waiting for the elevator, an elderly lady joined us. As we entered the elevator, she admired my tricycle and said she had been unable to find one to buy for her grandchild. So I handed over mine, on the spot. The elevator stopped at the fourth floor, she got out with my red tricycle, the door shut, and my tricycle was gone. My parents had stood by, stunned, and permitted the incident to happen. I told Donald that now, as a parent, I would say to the elderly woman, "That's a child. Why are you taking the tricycle?" I would have a long talk with my child about what is too little and what is too much to give. And, if I were that elderly lady's therapist, I certainly would not counsel her to develop her ruthless side.

Donald thanked me for telling him this story; he said it helped. At the next session, he said he had been angry at the old woman for taking advantage of my childish generosity. He then told me a story of his own. He had a friend when he was seven or eight and liked to visit that boy's home and play with his friend's GI Joes. He gave his friend his extra Erector set box to store the toy soldiers. Donald's mother discovered what he had done, became angry, and made him take back his box. He then secretly defied his mother and again gave his friend the box. Apparently, my story had evoked in Donald the lost memory of a childhood time when he had actively participated in a friendship. While it was understood that Donald and I could not be friends and he had protested our lack of common ground, he now met my story with one of his own. After telling me his story, Donald expressed some anxiety about violating my privacy by knowing something about me. After all, I had said earlier in his treatment that I would not talk about myself, although he had repeatedly indicated his need for a more personal sense of me. I inquired further about Donald's anxiety. Did he feel I had violated the boundaries of therapy with my story? Was I, like his mother, losing control and abandoning a position of responsibility? No. What Donald realized was that he had just gotten what he wanted, and getting what he wanted made him anxious. He wondered about his own manipulativeness. I asked him, "Are you afraid you've somehow manipulated me into handing over to you a red tricycle in the form of a story?" Yes, this possibility did make him anxious. He feared his own capacity for "aggressive manipulation" to get what he wanted. He was afraid to take responsibility for wanting, for self-interest. He was supposed to be the one who could give away and do without.

I was then able to link this pattern to his posture early in therapy of waiting in retreat for me, with my presumed omniscience, to intuit and provide what he needed to get going. I told him, "As we've said before, partly you didn't believe or trust what I gave was really meant if you had to ask. But, partly, we can understand now that you kept yourself passive out of fear of actively asserting yourself to get what you want." Following this interpretation came several sessions in which Donald expressed sadness—more an affect of discouragement, which he said was not despair now—that all his choices in life had been arbitrary and reactive; that he had never been guided by desire; that he had never developed a sense of his own needs; that he felt close to grieving now the absence of family conditions in which he could have found his "internal desires." He said he felt left with a handicap, that the best he could do was to fit in with others when he chose; but that he had no negotiating position of his own based on his internal standards.

In the months that followed, Donald took the first steps in years to overcome his sense of being stalled in his career. He began a job search and ultimately negotiated an improved position within his own company. He reported feeling that "categorical change" had occurred within him. He was feeling consistently "plugged in." He called it "structural change." I also saw structural change in Donald. For example, his defense against his anger and aggression was now not so much dissociation, passivity, and schizoid withdrawal. Recently he has shown evidence of higher order defenses, such as displacement. Reading Bollas's new book, which I had recommended (and which he admired), he said, "I read Bollas saying it's difficult to treat schizoid patients, and I think, 'You asshole. Try harder.'" Instantly, Donald recognized his displacement and with pride affirmed that he had noted it as quickly as I had.

Donald has taken a more active part in shaping our relationship. If I am late, he firmly asks, "Why were you late?" If my attention drifts, sometimes he says, "Where did you go?" And Donald has begun again to date. He reports that, rather than being overwhelmed by shyness and anxiety, he can now remain present and explore with a woman what they have in common and what they feel for each other. He affirms with pride that he can now "negotiate a relationship." He notes his ability even to break up, kindly yet firmly and straightforwardly, with a woman who was falling for him, because he felt too little potential for intimacy to develop between them. In treatment, when he tells me that what he needs now as the unfinished work of his therapy is a greater feeling of intimacy between us, he is not drumming his digital finger patterns; he is looking me in the eye and pointing his finger straight at me. We share humor; I can tell him, "I'm glad I finally recommended readings; when would you have ever gotten to the Ws?"

Donald still continues to question why his therapy with me took the path it has and the time and the pain. He wishes he had been able to push at me—"nail you to the wall"—during the long stretch when I frustrated his needs and he remained unable to convey himself to me. He quotes me to myself from our early sessions, and I feel appalled. Could I really have said that? We continue to wonder. We have considered how, in my reluctance to evoke the transference risks of being too much like his invasive mother and perhaps drive him away, I had exposed us to the transference risks of my being too much like his dead father, too absent for Donald, and thus had driven him into despair. Even so, my presence, perhaps evocative of his grandfather, was allowing for the experience of continuity, safety, essential protest, and metaphorical realization. Now Donald begins to wonder where his own love has lain hidden. He wants to feel that he can vitalize a relationship and not just weigh it down.

Donald says he is beginning to see what we were doing together. "The trouble is," he says, "I never had anyone in my past whom I could trust and depend on and who would be reliable and responsive and still be themselves. I had plenty of people in my family being themselves, but that's why I couldn't rely on them. I had you being responsive, but I didn't think you were being yourself. I needed something in the middle."

Something in the middle. Donald brings our attention back to that middle area of experience between analyst and patient, between the subjective and the external, between the repetition and the renegotiation—the Winnicottian area of illusion where two people may intersect and negotiate the paradoxical reality of the analytic process.

In summary, the product of a negotiation in the analytic process may be an agreement about fees, an arrangement about scheduling, or an adjustment about such delicate matters as the use of deodorant. These issues are important in themselves; they permit the relationship to continue. At another level, the product of an analytic negotiation may be the resolution of a conflict, a shift in the patient's representational world, or a mutually sensible narrative construction. At the level of transference–countertransference, the product of a negotiation may be a jointly accepted understanding of a patient's repetition or an analyst's failure. But the crucial function of negotiation in psychoanalysis is that it constitutes the intersubjective process that delivers the therapeutic action. While engaged in the process of analytic negotiation, the patient experiences his participation in a kind of duet. He uses his voice to render the imperatives and the potentials in his own subjective world and hears the analyst's voice offering other-than-me substance that, in moments of grace, he may find and use to effect transformations in the core of the self. The structure-building potential of this process lies in the extension, articulation, and elaboration of the patient's internal capacity to remain competently, genuinely, and creatively engaged in ongoing negotiations. Negotiation is never complete; it is a living process. In a "good-enough" analysis, we prepare ourselves for playing in life's duets by discovering our own musicality.

2

"I Wish You Were My Father!"
Negotiating Potential Space

On the morning of December 17, Donald approached my house for his analytic session. As he walked along the entry path flanked by high snow banks, he looked up at the bay window of my second-floor office. During that session he shared with me his fantasy that I was at the window waving, welcoming him home for Christmas. Earlier in his treatment, which I described in Chapter 1, Donald had painfully and persistently protested my failure to be a father to him and provide restitution for the loss of his own father to cancer when he was barely two. Over several years we had struggled together to meet on sufficient middle ground between his schizoid tendency to retreat and repel and my psychoanalytic tendency to wait and interpret. We had managed to negotiate the paradoxes of my being and *not* being what he required enough to engage a deep and nurturing analytic process. So, on this December 17 I was warmed to hear Donald's symbolic realization of his longstanding wish. In my associations it linked up with an image Donald had used several times in previous years, an image of the lonely young

Ebeneezer Scrooge (in the Alistair Sim version of *A Christmas Carol*) at the moment his sister rescues him from exile at boarding school, crying, "Father has changed, and says you can come home now!" (I myself had seen that film many times and cried each time at that scene.) I shared my association with Donald.

ILLUSION AND PLAY

I hope that these images and phrases from Donald's analysis illustrate my belief that the analytic process is a duet, a joining of two voices in a chamber work wherein the interweaving of tonalities and lyrics, of resonances and dissonances, establishes a potential space with modes of playing. I further believe that the analyst is responsible for the preservation of optimal potential in potential space for the analysand's personal use, and that this potential resides in the existence of paradox, which is, as Winnicott insisted, respected, tolerated, but never resolved. I would add that paradox is negotiated continuously through the intersubjective dialectic between analyst and analysand and that the straddling of paradox is potentiated by the analytic couple's capacity to dwell in illusion, accept ambiguity, and play in the precarious *Spielraum* located between fantasy and reality. In particular, I intend in this chapter to demonstrate the usefulness of metaphor and the subjunctive mode as instruments available to help analyst and analysand locate, articulate, sustain, and negotiate the vital paradoxes inherent in potential space.

To return now to Donald, in the session following his fantasy of my welcoming wave at the window, Donald remained remote and abstract until, when I pointed this out, he immediately jumped back to his vision of being at my house for Christmas and said that he knew he did not belong there, that he was not "good enough" and could not hold up his end of a holiday celebration. Then he suddenly pictured himself ducking and covering his head. I asked him what this might be connected with, and he reported picturing my wife and me fighting (Donald and his girlfriend had been consulting my wife for couple therapy during recent months). He then said that this image must be a memory of his grandmother and grandfather, who always fought at Christmas, with his grandmother perpetually looking for an excuse to close herself into her bedroom. His next association was to a comedy show he had recently seen in which someone fired a gun at a Freud-like figure and exclaimed, "I just shot the father of modern psychology!" Donald wondered where *that* image had come from. I asked whether envy of my Christmas was involved and suggested that the character who had just been shot might have asked Donald if he wanted to marry the *mother* of modern psychology. We shared a laugh. Toward the end of this session, I asked Donald about his decision to spend the upcoming Christmas alone, not even joining his girlfriend of nearly three years for the holiday. In the sessions that followed, Donald wondered whether my granddaughters had yet arrived for the holidays; he felt an impulse to grab a beanbag frog from the shelf over the couch and throw it across the room; he imagined that some other patient had posed the frog in some personally expressive way, and he felt like ruining it; then he felt guilty and imagined a war in which he would reposition the frog and the other patient would restore its pose; and now it seemed to him to be a kind of correspondence that pleased him.

On December 23, when Donald removed his shoes as usual before lying down, he was, for the first time ever, wearing no socks. As he placed his bare feet on the couch, he said he had no clean laundry at home, no socks, and also no heat. Lying on the couch, he reported feeling as if he were actually physically at my house for Christmas. He wanted to focus on remaining relaxed while still speaking, which was not easy for him. He said he felt he now understood why he had dressed down and forgone the use of deodorant for years: "I wanted people to accept me as I am." He went on to say, "Why package yourself when your body is basically deficient?" I told him that this reminded me of what he'd told me about his foot (which, because of a congenital orthopedic anomaly, had been operated on several times before he was five years old). Although Donald had mentioned this before, he now for the first time recollected in vivid detail his feelings of shame and fear that something was terribly wrong with his body and how no one had helped him to bear or to make sense of his painful feelings. He associated this with his development of a defensive "fog and sleepiness . . . to insulate myself from dwelling in my body." Then he said, "Do you know what's on my mind? I'm thinking how my fragmentary communication must make it hard for you to stay with me" [Does he mean, "accept me as I am"?]. I replied that I had actually felt close to him in sensing the potential to speak about his foot, which he had allowed me to see for the first time today, and that I noticed a smile on his face. The session was over, and, as Donald left, he asked if my granddaughters had arrived for the holiday. When I said yes, he added, "May it be as lovely for you as I expect it could be."

When Donald imagined me waving at the window, or when Donald went on to imagine his unfitness to join in my family holiday, or when he pictured my wife and me fighting (as a memory of his grandparents? as a wish? as his projected aggression? as his underlying disbelief in any abidingly loving partnership?), or when he indulged the fantasy of ruining another patient's (or my granddaughter's) use of the frog (and conceived of a communication between his analytic space and someone else's), or when he invoked the shooting of Freud (and I shot a Freudian salvo back at him), or when we looked together at the bare emotion that he had barely shared with anyone about the early history of his now-bare feet, Donald was coming into play with me in potential space. Winnicott (1971a) wrote, *"Psychotherapy takes place in the over-lap of two areas of playing, that of the patient and that of the therapist. Psychotherapy has to do with two people playing together"* (p. 38). As we can see, analytic play is not simply gleeful; it may be quite solemn and entail the representation of relationships or experiences fraught with such affects as anger, shame, sadness, hurt, or rejection, as well as satisfaction, kinship, or love. Analytic play, in its range from hilarity to high seriousness, entails an inter-subjective exchange of "squiggles" that mark, or re-mark on, the personal world of the patient and the shared world of analytic space. As Winnicott (1971a) emphasized, "If the therapist cannot play, then he is not suitable for the work. If the patient cannot play, then something needs to be done to enable the patient to become able to play, after which psychotherapy may begin" (p. 54).

The essential therapeutic mission of Donald's analysis may be seen in this light as the establishment (practically the installation) and creative elaboration of an intersubjective—and thereby an internal—space wherein Donald could symbolize, assemble, connect, feel, communicate, author, and share his personal experience. Indeed, the establishment, enlargement, and playful negotiation of potential space lies at the heart of therapeutic action in any analysis. I agree with Ogden (1986) when he points out, as

Winnicott (1963a) did, that the medium of dialectic that preserves and negotiates potential space is essentially verbal—to which I would add its symbolic language equivalent in kinetics and gestures. That is, potential space is described by communication that is explicit but "indirect," allowing in its very approximation of meaning room for personal consideration, reflection, the generation of personal meaning, and the experience of a self with authorship, agency, boundaries, and effectance in dialogue. The alternative to "indirect" communication is "direct" communication, which forecloses and collapses potential space. Ogden (1986) points out that the patient's form of direct communication is often a projective identification that, by its quality of concrete coerciveness, induces a state in the analyst and thus undermines the analyst's ability to register his inner state symbolically as a countertransference experience and thereby maintain a psychological dialectical process. The therapist's violation of potential space, according to Ogden, tends to take the form of interpretations proffered as statements of fact, which, by their very peremptory and Procrustean nature, eclipse the internal space wherein the patient might arrive at his own construction of personal meanings. The analyst's indulgence in authoritative interpretation—explaining the patient to himself and teaching the patient who he is—may be viewed, in its concretization of language and coercive power, as a variant of the analyst's projective identifications and a violation of potential space as well as of the patient's core self.

This is why I prefer to think of the analyst "squiggling" with a patient rather than mirroring the patient. Unlike Schwaber (1992), I do not believe that we can empathically know an analysand by listening from his or her perspective; we can only empathically imagine this other person as we straddle the space *between* our perspectives, honoring the paradox of our simultaneous separateness and relatedness. Developmental researchers have informed us that the mother's mirroring response is multimodal, that it organizes meaning; adjusts affective shape, intensity, and direction; and reaches toward linguistic exchange. As Meares (1993) has written, "The mother is not simply a mirror. In her responsiveness to her infant, she gives back some part of what the baby is doing—but only some part and not all—and also gives him something of her own" (p. 30). Sanville (1991) develops a similar thesis, when, invoking the Soviet literary critic Bakhtin, she writes, "Bakhtin's definition of interpretation is not based on the assumption that one person in the dialogue knows what the other really means; rather, it is essentially responsive understanding" (p. 126). Here again we are in the area of therapeutic potential space as defined by Winnicott, or Ogden, where the paradoxical intersections of subjectivity and objectivity, sameness and difference, knowing and unknowing, privacy and commonality require and promote the ongoing negotiations of a dialectical process. In this coconstructed space of psychoanalysis, reality and illusion are bridged in the particular ways that patient and analyst come into play together. The analyst engaged in negotiating potential space is not supplying the correct or corrective interpretation; rather, he is offering for the analysand's consideration and personal use an option for symbolically registering some aspect of self-experience. As Sanville further paraphrases Bakhtin, "while accuracy may be what matters in natural science, in human science it is depth that is essential" (p. 126).

I am not advocating a cavalier dismissal of clarity or reality; I am not suggesting that we cultivate mystification or muddle as a goal. Nor would I suggest that the analyst abjure his personal authority. (Indeed, I am reminded of a paper by Hoffman, 1996, aptly titled "The Intimate and Ironic Authority of the (Psychoanalyst's Presence.") Potential space is *not* arrived at by the analyst's creating a personal vacuum—by avoiding disclosure of the substance of the analyst's own countertransference experience, imaginative resonance, linguistic association, metaphorical elaboration, interpretative emphasis, personal limit, or affective response to the analysand. The analyst need not be tentative, sheepish, or apologetic about offering to the patient his squiggle (other-than-me substance), whether it constitutes inevitable enactment, parallel regression to primary process, or a necessary act of freedom to declare what the analyst holds to be a reality. The analyst does, however, remain consistently committed to an effort to bridge, within his or her own center of attention, positions of subjectivity and empathy, imagination and observation, knowing and unknowing, expression and reflection, disciplined technique and authentic responsiveness: in short, the analyst maintains the practice of concerted self-analysis while participating in the analytic dyad. Within this self-analytic practice, responsibly retuning the analytic instrument (musical, not surgical: more a cello than a scalpel), as a player in the analytic duet, the analyst may indeed exercise considerable "voice." And the analyst's workmanlike attention turns continually toward the integration of genetic themes, the consideration of patterns of transference, repetition, and reflection on character defenses and resistance. But it is our humility—as we bear in mind that our analytic provision is indeed provisional, that our knowing is approximate and selective, that our technique is molded by our idiosyncracies, that our very state of consciousness is awash on the waves of yet to be recognized transference–countertransference influences—that gives us the freedom, along with the responsibility, to keep potential space open for negotiation. Thus, in my work with Donald, I had recurrently noted his distance or abstractness and had developed with him a language for our noting together his cognitive and communicative style that resulted from splitting and dissociation: he described how initially he had seen only fragments of my office, never putting the whole picture together; I introduced the image of his looking out at the world through holes cut in a cardboard box, turning his head to see unconnected, discontinuous images; and I described his style of associations as islands enshrouded in fog, kept separate and isolated, awaiting the lifting of the fog to reveal one vast, continuous inner landscape. In the vignette I have related, you can see how Donald used the metaphor of the fog to reflect on the development of his defenses against intolerable affect, and how my comment on his abstractness was instantly used to bring Donald back to his wistful fantasy of belonging in my house for Christmas.

But I now want to revisit my exploration of Donald's bare feet on December 23 to illustrate how the analyst's squiggle-mark may not presume accuracy, although it may still contribute a useful depth to symbolic articulation in potential space. Recall that as Donald lay barefoot on the couch he associated to his history of "dressing down" and omitting to use deodorant despite his conspicuous body odor. He voiced his understanding that he was tacitly asking people to accept him as he was, and his further associations now turned to question, "Why package yourself when your body is basically deficient?" Then he noted his state of sleepiness, and reflected that he perhaps deployed sleepiness and "fog" as a defense against anxiety. It was at that point that I said I was thinking of his foot and its many surgeries during his early childhood. Useful as my comment may have been—allowing Donald to make contact with early feelings of fear and shame in the absence of relational support—how could we possibly know whether I had given a correct, or even an accurate, interpretation? After all, Donald was also lying on my couch as a sockless urchin, with no clean laundry and no heat at home. He was in my house, feeling deficient and unworthy of joining my family gathering at Christmas. And, given his longstanding concern about the issue of body odor and his habit of wearing two pairs of socks (or athletic socks) to insure against smell, were his bare feet on this day an angry "So there!" or a symbolic enactment of his being "at home" with me or, paradoxically, both? My own selective focus on the genetic aspect of his sense of personal deficiency could only be approximately relevant. What I believe occurred during this session, within potential space, is that Donald, who was alone in childhood with his painful body experience, was now with me in a way that allowed him to be connected with his own affective life; and, paradoxically, while I could not be with him in the actual present of Christmas at home, I was now with him in the metaphorical past as he revisited his childhood home in which the absence of affective dialogue had contributed to his schizoid retreat. Thus, within the intermediate space of transference–countertransference illusion, we had negotiated a symbolic realization of a father's presence, even as Donald faced the blunt boundaries that delimited our real relationship in this season. Both Loewald (1974) and Modell (1991) have emphasized the essential illusory and paradoxical transference relationship at the heart of the analytic process. As I would put it, in potential space, the analyst is what he is not for his patient. And the negotiation of this paradox constitutes the therapeutic action of a psychoanalysis.

METAPHOR

As analyst and patient come into play in the area of illusion, they create metaphorical renderings of the meaning of their shared transference–countertransference experience. The unique metaphors that arise in the course of a treatment in any analytic dyad represent each party's creative authorship as well as a degree of conjoint association. In my work, I have found that metaphor is a particularly useful analytic instrument for maintaining the area of illusion and for bridging the paradoxes of subjectivity and objectivity that govern the perspectives of analyst and patient. The aptness and utility of a metaphor—one coined by either analyst or patient but accepted by both as currency within that analysis—reflects the negotiation of approximate meaning that gives each party room to move, to feel recognized but not "had," and that is, in itself, pleasurable insofar as the symbolic range of potential space is conceived in "the marriage of true minds" (an intimate union allowable to both parties in that intermediate area within the constraints of an analytic framework). The analyst's occasional use of metaphor in the service of interpretation allows him, at times, to evoke, articulate, clarify, or even extend an emergent transference configuration while minimizing the potential for shaming the patient, invading the patient, or educating the patient, and thereby collapsing potential space. Indeed, I believe that metaphor describes a potential space within which separate meanings converge to inform, define, discriminate, oppose, and accent each other in an inherently dialectical linguistic form.

The juxtapositions of object and (usually) linguistic representation, the conjuring of a density of resonant (often simultaneous with dissonant or improbable) associations, inherent to the metaphoric structure, strikes me as the closest that secondary-process thought and communication can come to the protean richness and immediacy of primary process—that psychic realm wherein all combinations are possible, even the possible may be impossible, and a negation may be an affirmation. Metaphor locates the threshold between primary process and secondary process. It is competent primary process, combining condensation with craft. Metaphor calls attention to a space populated by more shades of meaning than could yet surface on the wings of words and in its poesy reflects the psyche's deep potential for playing.

Returning once again to Donald's analysis, I would like to trace the evolution of some central metaphors as they came into play between us. Donald reported that he had greatly enjoyed watching on television an episode of "Quantum Leap," a program in which a man is transported in time to some moment in the past in which he is in a position to rescue people from a crisis and then leaves them, in an attempt to return to his own time. As my mind flickered images of the lonely hero who cannot stay in people's lives, and as I tacitly recognized the life of the analyst in this mythic story, I blurted out, "That reminds me of 'The Lone Ranger.'" Then I wondered why I had intruded my own image into the one that Donald had already introduced. Donald's surprising reply was, "You know, I watched 'The Lone Ranger' all the time as a child. He was my hero. I identified with him. I think that's where I got my idea that a good life was to live alone and look for people's troubles that I could help with." I wondered aloud whether Donald thought that his own father might have been like a lone ranger, who rode into town long enough for Donald to be given life and then had to ride out, unable to remain and live with folks. Donald said he had indeed pictured his father alone at night at a campfire beyond the town. In the week that followed, Donald had a series of dreams in which he was in situations of danger, war, crime, adventure—sometimes alone and sometimes with an unspecified ally. Among his associations, he at one point remarked, "Oh yeah, I just remembered the Lone Ranger had Tonto!" This metaphor of a paradoxical hero, a man both alone and companioned, became a referent for existential questions such as whether Donald could envision himself settling into a committed domestic life, or transference questions as captured in Donald's playfully conjecturing that the Lone Ranger and Tonto may have been gay. Donald's implicit questions about the nature and purpose of closeness, partnership, and love bring me to another metaphor unfolding between us, which I will call the metaphorization of "holding" in potential space.

In the second year of Donald's therapy, as he questioned whether he would ever feel close enough to me for his treatment not to be futile, he told me that he doubted that he could ever feel what he needed to feel unless I would actually hold him. He said he knew that the rules of therapy would forbid this. I chimed in with, "That's right; no holding." In retrospect, I wince at my gratuitously flat-footed remark—indeed, a foreclosure of potential space. Again in a later year of Donald's analysis, the question of holding arose, as it had on several prior occasions. Donald said that he felt as if he needed to do a lot of crying, which he feared was beyond him in the absence of holding, and asked me directly why I had flatly said, "No holding." I told him I had been thinking of the boundaries that provide a safe space for feeling and that I was loath to imply to Donald a false hope for a form of enactment, which, at that time, I could not consider possible between us. I added, however, that I regretted my unnecessarily categorical dismissal of holding, and, because this felt like a different time between us, I suggested that, without our presuming the outcome, we might usefully leave the question of holding open between us without a priori assumptions, to see what this need might entail, what we might learn, and what might actually help him. Donald said that my statement had already helped him. He then said once again that, of course, the rules and ethics of analysis would forbid holding, and expressed anxiety at the thought of our breaking the rules. I mused, "What a sad paradox it would be if it turns out that to do what helps would mean violating your treatment, and for this to remain your treatment we cannot do what helps." Donald then fantasized that perhaps he should sign up for a psychodrama, where it *is* in the rules to hold people. He continued, "I could get an auxiliary to be you, and I could play out what it would be like. Maybe then I could cry like I need. But it wouldn't be with you." I asked what might be his conflict over crying *with me* versus breaking the rules. He replied, "The real issue is I'm split. I'm not one whole person. And I think I need to cry and be held to come to feel like one person." I responded, "You've been saying that in one way or another all along." "This is different," insisted Donald. "That was about being close to you. This is deeper. It's about getting close to myself. It's connection with myself, not another person. I need to feel like one whole person."

The following week, Donald reported an intense experience that had occurred during the weekend. He had been speaking on the phone with his girlfriend for several hours, a common happening as they thrashed out the fate of their relationship, and in a moment of feeling both closeness and anger, he had experienced an attack of terror and pictured hitting himself in the head. These terrors had occurred a few times recently, and in the throes of their severity he feared a breakdown. This time, he had imagined phoning me and coming to my office immediately, on a Sunday evening, where he would lie down on my couch and I would sit on the floor next to him and cradle his head as he cried. As Donald reported this fantasy, his fists went to his forehead and he complained that he now felt split again, as if his head were flying off his body. He again imagined hitting himself in the head. I asked if perhaps he was seeking some way for his head and his heart to feel the same pain together. With immediate, tearful relief, Donald said that my understanding startled him and helped him hold this experience together.

What I mean in this case by "the metaphorization of holding" is the progression from Donald's initial requirement of concrete, skin-to-skin bodily holding prior to the establishment of a potential space—first between us and then within him—to the eventual emergence of his inner capacity to symbolically register holding as a useful metaphor representing our relationship in the service of his self-regulation. Holding has moved from the imperative to the subjunctive. I will add, however, that I cannot know now that actual holding will never occur between us, because the paradoxical existence and negation of that possibility within our analytic frame now describes a potential space that remains in use. And notable among Donald's current uses of potential space is his dramatically increasing tendency to link his associations; to link a session with prior sessions, past and present, affect and idea, transference and concurrent life. The fog is lifting, and continuous internal ground becomes easier for both of us to see as it is held together.

One more permutation of the metaphor of holding: In the last session before the two-week vacation during which I would begin to write this essay, Donald objected that my interruption of our meetings could break the flow of more fluid associations and the emergent sense of wholeness that was making him feel hopeful that "something is breaking through." I asked Donald whether he thought our work would cease to exist during the time we were apart. In one of those moments in analysis that is both a surprise and not a surprise, Donald replied, "No, not this time. You've used the image of islands in the fog. I now think of all the separate rooms inside of me. Only now you are in a lot of those rooms. Not all of them; some of them are still dark." As I listened to Donald, one of the mysteries of potential space visited me in the following way: Donald's image of the dark rooms brought suddenly to my mind the memory of a disturbing dream I had early in my freshman year of college. In my dream, I was following Charles Laughton on the street, desperately trying to catch up with him as he sped up and eluded me, ducking into a building. I followed him into the building and found myself in a dark room, suddenly in terror. Now, sitting behind Donald, I sensed the existence, in the dark room of my dream, of some missing element in my relationship with my own father. I kept this piece of self-analysis to myself, receiving it as the gift an analyst may find as a participant in potential space. Amazingly, Donald went on to generate a fantasy of my relationship with my father and, wondering what a relationship between a son and father could be like, constructed images that he might hold inside.

This set of associations led to Donald's first recollection of a positive experience with his own stepfather: when he was between approximately the ages of three and eight, his stepfather would join him regularly at bedtime to hear his prayers ("Now I lay me . . ."). We then recalled together how the sequence of Donald's associations to "Quantum Leap" and our elaborations around the Lone Ranger (and Tonto) had been preceded by a period in which Donald had felt the magnitude of his loneliness in life and had said to me, "I feel like I drive around, go from place to place, park my car, come here, do whatever—and my life is all meaningless because I'm all alone and no one takes an interest in me; no one knows." Behind the couch, feeling Donald's despair and sensing the presence of the absence of his father (and probably experiencing my own countertransference pain and defensiveness in the face of his implied negation of my own presence), I responded, "Hearing you now, I suddenly think of the lines from Psalm 23: 'Yea, though I walk through the valley of the shadow of death, I will fear no evil: for thou art with me.' You miss that feeling."

By the end of that prevacation session, Donald returned to his distress over my "going away." He said he hated to think of me clearing my mind of him, perhaps glad to get rid of him just as he would feel glad to be rid of his family. He imagined that I would choose never to return to work, or I would retire or die. He then wondered if his own father's early death had involved his not really wanting to live in that family or to be Donald's father. I told Donald that during this vacation I would be writing an essay and that "we may even show up in it."

On my return from vacation, the representation of father registered some notable evolutions in metaphor, in memory, and in the immediate relationship between Donald and me. The first postvacation session began with Donald's reporting a feeling of relief during our time apart: "It was time off from the tension of being here." Donald elaborated on this "tension" as the recurrent feeling of deficiency he felt subject to in our sessions. He said that during these two weeks he had taken a kind of refuge in his work life as a "techie." He went on to declare that he felt disappointed in himself and in me. Indeed, on the previous day, spent at a park with his girlfriend, he had felt angry with me. He had wondered if his anger was due to my absence and imminent return. I reminded him of his prevacation transference feelings toward me as "father proxy." Donald then further considered his disappointment. He said he had projected his ideal for himself onto me. He went on to say, "I'm disappointed in you, and I'm disappointed in finding myself in you." Donald added that he felt like a machine, like a ghost in a machine, with no feeling. How, he protested, could anyone love him—how could his girlfriend love him—when "I don't love myself!" Then Donald's next association opened up an important doorway to one of his dark inner rooms, bringing some light to his cluster of feelings of anger with me and with himself, his disappointment in my usefulness as a figure for identification, and his machinelike lack of affect: Donald pictured his stepfather spanking him brutally over his knee.

During several subsequent sessions Donald's recollections of these beatings gained detail, dimension, and affective intensity. For example, Donald began that week's second session with a yawn. He said he had hardly slept because he was thinking about what was said the day before. He was preoccupied with feeling like "a machine." How could he become more of a whole person? He added, "Even the way I think about it is mechanical." He wondered how he could connect with his feelings. He remembered that as a young child he had looked at the world with a natural fascination, but that now, "I feel like I've lost my innocence. I'm angry, bitter, and not trusting." His thoughts turned to his girlfriend and his difficulty trusting her. He described her as someone "who was trying to control me; I've felt so helpless. There's no telling when she'll get angry." I told Donald, "That reminds me of what you began to describe yesterday—helplessly lying over your stepfather's knee, being spanked, submitting limply." Donald went on, "We were told that if we stiffened our buttocks to protect ourselves from pain we'd be hit more and longer." He protested, "Why did he hit us so hard? And so many times? We were young!" (Donald had been less than nine years old, and his younger siblings around five.) He recalled seeing his siblings unable to sit down after these beatings. I commented, "He didn't respect your natural self-protective responses.

This does not sound like discipline, but *assault*." Donald then said, "The only thing I could do was go elsewhere in my mind—like off to my grandparents." I noted how dissociation has been called the escape where there is no escape. And Donald added, "When the younger ones were spanked, I went to my room. I couldn't stand to watch. I was just helpless." I commented to Donald, "I wonder right now if I'm feeling my anger or yours." "I *guess* I'm angry," he replied, "but I don't feel it."

Later in that session I told Donald that I recognized my own anger at what I'd heard but that my anger might also be augmented by the anger Donald had not yet released. Donald responded, "What could I do with my anger? Go spit on his grave? Push the gravestone over? Kick dirt?" I asked, "Is the issue that he's not alive to feel it anymore?" "No," answered Donald. "The issue is *I can't feel my anger!*" At this I laughed. And Donald laughed. I quipped, "Pushing over the gravestone with equanimity?" "Well," answered Donald, "I do feel a twinge of anger." Then Donald turned abruptly to rationalizations: his stepfather must have been abused himself; it was the alcohol. Donald caught what he was doing and, with increased heat, asserted, "Why do I even think about that? He did what he did. What can a child do? Kick him in the knee? It's the helplessness I can't stand! I just had to go far away." I said to Donald that I thought his habit of going far away perhaps constituted a more pervasive injury than stinging buttocks and that his injuries extended to his feeling that he could no longer trust or idealize the man who had joined him at bedtime to say prayers. Donald cried as he again pictured himself helplessly witnessing his siblings' severe spankings. Then he remembered his stepfather threatening to burn him with cigarettes. And he connected with his feelings of rage and hate, and then shame, that after the loss of his innocence he had come to hate people and to seek to manipulate and control them. "I can be a monster," Donald added. "I feel like no one has loved me when I'm a monster."

Then Donald reminded himself that he would be away the entire following week on a business trip. He said, "I'm thinking tomorrow's Friday. Actually my thought was 'Tomorrow's Friday, you bastard!' Why would I be angry? *I'm* leaving, not you." Mindful of the anger and protest that had filled this session, and wondering which aspect of it to comment on, I simply replied, "I was just away for two weeks." Donald responded, "That feels like long ago right now. This feels more like it's about next week. I feel abandoned, even though I'm the one going. I wish—it's like going off to college—I wish I had someone at home to call home to, to talk about what I'm doing, to be proud of my work. I wish you were my father!" Then Donald added, "But you can't be. And I can handle it." And I commented, "You can handle it, but you feel what you feel." Silently, I noted how the ghost in the machine could find the voice to express feeling and even that Donald could risk calling me a "bastard," could risk being a bit of a monster and perhaps be loved. I felt the impulse to invite him to phone me from his trip, but I suppressed it.

Donald began Friday's session by saying, "I feel strangely placid." I responded, "An oxymoron, like uncomfortably comfortable." After a long silence, Donald said, "I hate silence." I asked, "Is this an empty silence, or are you in danger of being full of feeling?" Donald answered, "I'm feeling close to you. And my heart is pounding—to admit that I feel attached and dependent. Last night I thought, 'Now you've done it!' Now I feel attached to you enough so it will hurt when we have to part ways." I said, "Sounds like it's both the bad news and the good news." "Yes," Donald replied. "But it gives me a headache. My whole body aches now. My body is fighting me." I responded, "Headache, ducking your head, hit in the head, spanked over your stepfather's knee: How closeness gets infused with hurt." "Yes," Donald replied. "I'm afraid to trust. You could reject me—no, that's not real. But *something* could happen. I want to scream! I can't stand it anymore! I can't stand attachment! So much has gone wrong!" In response to Donald's outpouring of pain and dread at the threshold of his amplified feelings of attachment, and because he was about to go away on a trip, I tacitly chose to tell him a story, and thereby another metaphor emerged for his use.

I told Donald that his dread of something going wrong at the threshold of hope reminded me of what I called "the Bridge of San Luis Rey syndrome," after the novella by Thornton Wilder. In that story, several people in an Andean village, unknown to one another, reach a turning point in their lives of loneliness, poverty, defeat, or despair. For each person, the first act of hope entails crossing a mountain gorge by a rope bridge toward a new beginning in life on the other side. As they all converge upon the rope bridge, it collapses, and they plummet to their deaths. Donald's response to this story was to say, "Good image. I hope you and I both get across the bridge before it collapses." Then Donald paused for a long time of silence, after which he said, "I have a hard time allowing myself to feel my love for you. To feel it here, not just as a memory when I'm not here." "In real time," I replied. "Yes," said Donald. I added, "A step toward feeling whole." Donald smiled and said, "It's that we're in this together!" I responded, "That's an aspect of love: we're in this together." "Yes," said Donald, and then he continued, "I can't find the words. But it's about this affecting *you too*. It's not just like my earlier image of a doctor who would explain things to me or fix things in my life. It's more that we're both struggling." I asked Donald what the verb "struggling" referred to, and he said, "I can't find the words. But we're both crossing the bridge. I can't quite find the words. It's here, right now between us. But I can't quite find the words because I can't fully feel it. That's it! I can't fully feel it yet."

As Donald departed for his business trip, I privately reflected on his passage across his bridge amid his dread of a plunge and his hope of a crossing. I thought of our straddling together the paradox of my being what I was not for him, so that he could experience the essential absence and the essential presence of a needed relationship and the hindrances—external and internal, past and present—to the lived experience of a relational connection ("for thou art with me"). Together we had been bridging potential space through play, illusion, metaphor, and the negotiation of paradox: as Donald put it, we were both struggling, "both crossing the bridge," in a dialectical process. The therapeutic yield of this process, incomplete as it is at this point, can be seen in Donald's increasing ability to bridge his own internal self-states, with their state-dependent features of memory, affect, and wish. Thus, the separate islands enshrouded by Donald's internal fog—his aloneness, despair, pain, helplessness, rage, hate, frustration, shame, and love—are becoming more accessible as continuous inner terrain. And memory, affect, and current relational experience bridge together in the "struggling" Donald shares with me in potential space.

THE SUBJUNCTIVE

Returning now to the moment when Donald exclaimed, "I wish you were my father!" I would like to shift our attention to the usefulness of the subjunctive mood at moments in potential space.

That single sentence, "I wish you were my father," accomplished the statement of a paradox: while negating me as father in the indicative mood, Donald was conjuring me as father in the subjunctive mood. Thus, I take his statement to be simultaneously both vehement protest at what *is not* between us and affirmation of what *is* between us in our analytic relationship. The subjunctive in analytic potential space is of value specifically because it is the linguistic modality, in English, for rendering the "counterfactual conditional"—not what *is* or what *was*, but what *might be*. In short, the subjunctive is the verb form used in English to convey the optative—a wish or desire—as well as the conjectural—the realm of potential. Thus, the subjunctive mood strikes me as a particularly apt linguistic form for entering dialogue in potential space, wherein the analysand's (and the analyst's) subjectivization of object-related experience is constituted by the interplay of the wishful or conjectural deconstruction of the object (the object subjectively conceived) and the recognition of the object as a separate being (the object objectively perceived). This playing out of what might be, without losing sight of what is or what was, describes the essence of potential space in the analytic transference–countertransference exchange.

As linguists know, most languages distinguish between "realis" and "irrealis" through their verb forms.[1] The realis is conveyed through the past or present indicative mood of the verb; the irrealis is conveyed through the future indicative or the "counterfactual," which includes the subjunctive. The subjunctive mood varies cross-culturally; there are no universal set rules, and not all languages use a distinct subjunctive, or counterfactual, linguistic marker. Bloom (1981) conducted cross-cultural research on the linguistic shaping of thought and reported that, whereas English-speaking subjects readily identified and navigated the realm of the "might have been," Chinese speakers notably failed to recognize "counterfactual" statements and even refused to shift into the counterfactual realm, "brand[ing] questions that called upon them

---

[1] I am grateful to Andrea Massar, and to George Goethals and Roger Brown, for introducing me to linguistic concepts. I particularly thank Xiaolu Hsi for her careful reading of this manuscript and for directing my attention to the ambiguities in Bloom's study of the Chinese language, and Professor Isabelle Mao for her clarification of the form of the subjunctive in the Chinese language.

to do so characteristically un-Chinese" (p. 16). Bloom attributed these findings to the difference between English and Chinese linguistic structures. The Chinese written language uses ideograms, and, hence, Chinese verbs are without conjugation or tense markers. The subjunctive verb (irrealis) in Chinese is the same as the present indicative verb (realis), but the Chinese use modifiers elsewhere in a sentence and rely more heavily on their prior knowledge of the context of a linguistic act in order to render the counterfactual meaning of a statement. Bloom assumed that this more complex system of modifying the present indicative verb to convey the subjunctive would account for his empirical findings. Others[2] have questioned Bloom's interpretation as too zealous a defense of the Whorfian hypothesis (that language determines what can be thought in each linguistic or cultural group) and have proposed alternatively that, while the Chinese language adequately builds the subjunctive into its structure, use of the subjunctive has been suppressed by centuries of Chinese cultural tradition, which discourages wishful thinking or dwelling on what is not actually so. But, whether Bloom's data reflect differences between the Chinese and English languages *as structured* or *as practiced*, it is evident that cultures vary in their relative articulation of the counterfactual conditional, or subjunctive, realm.

Bloom's (1981) study drew important inferences concerning the interconnectedness of linguistic development and general cognitive development and concluded that

> distinct languages, by labeling certain perspectives on reality as opposed to others, act (1) to encourage their speakers to extend their repertoires of cognitive schemas in language-specific ways and (2) to define for their speakers that particular set of schemas they can make use of to mediate their linguistic acts and to establish explicit points of mental orientation for giving direction to their thoughts [p. 83].

Thus, the Chinese-English bilingual subjects in Bloom's study were significantly more adept than the monolingual Chinese at understanding written materials couched in the Chinese rendering of the subjunctive—the bilingual subjects alerted themselves to the counterfactual meaning of the Chinese paragraphs they

---

[2] For a balanced and scholarly discussion of the critical responses to Bloom's linguistic studies, see Lucy (1992), especially pp. 208–252.

were reading by writing in the margins, in English, the words "would have."

I believe that this brief excursion into cross-cultural linguistics may suggest valuable implications for clinical psychoanalytic discourse. Consider that the subjunctive is our English-language vehicle to communicate the counterfactual conditional, whereby we may say that something is not true but then make a condition for entertaining it. Thus, the subjunctive is an inherently paradoxical modality: in the subjunctive we negate something and simultaneously consider it in terms of "what if," "how might," and so on. The subjunctive mode, then, is a part of how we are equipped linguistically to dwell in the paradoxes of potential space, to entertain desire or want or conjecture without coercing a foreclosure or conflation of subjectivity and objectivity. Modell (1991) has argued that the therapeutic relationship is a paradoxical experience that exists concurrently within multiple levels of reality—the "ordinary life" human relationship, the iconic transference, and the transference–countertransference quality of the therapeutic frame. Modell declares that "it is essential that the analyst or therapist demonstrate capacity to shift playfully from one level of reality to another" (p. 13).

In an earlier essay, Modell (1989) suggested that a patient's inability to accept and use paradox might be the basis for an interminable analysis. Could there be an analogy between those analysands or analysts who lack a facility for negotiating paradox and the Chinese in Bloom's research who resisted thinking in the realm of the counterfactual conditional? If language development facilitates cognitive development, might the employment, and practice, of the subjunctive in analytic discourse widen the area of potential space, sustain its paradoxes for consideration, and provide a medium of articulation that could foster such ego development in the analysand as would augment his capacity to tolerate paradox and use it therapeutically to conjure dimensions of subjective experience? Might the analyst's use of the subjunctive mode help to avoid those foreclosures of potential space that result, as Ogden (1986) indicated, from the analyst's proffering of interpretations as statements of fact (the realis)? Perhaps the analyst's use of the subjunctive might relate tactfully to the patient's resistance, based as it is on the patient's anxieties over the prospect of destabilizing internal changes coerced in the analytic process. The subjunctive mood permits analyst and patient to engage together in fresh considerations regarding the patient's subjectivity, while affording the patient some experience of wiggle room—some empowerment to negotiate the passage of internal change—that would not seem as available in the face of interpretive declarations.

Here are some analytic situations that illustrate ways in which the use of the subjunctive might enlarge the analytic repertory: One patient, exploring his resistance to being fully open throughout several sessions, stated his fear that I would be angry with him because he was choosing not to share a small inheritance with his parents as he compared his needs with theirs. I considered asking why he thought I would be angry, but I elected not to because I did not want to imply a presumption that the issue must lie within him alone. (I recognize that asking "why" does not necessarily indicate dismissal of a two-person field of relationship with mutual influences; however, I do believe that the tilt in asking "why" tends toward the doctorly inquiry into the patient's psychic reality, a more one-person emphasis.) Incidentally—and, indeed, not so incidentally—I did not know if I was angry with him at that time. I was not aware of feeling anger toward him, but perhaps he was aware of feelings somehow manifested in me without my yet registering them. I chose to address this patient's concern by giving us both room to consider together how his fears were generated in our intersubjective field, without a foreclosure of potential space. I asked, "If I were angry with you, how might I express it, and what would it reflect between us?" His first response was that, because he had made of me his "superego" (which we occasionally referred to as Jiminy Cricket), he awaited my judgment on this conflict of conscience. He feared I would judge him to be lacking in conscience and that I would therefore reject him. He thought I would enact my rejection by withholding my responses, subtly distancing myself, and abandoning him to silent isolation on the couch. He then pictured me envying him his inheritance and begrudging him what he has, and thus he imagined my hostilely withholding from him what I have that he wants. From there he was able to recognize his recurrent envy of me, his chronic sense of personal impoverishment, and his anger with his parents, and with me, for all that he has missed. I believe my choice of a question posed in the subjunctive widened the space within which this patient could entertain a range of potentially important relational issues. By my neither negating nor affirming my anger, but instead simultaneously doing both within the subjunctive mood, this moment of his defensiveness yielded to more open and risky associations.

Another analysand, a shy, scholarly, and inhibited woman in her fourth year of analysis, became able, and moved, to express transference love directly and emphatically. On one occasion, she said, "Will you leave your wife and run away with me?" How to respond to such a question?! This frontal challenge placed us at the very heart of the issue of boundaries, love, mutuality, power, and vulnerability in this analysis, as happens in so many analyses. It would not do (it would never do) to say or imply "yes"—seductive exploitation of love has no place in analysis. But would it do to say "no"? Sometimes, with some patients, the only answer for the safety of the patient, or the therapist, or the viability of the treatment, is to declare a definitive "no." However, it is often—as in this instance—safe enough to explore the question in potential space, as long as the paradox of negation and consideration might be mutually tolerated and sustained. In my relationship with this analysand I did not want to ask her why this question was arising now or what feelings lay beneath it. I did not even want to confront the teasing element that I experienced in her question, because this more emboldened foray of hers into passionate and free communication could too easily be routed back into hiding in the thickets of her shame and inhibition. She was venturing a risk with me, playfully exposing her earnest feeling; she was out on a limb, and I believe it would have been hurtful to leave her alone on that spot. Instead, using the subjunctive mood, I asked, "If I were to run away with you, how might we reconcile it with my being your analyst?" By joining this woman in entertaining a potential scenario, while tacitly invoking the negation of it implicit in English in the counterfactual mode, I placed the question between us as a shared dilemma. She then expressed her pain at the "impossibility" of her position with me and her frustration that our relationship was both so "real" and so "unreal" at the same time.[3] She laughed with delight at her freedom to ruffle me, and her enjoyment of our mutual impact on each other.

---

[3] This analysand's very personal outcry and wonderment at the simultaneously "real" and "unreal" quality of love between us in our transference–countertransference relationship is reminiscent of Freud's (1915a) implicit grasp of the paradoxical nature of transference love—its "genuineness" as well as its status as resistance and repetition.

As noted earlier, when Donald exclaimed to me, "I wish you were my father," his use of the subjunctive served to bemoan that I was not his father while simultaneously affirming that it was precisely because I *was* his father in symbolic realizations within our analytic potential space that he protested that I was *not* his actual father. Donald's counterfactual statement indicated to me his increasing competence in making creative use of the paradoxical levels of reality within our analytic relationship. Earlier, when I said to Donald "no holding," I had failed to negotiate a potential space within which Donald's needs for holding could be articulated, recognized, and somehow addressed. It was only when I placed the issue of holding into the subjunctive by inviting Donald to consider with me the question of my actually holding him, to see what that might entail, that Donald pursued his more metaphorized use of the potential in his analysis for holding his dissociated islands of experience together in the service of establishing a sense of being "a whole self." Subsequent to those sessions, Donald chose to locate and bring in to show me the only tangible memento he owns of his own father: a photo of himself, barely a year old, being held in the arms of his father shortly after his cancer was diagnosed. Through the use of play, illusion, metaphor, and the subjunctive, Donald has grown increasingly able to bridge memory, perception, desire, and feeling in our analytic duet.

3

Multiplicity, Paradox, and the Creative Self

In his poem "Song of Myself," Walt Whitman writes:

> Do I contradict myself?
>
> Very well then I contradict myself,
>
> (I am large, I contain multitudes.)

Whitman's lines capture the dilemma and celebrate the creative potential of the person faced with the inherent multiplicity of lived experience. In this chapter, I speak from a perspective that believes in the irreducible multiplicity of both subjective and relational experience. I agree with Winnicott (1971c) that we dwell psychically within unresolvable paradox. I further believe that our continuous, lifelong struggle is not only, as Winnicott suggested, to keep inside and outside separate yet interrelateded. Our ceaseless challenge is also to keep *inside* and *inside* separate yet interrelated. We are all individual, yet always bridging to a relational context. This duality implies a binary model of psychic reality versus external reality. And we are all individual, yet always bridging a *divided interior*. Here, a binary model cannot apply. Psychic reality is not a singular island of subjectivity set off from the mainland of objective reality. Rather, psychic reality exists as the bridging of separate islands of subjective experience, an infinite latticework of causeways that span the islands of affect, memory, desire, introject, representation, word, metaphor, idea, mood, fantasy, and vision that constitute the multiple components of self-experience. Thus, psychic reality can be viewed as the mind's integrative process, yet not an integration; a bridging process, but not a bridge. And our psychoanalytic model of the mind needs to account for the universal presence of dissociation—or complex, nonlinear organizations—in health as well as in illness. We need a model of the self that is decentered and dimensional; a self that, as Whitman put it, contains multitudes; a *distributed* self. Transitional space lies not only between internal and external realities, but also between multiple—and even contradictory—*internal* realities. Our creative potential lies in the preservation and exploration of transitional spaces between otherwise dissociated elements of the self—in this sense, the creativity of everyday life, or of a psychoanalytic process, does not differ from the creative process of the painter or poet. Wellness lies in the capacity to straddle paradoxes within the self. Creativity lies in the fresh negotiations of paradox within the self as well as between the self and the material and relational outside world. Therapeutic action lies in the cultivation of interior potential space—a bridging of disparate self-experiences—through the negotiation of analytic potential space. As Bromberg (1993) has written, "Health is the ability to stand in the spaces between realities without losing any of them. This is what I believe *self-acceptance* means and what *creativity* is really all about—the capacity to feel like one self while being many" (p. 166).

I am not speaking here of multiple personality disorder when I assert that we are all inherently multiple selves. Pathology reflects the failure to contain, tolerate, or mediate multiplicity—and, thus, the degree of dissociation, fragmentation, or foreclosure of internal potential space. Multiple personality can be seen as the failure to communicate between self-states, the burning of bridges between islands of psychic reality (thus, one person with multiple personality told me that paradox was a nonexistent concept for her). Neurotic defenses, and character defenses in analysis, can be seen as the foreclosure of internal potential space by coercing a solving of paradox within the self; requiring the repudiation of contradictory self-experiences, the eclipsing of inner conflict, and such relational mechanisms as projective identification that seek to preserve the illusion of a nonparadoxical self.

In contrast, the creative process *plays* with the paradoxical nature of a multiple self and its multifaceted relationship to the external world. The creative artist sees, hears, or names the paradoxical welter of experienced living. Indeed, our criteria for recognizing a work of art, in contrast to a work of talented craft, may be in our sensing the rich, unintegrable, and paradoxically self-contradictory density of the artist's subject gathered, selected, and rendered by the artist in a way that allows us—viewer, listener, or reader—to hold together, in a focused manifold, the essence of a paradox preserved in its multiplicity. The poetic metaphor that forecloses paradox is sentimentality; the painting that forecloses paradox is greeting card or tourist art. In the product of a creative process, we find preserved the essential unresolved paradoxes that represent the scale and texture of life, yet negotiated by the artist's handling of the elements in a way that provides a sense of combined focus and completeness—the world registered subjectively: received, respected, destroyed, and created.

The psychoanalytic process, when it is creative, is also located in that area of play shared between analyst and analysand. Within this potential space between two participating subjectivities, analyst and patient negotiate a mutually meaningful language, invent metaphors, coauthor a plausible narrative, develop portraits of the analysand's object world, and engage together in the full tonal range of a relational duet. Winnicott (1971) pointed out that, if the analyst is unable to participate in such play, he is unsuited for the work; and that if the patient is unable to play, he must first be helped to become able to play, after which the work of analysis could begin. From this perspective, the analyst's task is to notice, illuminate, and counter the ways in which the patient, recoiling from the pain and anxiety of internal or relational paradox, seeks to foreclose potential space along familiar, repetitive patterns of internal defense and relational coerciveness. Thus, the therapeutic mission is to keep analytic potential space—and thereby, or eventually, the patient's internal potential space—optimally open for ongoing negotiation.

This chapter was written originally as an invited paper for a panel on "Psychic Reality and Creativity" at the 39th International

Psychoanalytical Congress. In that paper, I had hoped to illustrate these ideas with clinical material from the treatment of an artist, focusing on one of his self-portraits and a dream we had used in one session to explore multiple facets of his subjectivity. I had intended to contrast this artist with the autistic savant artist Stephen Wiltshire, as described by Oliver Sacks (1995), and thereby consider the relationship between psychic reality and creativity by this juxtaposition. I felt enthusiastic about this elegant contrast as the basis for my remarks on the central role of interiority, potential space, and the straddling of essential paradoxes in the creative process. I was pleased to have found such a nifty way to ask what psychic space might be required for creativity to occur. But, true to the best laid plans, in the weeks just prior to the brief vacation I would take in which to write my paper in the face of an imminent deadline for distribution among the IPA panelists, my patient began to express anxieties about being thus used in a paper. I decided, in the face of his anxiety, to not complicate the treatment in this way and confidently declared that I would write this paper with alternative material. My patient expressed relief.

I, however, was not so relieved. Suddenly without the clinical material vital to the very structure of my paper as it had already crystalized in my mind, I panicked. That night, I had three dreams:

In the first dream, I am sitting with someone at a picnic table. Eating a granola bar, I am mostly feeding it to the birds. Suddenly I am aware that granola bars are now being made with less nutritional material and that people are inadvertently starving the birds because of feeding them the same *amount* of granola bars by volume, but containing less nutritional value. I crumble the rest of my granola bar on the grass so birds may come and have more, but now I feel worried.

In my second dream, my wife, Barbara, and I are checking out of a fancy hotel after a conference. I have allowed ample time to drive to the airport for our flight home. With the sense that everything is in hand, I ask the doorman to get us a cab. This confidence crumbles as time elapses and no taxi comes. I start to worry, and ask the doorman to keep trying. A taxi comes, to my relief, and lets people out at the hotel. I run to ask if he has come for "Pizer," but the driver is leaving his cab and says "No." He is through working. Now I am quite upset. There is barely enough time left to make the plane. We need a taxi immediately. I shout for the hotel's "top manager" and tell him, "Your doorman hasn't yet gotten us a taxi, and we're late for an international flight!" The manager, after several attempts on a portable phone, finally reaches a taxi company. The taxi dispatcher needs information from our tickets, which my wife has in her purse. She is now in a building opposite the hotel driveway. I run there. It is a library reading room, and I cannot see her in the crowd and clutter. I call her name: "Barbara!" Several women stand up. I realize that all women there named Barbara have stood up. As they crowd forward, I see my wife among them. Embarrassed, I call out, "I'm sorry, but we're late for a plane and I had to locate her." I wake up feeling very upset and angry with the hotel, the taxi driver, and also Barbara for delaying us. My first waking thoughts are: I've lost time; I'll never get my paper done; time is running out, and nothing is working. My immediate association to the library building is the hospital annex building where I had accompanied my wife during the preceding six months for her chemotherapy for breast cancer.

I go back to sleep and have my third dream. In this dream, someone else and I stand looking at a huge, house-size bird cage. The interior of the birdhouse is multicompartmented, with several levels and an irregular pattern of separate chambers. In the top left chamber, a man is sitting like a reader in a reading room. Next to him in this chamber of the birdhouse is a small bird cage with a small young bird inside. I recognize that the man is preoccupied with his reading and even seems asleep over it. The little bird is being neglected in its cage and is not fed. I exchange with my companion the worry that this bird will come to harm, left forgotten and undernourished. Then we notice an adult bird arrive and, like a concerned mother bird, alight at the top of the large birdhouse and perch there waiting and worrying. This bird then extends its legs and stamps on the roof bars of the birdhouse to summon the attention of the man inside. But he doesn't notice. We share a sense of concern and feel this mother bird's distress. Then, with a revelatory feeling, I tell my companion, "Watch now what the bird is going to do!" With a sense of anticipation and then wonder, we watch as the bird flies up and then does a remarkable parabolic flight, instinctively and perfectly executed with miraculous acrobatic ability. The mother bird flies up from the roof and circles back down and around the cage, entering a small port hole at the back, then proceeds in a sure and uninterrupted flight straight through another hole in the bars of an interior separator wall, then up through a hole in the flooring of the next chamber and across and up and back and through more holes—never touching the metal bars of the cage—and finally up through the floor of the chamber with the man still reading. Circling around the small cage, the mother bird enters it to save the young bird inside. I feel amazed and relieved that the little bird will now be safe. I awake with this thought: my dream is my mind's reassurance that I *will* somehow find a way to write this paper.

Over breakfast I tell my three dreams to Barbara, who is also an analyst. She says, "It's clear what the dreams are about." I say, "I'm afraid I won't get my paper done in time." She says, "What kind of flight is it, an International flight?" "The *International*, of course!" I reply. I then express intense worry about writing this paper. I admit that I tend to feel anxiety before any new paper crystalizes in my mind. But, this time I feel less prepared. My mind has not been free lately for intellectual work. I do not have the months I usually take to read, sift, and take copious notes; and I feel thrown by losing, at the last minute, the elegant focus of my artist patient and the artist savant. Here is the dialogue that follows between Barbara and me:

Barbara: You have to stop reading and just start writing.
Stuart: I can't do that.
Barbara: You *can* do it.
Stuart: I can't! No way!
Barbara: Your dream tells you that you can.
Stuart: My dream tells me that I'm running out of time. I'm late for the International! And the birds are underfed! [I begin to notice that I am speaking from only one island of feeling within myself, but I remain entrenched in my despair.]
Barbara: What does the *bird* tell you?
Stuart: Oh. I see that I'm reassuring myself that I will manage a last minute rescue.
Barbara: Yes. What poem do you know with a bird?
Stuart: My first thought is Yeats's "The Second Coming":

Turning and Turning in the widening gyre
The falcon cannot hear the falconer;
Things fall apart; the center cannot hold

[I associate to my loss of a paper focus—it's all falling apart.]

Barbara: OK, that's one bird poem. What else?

Stuart: I think of "The Raven," "Ode to a Nightingale," "To a Skylark." [I realize I'm moving from the grim to the defensively intellectualized.]

Barbara: What's the poem with the father and daughter, and a bird, that we like?

Stuart: [with the feeling of a lightbulb going on] Oh! "The Writer" by Richard Wilbur! Oh, that's the one with the bird that's trapped in the room and they watch as it struggles, until finally it finds its way out the window, "clearing the sill of the world."

Barbara: Yes, "The Writer."

Stuart: So, the bird is the writer's inspiration, struggling to get out, to be released.

Barbara: Isn't that what's in the poem?

Stuart: Yes! So the bird is the Muse, inspiration, or the phrase I used in my last paper: "the wings of words." The flight of the bird is the very opposite of "things fall apart." This bird interweaves the interior chambers by the path of its flight—like the separate islands of the self—multiplicity and paradox being spanned, as I'm writing about! Like the separate chambers in the mind and self of Donald [the patient I've written about], and analysis as a "chamber" work, or duet. And multiplicity—paradox—is being joined, not by a solid and constant bridge, but by the flight of the bird in motion; a process. It's a connector—my central ideas about bridging paradox!

Barbara: This is a better case to use in your paper: your own self! [Suddenly I think of Kekule's dream of the snake swallowing its tail, which informed him that the structure of benzene was a ring; and again I picture the serpentine flight of my dream's bird.]

Note how, over breakfast coffee, my wife functioned as analyst in a creative duet. First, just by *being there*, her presence defined a potential space framed by our relational space, affording me the experience of a context, a holding environment for my muddle. Then there were her several specific acts of holding the moment and the process together with me. She asked questions—about the "International flight," the "bird poem"—that, like any good interpretation, focused and deepened my associations. She has learned how to speak to my defensive acts of foreclosure and to sustain a duet with the moods of my several self-states. She carried within her own working psychic space the history of my significant images and metaphors and even cherished poems, thus bringing into play between us juxtapositions that my own mind could use; she shared a potential space, associating along with me in a verbal "squiggle game," but organizing her associations around what she has come to know about *my* psychic reality, keeping a psychic space optimally open as she offered me pieces of approximate meaning to pick up for my own potential use. Barbara was helping me to bridge from one internal chamber to another, to span my own internal multiple and paradoxical positions as a writer, to release my bird from its confinement.

A final question: Was Barbara *right* about the Richard Wilbur poem? Who knows?! Was hers a correct interpretation, correcting my skewed psychic reality? Or was it an offering from the participation of a separate yet connected psychic reality; a timely element that could be played with in the dialogue of a shared potential space, evoking from my own interior something of my imperiled creative potential? As in any good psychoanalytic dialogue, psychic reality may not be uncovered, revealed, exposed, illuminated, or corrected, so much as it is created through an intersubjective negotiation.

"The Writer" by Richard Wilbur

In her room at the prow of the house
Where light breaks, and the windows are tossed with linden,
My daughter is writing a story.

I pause in the stairwell, hearing
From her shut door a commotion of typewriter-keys
Like a chain hauled over a gunwale.

Young as she is, the stuff
Of her life is a great cargo, and some of it heavy:
I wish her a lucky passage.

But now it is she who pauses,
As if to reflect my thought and its easy figure.
A stillness greatens, in which

The whole house seems to be thinking,
And then she is at it again with a bunched clamor
Of strokes, and again is silent.

I remember the dazed starling
Which was trapped in that very room, two years ago;
How we stole in, lifted a sash

And retreated, not to affright it;
And how for a helpless hour, through the crack of the door,
We watched the sleek, wild, dark

And iridescent creature
Batter against the brilliance, drop like a glove
To the hard floor, or the desk-top,

And then, humped and bloody,
For the wits to try it again; and how our spirits
Rose when, suddenly sure,

It lifted off from a chair-back,
Beating a smooth course for the right window
And clearing the sill of the world.

It is always a matter, my darling,
Of life or death, as I had forgotten. I wish
What I wished you before, but harder.

4

The Capacity to Tolerate Paradox
Bridging Multiplicity Within the Self

Minutes before her scheduled appointment with me, Joyce telephoned my answering service to say she could not come because the babysitter for her three-year-old daughter never showed up. Joyce had been in twice weekly therapy for four years. A European émigré in her early 30s, the only surviving child of a depressed and narcissistically self-absorbed mother, she had been working determinedly to extricate herself from her mother's psychologically abandoning, controlling, and emotionally demanding orbit of influence. But Joyce did not want to abandon her mother altogether. Across great geographic (and empathic) distance, Joyce had dedicated herself to negotiating a mutually viable relationship with her mother that would maintain their active kinship; and she had used her treatment to buttress her own ability to receive her mother's "poison messages" without succumbing yet again to despair and depressive collapse. In the course of our work together, Joyce had established a positive and trusting relationship with me and was able to link her recurrent feelings of hopelessness to the pervasive affective tone of her lonely childhood. She had brought us vividly back to those interminable afternoons at home, her mother in the next room not to be disturbed at her desk, and her father, out of economic necessity and marital alienation, spending long hours at work. We sat together as Joyce remembered her young self sitting alone on the floor of the vestibule surrounded by the disarray of objects she had pulled out of drawers. She'd recalled the night she had been spanked for going to her parents' bedroom seeking comfort after waking from a nightmare (in which she had found her mother all in pieces). Thus using her therapy to help moderate her desperate, suicidal sinking spells, Joyce had been able to make affirmative life choices to improve her work situation, to marry, and to become a mother.

On this particular day, when I received Joyce's message that she would have to miss her session, I phoned her to check in. Joyce answered the phone with a tense voice. She was distraught. She said she felt angry at her thwarted session, trapped by her daughter's dependence on her; and she took all of this as a sign of the impossibility of her life. Hoping that we might find a way to help Joyce transition out of her tumbling mood, I asked her if she would like to have her meeting now, over the phone. She questioned how she could do this with her daughter present, so insistent and interruptive, and requiring her attention. I suggested we give it a try.

As we proceeded to talk, it became clear indeed that Joyce's wonderfully assertive three-year-old was indifferent to the therapeutic frame. As Joyce repeatedly broke off from her dialogue with me to address her daughter, she would report to me, "Now she's got my lipstick and wants to draw on our faces," or "Now she's found the chocolates and is taking them all out of the box—No, Emily! You can have only one now!" Joyce paused to gather crayons and paper for Emily, and we were allowed a few minutes of conversation, until Emily came to sit on Joyce's lap. "See," exclaimed Joyce, "this is hopeless." But then, taking a breath, she asked me to hold on while she selected a videotape to play for Emily. I heard Joyce as she started the video and invited her daughter to sit next to Mommy on the couch. "Maybe this will work," said Joyce, "it's one of her favorites."

Now, with jingles and laughter in the background, Joyce attempted to pursue her therapy session with her arm around

Emily. "This seems to be okay for now," said Joyce. "But I don't know what we can do. I don't know. I don't see how we're ever gonna fix me. What can we do? I'm never gonna be okay!" I said to Joyce, "I'm not sure what we may yet do. But I picture something that you need, and I don't know how you might find it. You need something like what you just did for Emily, helping her with her own state of need and disarray. You found a way to include her and managed to settle her and provide for both of you at the same time. Picturing you at Emily's age, it seems to me like that's just what you were missing, and it's what you're missing even now: someone to just be with you when you're in a mood, so you can make your way to a new feeling." Joyce was silent. I added, "And, I think you're right; we don't yet know when or how you may find something like that for you, or within you." With that, Joyce reported feeling better. For this day, this moment, we had managed to negotiate for Joyce a bridge that conducted her from the island of despair to the island of hope.

THE TOLERANCE OF PARADOX

Now, picture this everyday occurrence: toddler practices exultant new feat of walking to mother while mother's face, arms, and voice open wide in welcome; then toddler tumbles along the way and looks up at mother with face all scrambled at the brink of outcry; and mother executes an adroit parabola of affect, beginning with a subtly furrowed brow and a crooning "oooh" that meets the child's disconcertedness like a gentle wave and sweeps on into a renewal of openfaced singsong: "Baby go BUMP!" Baby's incipient wail yields, perhaps through a pout and a moment of quizzical hesitation, to the resolution of a startled reaction, and the wave sets him down with a watery smile. The mother, as "transformational object," is not only a mirror; she is, as Bollas (1995) vividly illustrates, a humorer! Mother deftly transports her child to "the other side," domesticates the vertiginous "far side" into a familiar space within their shared orbit of mastery, and—importantly—sponsors feelings of pleasure, delight, or joy in these moments of bridging between worlds (e.g., the "exultant walk world" and the "tumble to earth world"). She certainly meets her child at the affective moment, but she does not take the plunge with him—or, if she does, it becomes an enchanting pratfall that clinches the shift from a startle state, through self-righting, to a potential restoration of play.

This caregiver function of affect regulation (or "ego coverage" in Winnicott's term), in its agency of organizing the intensity, totality, timing, flow, and concertedness of affect, would be aptly described by another metaphor to replace mother as "mirror": the mother as *conductor*, or *transitional mirror*. As a conductor, the good-enough mother is not an embodiment of the Toscanini school, a martinet whose baton can marvelously compel all players to comply their way into a disciplined unison and produce a performance gem. Mother-the-conductor does not coerce, or coax, a false-self yielding, or shielding, of an authentic state in her child. Rather, she engages a subtle and delicate negotiation of affect and intention, allowing her child the time and space to hesitate, to subjectivize, and potentially to own her transformational gesture; and she and her child both find their way to tolerating those moments in which a negotiated harmony or transition is beyond their mutual reach. The conducting, or bridging, function of the caregiver is a version of mirroring that meets the child's affect, mood, or intensity state and sponsors a transition along toward intensification, relaxation, resolution, or shifting of state. Thus, the mirroring must be both empathic (attuned) and inexact (different). Transitional mirroring is a negotiation of state regulation. Mother-the-conductor is serving as a transitional mirror.

So, mother, or other caregiver,[1] helps us to tolerate surprise and startle, helps us to bear sudden state shifts, helps us to manage transitions of state and affect, helps us to accept discrepancies, to feel that what may be beyond our comprehension or our competence may still be OK to live with. I mean to suggest by this metaphor the ordinary, everyday experiential basis for each child's developmental attainment of an affective tolerance for disjunctive, discrepant—paradoxical—juxtapositions of state. The key to feeling OK amidst the disconcerting multitude of internal and relational states is to be found in lived moments of affective exchange that constitutes, and establishes in the mind, *an experience of bridging*. By means of such negotiations of state and state transitions, sponsored in the parent–child relational dialogue, each

---

[1] This exposition is not intended to exclude fathers, or grandfathers, for that matter.

person develops the competence to bridge a multiplicity of contradictory and paradoxical experiences of self and self-with-other
and to contain them within.

Is the negotiation of paradox—in the process of living, creating
a work of art, or a psychoanalysis—qualitatively different from
other kinds of negotiation, such as the negotiation of (intrapsychic
or interpersonal) conflict? Emphatically, yes. Is this difference a
matter of importance? Indeed, yes.

Here I will elaborate on the particularly compelling nature of
paradox and attempt to discriminate what sets paradox apart from
conflict. I will explore, in particular, how the tolerance of paradox
becomes a developmental achievement that provides for the ability to straddle the multiplicity of private and relational experiences
while preserving a sense of personal integrity over time. I consider
the specific contributions of the caregiver toward the infant's mastery of paradoxical experience and the establishment of the affect
accompanying the acceptance of paradox: the feeling that the existence of the impossible is OK, even as it strains the accommodating embrace of mind.

Negotiation of paradox and negotiation of conflict can be dis-
criminated as subjective experiences. Conflict connotes dichotomous (or "trichotomous," and so on) interests or tugs between
people or groups; or, in individuals, between divergent tendencies
within a bounded nucleus of the self. On the other hand, paradox
resides in the multiplicity of bounded nuclei within the self, where
simultaneously coexisting nuclei (self-states, affects, self–other
representations, and so on) reciprocally contradict or negate each
other. Conflict can be resolved through interpersonal negotiation
or mediation (you give a little and I give a little, or we are both
helped or required to make concessions, and we arrive somewhere
we can both live with or even codify by contract or treaty).
Intrapsychic conflict may be resolved through choice (I'll accept
this college) or renunciation (I'll let Dad keep Mom) or repression
("and never was heard a discouraging word"). On the other hand,
paradox cannot be resolved (Winnicott, 1971c); mutually negating elements continue to coexist, and the negotiation of paradox
yields not resolution but a straddling, or bridging, of contradictory
perspectives. At this point a metaphor may help to illustrate the
contrast between conflict and paradox.

Imagine you are watching on a television channel an old rerun of Jimmy Durante at the piano. Head cocked, proboscis at a tilt, and gesturing with his squashable hat rapidly placed on head, on piano, on head again, he sings: "Have you ever had the feeling that you wanted to stay, and then you had the feeling that you wanted to go? You started to go; decided to stay. Started again to go, and decided again to stay. Have you ever had the feeling that you wanted to go. . . ." Here is ambivalence par excellence; you want it both ways—a true tug-of-war conflict unto comic obsessionality. Now go channel surfing. You switch your television to a channel showing a soap opera: a woman sitting over lunch with her confidante wonders if she should tell her husband about her affair. She fears his retaliation, or loss. She doesn't want to hurt him, or the kids. She needs passion, but she needs security. How long can she bear the guilt, the secrecy? Change channels. On the news a correspondent questions the chances that the Bosnian Serbs and Muslims will finally accept a UN-mediated ceasefire. Change channels again. Now, on a sitcom the mother wants her children to go to bed so she and her husband can finally cuddle, but the kids want to stay up and use the grownups for rambunctious sport. Mother offers a deal: if the kids brush their teeth and clean their rooms, they can return for 15 minutes of story time. On each channel we have something familiar: conflict. There is divergence, parent –offspring clash of interests, someone wanting it all and postponing renunciation or grief, paroxysms of guilt, and the divisions of tribal ethnocentricity. Some conflicts are resolved easily enough; a deal is made. Some conflicts are resolved with painful consequences. Some may never be resolved, and decades of blood feud, squandered energy, and heavy casualties may drag on. But, however complicated or delicate the negotiation may be, however strained the mediation, none of the conflicts strains our logic—our patience maybe, our stomachs, or our hope; but not our logic. On each channel, our minds can hold the conflict, shift from side to side, contain centrifugal vectors of intention and feeling, and apply linear laws of logic ("If this, then. . . ;" "Either this, or . . . ").

Now, instead of watching one of these television channels, imagine that you *are* the television set and you contain all the channels. Now we approach the multiplicity of self-states, each with state-dependent memory, affect, intention, perception, bodily adjustments, judgment, fantasy, and conflict. Now let's carry the metaphor a step further. Imagine you are in a large electronics store buying a television set, and every model is there on display, each one showing a different channel. And they are all you. Now we approach the experience of *paradoxical* multiplicity. How do you watch all these screens, follow their separate internal continuities, and hold the moment together? How can you find yourself on all these channels at once and retain an undemolished sense of being personally centered, with a unitary consciousness? We are doing just this all the time. Only the most dissociated personalities among us are strangers in paradox.

Turning from metaphor to logic, we can understand the compelling power of paradox by virtue of its violation of the law of the excluded middle—that a proposition cannot be both true and false at the same time (Paul Russell, personal communication). As Sainsbury (1988) writes, paradoxes "immediately provoke one into trying to 'solve' them." And, indeed, philosophers and logicians, as well as jokesters, have devised solvable paradoxes along with unsolvable paradoxes. Life hands us the unsolvable paradoxes. According to Sainsbury, paradoxes are "fun" and they are "serious." He classifies paradoxes on a continuum from "weak or shallow" to "cataclysmic" and offers his own definition of paradox: "an apparently unacceptable conclusion derived by apparently acceptable reasoning from apparently acceptable premises" (p. 1). He then argues: "Appearances have to deceive, since the acceptable cannot lead by acceptable steps to the unacceptable. So, generally, we have a choice: Either the conclusion is not really unacceptable, or else the starting point, or the reasoning, has some nonobvious flaw" (p. 1).

Sainsbury's argument honors the constraints of logic, the domains of philosophy and mathematics. But, in psychoanalysis, when Winnicott writes of the essential acceptance of paradox, he is not arguing a matter of logic but a matter of subjectivity, intersubjectivity, noninvasive human relating, transitional phenomena, and affect. A paradox that is logically unacceptable may *seem* acceptable to us while remaining cognitively unsolved. As Tagore[2] observed, a mind all logic is like a knife all blade; it cuts the hand that uses it. I will consider how a person attains, in the course of development, a tolerance for paradox, a feeling that paradox is OK even as it violates the accustomed laws of sequential thought; but,

---

[2] I am grateful to Lane Conn for this reference to Tagore.

first, I want to convey more of the magnitude of tantalizing challenge issued to the mind by paradox.

A few examples: One of the hardest paradoxes, though deceptively easy to state, is the Liar Paradox: You are asked to consider the man who asserts, "What I am now saying is false." Is what he says true or false? If it is true, it is false; if it is false, it is true—and then it is false. According to Sainsbury (1988), this paradox was the nemesis of many ancient logicians and is even alleged to have caused the premature death of Philetas of Cos. One more classic paradox brings us closer to the flavor of a relational dilemma. Sainsbury refers to it as "The Gallows," and renders it thus: "The law of a certain land is that all who wish to enter the city are asked to state their business there. Those who reply truly are allowed to enter and depart in peace. Those who reply falsely are hanged. What should happen to the traveler who, when asked his business, replies, 'I have come to be hanged'?" (p. 145).

How do we respond upon encountering such a paradox? Immediately we feel intrigued, beguiled, disturbed, and incited to reconcile the conundrum. The mind is magnetically attracted to struggle in the space described by such categorical disparities. Chaos theory tells us that paradox is "a fundamentally chaotic process" (Abraham, 1995, p. 165) that generates a centripetal "attractor" in truth space. How do we handle this unsettling attraction? In the case of the Liar Paradox, we feel our minds straining, generating great heat while shedding no further light; we feel incipient mental meltdown. We become vexed, perhaps enraged; or we find ourselves suddenly very tired—somnolent detachment (Sullivan, 1953). We may dissociate if we don't repudiate this *instigus*. The Liar Paradox may have been truly traumatic for Philetas of Cos. We live more easily with the Gallows paradox. It lies further from the cataclysmic end of Sainsbury's scale. We may even enjoy rolling it around in our minds (perhaps the atmosphere of mythic and geographic distance helps). We sense that we can carry the Gallows paradox around with us, leave it unresolved, perhaps save it for a revisit later. We can play with it, use its challenge for mental exercise—a scratching post for the kitten claws of thought. We may propose, following Sainsbury, that the starting point has "some nonobvious flaw": perhaps it matters that the paradox omits to specify that "all" who reply truly are allowed to enter and depart in peace; or perhaps *not only* those who reply falsely are hanged; or possibly this traveler is a jester who understands the play of paradox, and his timing and delivery "crack up" the city's authorities (maybe then the presumed conclusion is flawed, and this traveler does not "enter and depart in peace" but, rather, is invited to remain there in peace as Secretary of Pranks). Bollas (1995) describes how the comic helps us to delight in chaos, have fun with the disconcerting, find pleasure in violations of the order of nature (or of thought!), and transform the tragic to the amusing. Paradox and humor are kindred in structure: novel, surprising, or startling juxtapositions (of word, image, gesture, causal sequence, meaning, context, relationship, state, affect, etc.) disquiet us and relieve us simultaneously. We face the alien, the preposterous, or the impossible, and it feels familiar. We are startled but tickled; we are played with but we are still playing. We are taken over ("He got the best of me") but in "getting it" we sustain our feeling of mastery. We laugh. Paradox provokes. Humor transports. We feel OK. Winnicott (1971b) told us that play is always precarious, always at the edge of overexcitation; "cracking up" is one thing, but "flying into pieces" is quite another. Bollas's (1995) mother-the-clown is also his mother-the-transformational-object, skillful in her delivery (introducing "the world in small doses"), and intuitively on the mark in timing and spacing (empathic conjunction, affective attunement, and intersubjective tactfulness) like the good-enough stand-up comic. Here again is our metaphor of mother-the-conductor.

Now let's further examine the paradoxes of everyday life in the matrix of familiar object relationships, wherein the multitude of self-experiences, and the spaces between them, are being registered, distributed and, with varying success, bridged. What about the following paradox?

Mother is the person I run to when someone hurts my feelings. Mother is the person who hurt my feelings.

I believe that no developing child escapes experiences of such paradoxical relational truths. Each good-enough mother of the average-expectable family environment will present each child with her array of self-states, ranging in relative attunement, complementarity, harmony, or dissonance. The parent–offspring conflict paradigm in modern evolutionary biology (Slavin and

Kriegman, 1992) predicts the inevitability of multiple vectors in every parent–child relationship. And then there is always the inadvertent or the circumstantial cause of disjunctive relational experience (that is, accidents and setbacks will befall even the best of parents). Each child, barring extremes of interaction, learns to straddle the multiplicity of mutually negating experiences of self-with-other. Perhaps the child senses that mother's state changes when she registers her child's hurt feelings and her tenderness reemerges. Perhaps the child tacitly recognizes that mother did not seek sadistically to hurt his or her feelings. Perhaps eventually there is a poignant reunion in sharing a soothing moment after an emotional storm (the foundation for refinding later in life all object experiences of "kiss and make up"). On the other hand, quite possibly the discordant representations of mother as soother of hurt feelings and mother as provoker of hurt feelings have begun to distribute in the child's mind into a Fairbairnian (1944) endopsychic structure: the frustrating mother, the overexciting and rejecting mother, or the mother of attachment aligned with the central ego. While developing the capacity to tolerate paradox in vital human relationships, the child is handling such discrepant self-object moments (RIGS in Stern's, 1985, theory) by storing them under different "affect categories" (Edelman, 1992) in the mind; and the multiple and contradictory quality of self- and object representations, the distribution of segregated aggregates, or islands, of self-experiences clustering around memories of affect, state, percepts, fantasies, somatic intensities, and intentions, has been laid down for life. As Mitchell (1993) has written:

> Earlier developmental theorizing portrayed the infant as swamped by multiple, discontinuous images of the mother, forming a consistent sense of "object permanence" only slowly over time. Some more contemporary authors suggest that the infant is capable of perceiving both self-invariance and invariance in others from the earliest months (Daniel Stern, 1985). Yet both young children and adults have difficulty throughout life reconciling different experiences of others, different "sides" of caregivers and other significant others. Not necessarily on a cognitive or perceptual level, but rather on a deeper emotional level, children have very different and often discontinuous images of those closest to them: angry father, gentle father, excited father, and so on. In one sense, these are all the same father; in another sense, these are quite different fathers, and will always

remain so. From the earliest interactions between infant and care-giver to the complex relationships between adults, experiences of others, like experiences of self, operate in a perpetual dialectic between multiplicity and integrity, change and continuity [pp. 116–117].

If multiplicity of relational experience is the rule and not the exception, and the unitary self-in-relation is a necessary illusion, how does the child become able to straddle this multiplicity of intimate object relationships and internal object representations? If the infant is capable, early on, of "perceiving both self-invariance and invariance in others," how is the mind's inherent faculty for negotiation of paradox cultivated in development? We have considered the caregiver as transformational object, mirror, or conductor. But we need to look more closely at how the polyphony of affect and the cacaphony of parental voices are orchestrated within the musicality of the child's mind. And we must focus more closely on the consequences for self-experience when "the shadow of the object" that falls upon the ego is more accurately a shadow show of shifting silhouettes, leaving lasting traces of discrepant shades of meaning and affect that cluster around separate islands within each person's internal universe. When we tolerate the "mother hurts my feelings" paradox, we exercise the self's competence at bridging from the island of "mother soothes" to the island of "mother hurts," while maintaining the feeling of unruptured unity of self and relationship. Most such paradoxical gaps between self-object relational nuclei are bridgeable. But, just before considering further models for understanding the capacity to tolerate paradox, and the paradoxically multiple-yet-bridgeable structure of the self, I want to introduce a different level of paradox (closer to the cataclysmic end of Sainsbury's spectrum), one that overwhelms the mind's capacity to bridge. We could name this the paradox of "Father's Lap," one version of which would be, "Father's comfy, protective lap presents an erect penis."

Paradoxes of this severity may not be tolerated within the mind. The effort to bridge intolerable paradox places a demand on the mind to work on overload. Indeed, we shall see how the child's mind, defending against psychic meltdown, resorts to dissociative defenses that are tantamount to the death of the self as constituted up until that traumatic moment. (I do not mean to suggest that intolerable paradox is exclusively a function of the severity of environmental, or relational, contradictions. The strain entailed in an internal multiplicity of intentions, desires, needs, identifications, purposes, and self-states may render an "identity diffusion" [Erikson, 1968], a difficulty bridging inherent multiplicity *within the self*.)

Again we reflect on the universal structure of the human psyche: a virtually infinite multiplicity of nuclei, or islands, of self-state gathering, and variously organizing, elements of percept, memory, personifications, fantasies, physiological adjustments, mood, metaphor, and lexicon clustered around intentions, impingements, and affects that arise during relational experiences that inherently pull for distribution into such mental categorizations (see Edelman, 1987; Mitchell, 1993; Modell, 1993; Bromberg, 1994; Bollas, 1995). These islands each contain conflict consistent with Freud's (1923) structural model of the mind as well as levels of consciousness consistent with his (1915b) topographical metaphor. But the primordial structure of the mind is constituted of multitudinous islands, and an "aerial map" of each person's mind would indicate these islands and the bridges between them. Some of the bridges connect closely allied islands, and their solid, multilane construction allows a steady commute in both directions. Other bridges are paradoxical, with their stanchions on either end rising from islands that mutually negate the reality of the other; and yet the capacity to negotiate paradox permits the self to tolerate this straddling and sustain constructive or creative commerce along the span. One can set out from the island of "mother hurts feelings" toward the island of "mother soothes feelings," and, despite the warnings of some inhabitants that from the perspective of this island the other one could not exist, the bridge is crossed with trust that it will hold and extend to a tenable location—and so the paradoxes of everyday life are tolerated with an OK feeling.[3]

Then there are those islands—more rare and, fortunately, showing up on fewer maps—that have no bridge between them.

---

[3] I believe Loewald (1960, 1980) was advancing a similar model of the healthy psyche, while hewing to the metaphorical framework of Freud's (1915b) topographical model, when he described the person's to-and-fro commute between regressive and progressive poles of ego organization: between the structurally simple and the structurally complex; the primitive and the mature; the passionate and the articulate; primary process and secondary process.

Like the two islands of the "Father's Lap" paradox, all bridges have been destroyed and commerce is forbidden, a proscription strictly enforced by vigilant dissociation. An aerial view may show stanchions and incomplete ramps left suddenly abandoned during construction, with the skeletons of some workers crushed by collapsing structure and buried forever under debris. An occasional catamaran from one island strays inadvertently near the other island, senses the pull of a cataclysmic "black hole" and flees. Bromberg (1994) aptly describes this intrapsychic state of affairs:

> Where drastically incompatible emotions or perceptions are required to be cognitively processed within the same relationship and such processing is adaptationally beyond the capacity of the individual to contain this disjunction within a unitary self-experience, one of the competing algorithms is hypnoidally denied access to consciousness to preserve sanity and survival. When ordinary adaptational adjustment to the task at hand is not possible, dissociation comes into play. The experience that is causing the incompatible perception and emotion is "unhooked" from the cognitive processing system and remains raw data that is cognitively unsymbolized within that particular self-other representation, except as a survival reaction [p. 520].

Here, in Bromberg's explication, we see the extreme case of severely discrepant relational experience not only violating the usual laws of thought, but violating the mind's capacity to tolerate and bridge a range of paradox, forcing recourse to a dissociative damage control that leaves islands of relational experience epistemically expunged from each other's register. Elsewhere, Bromberg (1995), presenting the implications of such defensive dissociation for the analytic process, quotes Laub and Auerhahn's statement that "trauma overwhelms and defeats our capacity to organize it." Bromberg asserts that

> it is the more primary nature of trauma to "elude" our knowledge because of what they [Laub and Auerhahn] call a deficit—a gap that has to do with the formation of psychic structure into "me" and "not me"—a dissociative gap, by virtue of which the experience of original trauma is relegated to a part of the self that is unlinked to that part of the self preserved as a relatively intact "me." It is not the "contents" of the mind that are primarily at issue; *it is the dissociative structure of the mind itself ("me" and "not me") that resistance*

is most fundamentally addressing, at least during much of the
ongoing treatment [p. 183].

Yet elsewhere, Bromberg (1994) maintains, "Dissociation is not
inherently pathological, but it can become so. The process of dissociation is basic to human mental functioning and is central to
the stability and growth of personality. It is intrinsically an adaptational talent that represents the very nature of what we call 'consciousness'" (p. 520). I wish to emphasize here the distinction
between dissociation as an "adaptational talent" and dissociation
as a defensive recourse, and the implications for the origins of
mental structure in development. I also wish to emphasize a distinction between the *distributed* self and the *dissociated* self.

I believe that the more universal nature of "consciousness" is
its multiplicity, not necessarily brought about formatively by dissociations. That is, as I understand it, such experiences as "mother
soothes" and "mother hurts" occur originally as disparate events
(or RIGs, schemas, or narratives) that become gathered into relative orchestration only as the developing mind's synthetic capacities establish the bridges between these intrinsically distinct
islands and produce what Bromberg calls the necessary illusion of
being one self. Hence, the more universal nature of consciousness
is its inherent *distribution* into an archipelago of multiple meaning-and-affect centers that come to be more bridgeable than not
as the mind develops in health. I suggest, then, that when traumatic overload forces the mind to deploy a defensive dissociation,
the network of connections that have been formed to span multiple meaning-and-affect centers suffers catastrophic breaches in
communication, the demolition of bridges between the mind's
islands of associated self–object relational representations. It is
under these conditions that the distributed multiplicity of self
yields to a dissociated multiplicity of self. Hence, I would agree
that the "dissociative" process by which consciousness is selectively focused, and attention is adaptively concentrated, reflects
the operation of basic "human mental functioning." I would stress,
however, the distinction between dissociation as a process of selectively focusing attention and dissociation as an organization of
unlinked mental structure persisting over time. Davies and
Frawley (1994) provide this cogent definition of the dissociatively
structured personality:

Dissociation is the process of severing connections between categories of mental events—between events that seem irreconcilably different, between the actual events and their affective and emotional significance, between actual events and the awareness of their cognitive significance, and finally, as in the case of severe trauma, between the actual occurrence of real events and their permanent, symbolic, verbal mental representation. . . . Traditionally, . . . dissociation is defined as a process by which a piece of traumatic experience, because it is too overstimulating to be processed and recorded along the usual channels, is cordoned off and established as a separate psychic state within the personality, creating two (or more) ego states that alternate in consciousness and, under different internal and external circumstances, emerge to think, behave, remember, and feel. Such dissociated states are associatively unavailable to the rest of the personality and, as such, cannot be subject to psychic operations or elaboration [pp. 62–63].

I think Winnicott (1962b), in his uniquely poetic condensation of wisdom, was addressing these very phenomena in terms of the process of "ego-integration" fostered by that devoted "ego-coverage" of the mother which spares her infant the "unthinkable anxieties" of going to pieces, falling forever, depersonalization or derealization. Winnicott wrote:

It can be said that good-enough ego-coverage by the mother (in respect of the unthinkable anxieties) enables the new human person to build up a personality on the pattern of a continuity of going-on-being. All failures (that could produce unthinkable anxiety) bring about a reaction of the infant, and this reaction cuts across the going-on-being. If reacting that is disruptive of going-on-being recurs persistently it sets going a pattern of fragmentation of being. The infant whose pattern is one of fragmentation of the line of continuity of being has a development task that is, almost from the beginning, loaded in the direction of psychopathology [pp. 60–61].

Winnicott then offered a critical distinction between "disintegration" and "unintegration" that, I believe, captures the difference between dissociated and bridgeable multiplicity within the self. He suggested:

The opposite of integration would seem to be disintegration. This is only partly true. The opposite, initially, requires a word like unintegration. Relaxation for an infant means not feeling a need to integrate, the mother's ego-supportive function being taken for granted. The understanding of unexcited states requires further consideration in terms of this theory.

The term disintegration is used to describe a sophisticated *defence*, a defence that is an active production of chaos in defence against unintegration in the absence of maternal ego-support, that is, against the unthinkable or archaic anxiety that results from the failure of holding in the stage of absolute dependence. The chaos of disintegration may be as 'bad' as the unreliability of the environment, but it has the advantage of being produced by the baby and therefore of being non-environmental. It is within the area of the baby's omnipotence [p. 61].

I believe Winnicott's articulation of unintegration and disintegration, even in its Kleinian, object-relational antiquity, presaged more current infant observational reports (e.g., Trevarthen, 1979; Stern, 1985; Beebe and Lachmann, 1992; Beebe, Jaffe, and Lachmann, 1992), and the contemporary literature on the self and on trauma and dissociation. I read in (perhaps into) Winnicott's language the distinction between an "unintegration," in which the natural welter of self-states experienced in a relational holding context are not forced into a conglomerate psychic unity but, rather, are tolerated in their multiplicity, with unresolved paradoxes accepted under the supplemental sponsorship of the caregiver's ego-coverage (transformational object function); and, on the other hand, a "disintegration," which reacts to stimulus overload, object impingement, or cataclysmic-level paradox by a defensive dissociation that seeks to establish internal mastery over external assault. In Winnicott's portrait of the infant basking in the hammock of unintegration, we may also discern the origins of the infant's spontaneous gesture, the creative bridging of internal islands, and negotiations of paradox that extend the individual's stamp of personal agency into interpersonal existence. We can picture the infant, in a quiet-alert state, participating as active agent in mutual regulatory exchanges with mother, negotiating facial squiggles on camera. In contrast, we can picture those children whose only relational recourse is the highly compromised mastery of rupturing connection, whose only prospect for internally authored meaning is an enforced absence of bridging.

Modell (1993), in his exploration of "the private self" as agent of continuous elaborations of personal meaning, offers a contemporary rendition of the infant's quiet-alert state of positive "unintegration" sponsored by resonant maternal mediation:

> It is not unreasonable to suppose that the confirmatory responses that validate the infant's affective states are internalized in healthy development and will contribute to the child's capacity to bring affective experiences within the domain of the self—within the domain of the personal. This synchrony of the affective states of mother and infant is bound to enhance the sense of continuity of the self in the infant, who is constantly experiencing rapid changes in mood and affect states [p. 29].

In such a facilitating environment, the infant finds his or her own way toward gathering and weaving a personal destiny out of these "rapid changes" in the experience of being-in-the-world. Each individual's intrasubjective personalizing of life's "blooming buzzing confusion" (William James, quoted by Myers, 1986) establishes the efficacy (White, 1963) of the "true self" (Winnicott, 1960) to structure, and commute across, bridges that straddle the paradoxical multiplicity of relational experience as memorially stored in the mind's cumulative and epigenetic categories, labeled according to affect, mood, and intention. Thus ensues creative living that keeps "inside and outside separate yet interrelated" (Winnicott, 1971c) according to the self's negotiation between its inherent "idiom," or aesthetic intelligence (Bollas, 1989), and the logic governing parental patterns of being and relating. For Modell, creative living is the prerogative of "the private self" in health and consists of the capacity to reconcile the evanescence of consciousness with the stability of personally encoded memory, yielding a singular authorship of emergent "meaning." As Modell (1993) asserts:

> One of the functions of the self is to reconfigure time, to juxtapose past and present experiences. Thus, according to Freud's theory, the failure to translate memories from successive developmental periods results in psychopathology. I suggest, as well, that such a failure of translation (recategorization) results in a loss of meaning. I view the creation of "meaning," in the broadest sense, to be synonymous with what Winnicott called the "creative apperception of the world that more than anything else makes the individual feel that life is worth living" [p. 161].

Modell's use of the word recategorization links his concept of "meaning" as based in translation (Freud's *Nachträglichkeit*), and

Winnicott's "creative apperception," to Edelman's Neural Darwinism, in which "recategorization" refers to the mind's work of "matching" real-time perceptions with personally coherent memory storage defined in terms of the brain's processes of Neuronal Group Selection. Modell, building on Edelman's model, pioneered the bridge between psychoanalysis and neurobiology. Edelman (1989, 1992) has contributed a theory of self wherein he grounds the human capacity to create meaning in the neurophysiological mechanisms entailed in neuronal group selection (a Darwinian model of preferentially established networks of neuronal pathways).

EDELMAN'S THEORY OF NEURONAL GROUP SELECTION

Edelman's theory recognizes the adaptive advantage enjoyed by creatures that can discriminate self from nonself, coordinate homeostatic and environmental regularities and novelties, and selectively attend to impingements in order to deploy efficacious motor responses. He defines a complex dynamic systems model of neurobiology that he calls "the matter of the mind" and describes the complex reciprocal pathways whereby the genetic, molecular, synaptic, and structural realms, as well as the developmental and experiential, affective and appetitive, intersubjective and socially constructed, conceptual, semantic, and linguistic realms, all converge and interact to produce human mental activity.

According to Edelman, all animals possessing *primary consciousness* can correlate properties of environmental objects, coordinate the perceptual input of an object or event across multiple sensory modes (e.g., visual, auditory, kinesthetic, and so on), and cross-reference these perceptual elements against memories of previous experiences. Hence, an animal capable of primary consciousness can encounter a novel object or action in real time and rapidly juxtapose its perceptual impressions with those cumulative experiences that have been learned and remembered. While not necessarily being conscious of doing so, such an animal has a discriminant sense of being a continuous self differentiated from the immediately encountered environment or event. Thus equipped to mobilize a selective response repertoire, such animals gain in survival fitness through their ability to distinguish internal continuities from external discontinuities. Humans, while also possessing a primary consciousness, have further evolved a *higher order consciousness* capable of complex conceptualization, symbolization, language, and communication. The processes of juxtaposing, matching, or correlating properties of objects or actions can be exercised within a person's mind free of immediate real-time events. Humans, by use of metaphorical matches, and a self-awareness with respect to their internal perceptual and conceptual mappings, can place themselves in past, present, or future and execute complexly orchestrated plans, revisions, or negotiations, according to personally coherent meanings and values.

In Edelman's theory, the existence of a self that can keep inside and outside separate yet interrelated (as Winnicott put it) is predicated on the biologically based mapping of *value* within the individual's dynamically functioning neurophysiological system; and, in humans, is additionally predicated on the more complex coordination of neurophysiological mapping groups that supply symbolic, metaphoric, and linguistic meaning. Edelman describes the brain as a correlating system that builds mental life out of its vast capability for scanning relative matches and mismatches. It is always in our survival interest to match the environmental factors facing us against our own needs, desires, and affects. As Edelman (1992) writes, "The sufficient condition for adaptation is provided by the linkage of global mappings to the activity of the so-called hedonic centers and the limbic system of the brain in a way that satisfies homeostatic, appetitive, and consummatory needs reflecting evolutionarily established values" (p. 100). Thus, *value* is an evolved property of neuronal "hard-wiring" that exerts a bias on perception consonant with individual and species survival[4]; and the adaptive benefit of value is in the selection and guidance of appropriate motor behavior. Value confers on the individual the potential for intentionality and agency—and, indeed, for the very consciousness of selfhood. Value and categorical memory underwrite the continuity of consciousness (Winnicott's going-on-being?) as the individual negotiates the discontinuities and novelties of each perceptual moment. Edelman (1989) summarizes:

---

[4] I am grateful to Arnold Modell for his help in clarifying this point.

Primary consciousness may thus be briefly described as the result of
the ongoing discrimination of present perceptual categorizations by
a value-dominated self-nonself memory. Inasmuch as such a memory
is built by relating previous perceptual categorizations to values, primary consciousness is accomplished by continual bootstrapping of
current perceptual states into memory states. Current perceptual
events are recategorized in terms of past value-category matches. It
is the *contrast* of the special linkage of value and past categories with
currently arriving categories, and the *dominance* of the self-related
special memory systems in this memorial linkage, that generate the
self-referential aspect of consciousness. Multiple parallel inputs from
different modalities are correlated in this fashion, and their salience
is altered mainly from within, depending upon previous value-category matches [p. 102].

Edelman's model could be visualized metaphorically by anyone
who has used the Paris Metro. In each Metro station, a traveler
who needs to select his route to a distant Metro station may con-
sult an electronically powered map and locate on a panel of but-
tons the one corresponding to his destination. When that button
is pressed, the map of the entire Metro system then lights up selectively to indicate just those lines and stations that get you there
from here. This selective lighting up of a pathway linking a new
element to an existing system from an established perspective
approximates for me the neurophysiological substrate of "value-
category matches" in Edelman's theory. How consonant this model
is with Loewald's (1960) representation of "transference" as originally conceived by Freud (1900), whereby latent meaning may
ride piggyback on the fresh manifest element of the day residue
yielding those dream-image condensations that bridge from unconscious to conscious recognition.

A thorough presentation of Edelman's complicated and detailed
Neuronal Group Selection theory is beyond the scope of this chapter. However, one critical element in Edelman's dynamic systems
model of consciousness is germane here: the process of *reentry*.
Edelman's term reentry refers to the large-scale criss-crossing of
multiple neuronal activations along selectively energized linkages
between salient neuronal groups (or local "station" maps). Reentrant signaling conveys raw perceptual features to those neuronal
clusters specific to processing each perceptual property (e.g.,
linear edges, color, movement, and so on) as well as those local

neuronal maps linked to the hedonic centers and the limbic system; and, in higher order consciousness, to global maps of conceptual, symbolic, and linguistic meaning. Edelman's model, without positing the existence of a supervisory homunculus within the mind, thus accounts for the shuttling of synaptic currents in a recursive system of perceptual category and value centers— islands of remembered experience and instinctual or affective charge—aggregated and coordinated through adaptive selection. By myriad reciprocally modifying correlations signaled along reentrant loops, the mind transforms the objects of immediate perception into personally meaningful experiences and simultaneously adds further shades of meaning to its memorial mapping system. Each person develops a unique topographical and functional mapping system whereby the self's perceptual categories, instincts and affects, and socially constructed meanings converge on the moment of present perception. This neural system seems to be capable of a dizzying number of couplings or correlations passed reciprocally across reentrant loops linking localized areas of brain/mind activity. In this sense, the dynamic process of reentry that recategorizes immediate perceptions and renders them meaningful, thereby shaping the basis for responsive behaviors, constitutes in itself a kind of neurobiological *negotiation* among inputs from the environment and from internal value-category clusters. In this negotiation, the impinging environmental event may claim salience (as in looking up from a reverie to notice the curtains on fire), or the internal value, or meaning, may be relatively more predominant (as when a saint accepts death at the stake rather than betray his faith).

Edelman applies his model of reentry to explain neurological and psychological disorders in terms of interrupted reentrant loops. For example, he suggests that blindsight, a condition in which a person has no awareness of vision yet can locate objects in space when tested, is caused by a disruption of reentrant loops necessary for primary consciousness regarding visual input. Similarly, Edelman considers schizophrenia "a generalized disease of reentry," in which communications between reentrant maps may be disabled in areas responsible for synchrony between maps, coordination between perceptual modalities, assignment of predominance to image versus percept, or in linkages between conceptual or semantic centers. We might then conjecture that Edelman's model of pathology as breached reentrant loops provides a distinct neurological basis for the more metaphorical notion of the demolition of bridges between islands of inner experience—dissociation in the mind must correspond to a neurophysiological event. We may also conjecture that the human affect tolerance for paradoxical experience confers an evolutionarily adaptive advantage, sustaining a continuity of self amidst contradictory, or mutually negating, mappings of concept, affect, and meaning; and, thus, that higher order consciousness has evolved a capacity to handle paradox, up to a point, during the negotiated reentrant signaling of disjunctive value-category matches.

Circling back to Modell's (1993) linking of recategorization and *Nachträglichkeit*, we recognize the universal occurrence of transference intrinsic to value-category matches correlated with each perceptual act. And, in the dynamic systems adjustments attendant on each reentrant process, we can see how novelty (the new analytic object) can slowly, over time, accrete modifications in the mind's preferential memorial mappings (representations of old objects): in essence, the working through of transference. Might not the analytic dialogue itself build bridges by way of the fresh accentuation of critical reentrant loops? As Modell writes, "the memory structures that generate the sense of self must be continually updated" (p. 163).

I am struck here by the remarkable resonance with Sullivan's (1953) conception of the "self-system," created without the benefit of contemporary developments in neuroscience, with its survival-ensuring gradient map of the anxiety potential in relational experience and its critical personifications and crucial dissociations. As Sullivan wrote, "the person has the sign." And, as he observed, the self-system is modified by each new experience, which, in turn, has been shaped through the patterns of the self-system. Although Sullivan's theory is more interpersonally accented, emphasizing linguistic syntax and consensual validation rather than a more one-person "private self," we could picture the dynamisms of the self-system operating in Edelman's neuronal group selection. And, interestingly, this model was anticipated by William James, as quoted by Myers (1986):

The knower is not simply a mirror . . . passively reflecting an order that he comes upon and finds simply existing. The knower is an actor. . . . He registers the truth which he helps to create. Mental interests . . . help to *make* the truth which they declare. In other words, there belongs to mind, from its birth upward, a spontaneity, a vote [p. 8].

As Myers elaborates, "Subjectivity figures not only in the search for truth and in its definition but also in its creation" (p. 8).

We could revisit Edelman's (1989) statement that "current perceptual events are recategorized in terms of past value-category matches" (p. 102) and now ask what happens when trauma "unhooks" certain relevant islands of "value-laden memories" and relegates them to exile by defensive dissociation (interrupted reentrant loops). We can see why Russell (unpublished) invokes Freud's observation that "consciousness arises instead of a memory trace" as the posttraumatic residue governing the repetition compulsion: the impossibility of completing the bridging between dissociated islands of "value-laden memories" maintains the perseveration of "meanings" hostage to "real time," because access to full "recategorization" has been cut off by the unbearable affect signals associated with the approach to those "black hole" islands where intolerable paradox made its violent appearance. Hence, cut off from the mind's full potential for metaphoric recategorization consonant with a coherently continuous self, what "arises" instead is a split-off, and therefore concretized, enactment of an unmodifiably dissociated self–other percept telescopically encoded for "survival reaction" only. In James's (1890) terms, the mind is disenfranchised of its spontaneous "vote."

Now we have circled our way back to Bromberg's (1994) model of the person dispersed into multiple self-states through dissociations forced by "drastically incompatible emotions or perceptions." I, however, suggest an emendation of Edelman's (1989) model to account for the universal *multiplicity* of self, within the *integrity* of "value-laden memory" systems, under nontraumatic environmental conditions of development. I propose that what Modell (1993) describes as the language-equipped self's "ability to create a coherent internal model of past, present and future" (p. 158) is an ability to *bridge separate islands of self-state and self-relating memory categories.* Thus, the coherent self is paradoxical not only in bridging the continuity of memory and the discontinuity of consciousness, but also in bridging the multiplicity of self and self–other experiences, even reciprocally negating juxtapositions of experience, while preserving the "coherence" of a singular identity over time. As I suggested earlier, perhaps the bridges I describe in my portrait of the internal world are themselves translatable into the relatively selected and deselected neural pathways of Edelman's model: constituting the self's potential for straddling intrasubjective *systems of systems*.

Bromberg (1994) also emphasizes a model of the psyche that "does not start as an integrated whole, but is nonunitary in nature" (p. 521)—and, as I see it, such an original mental structure would not be the result of dissociation; that is, a process of *un*linking or *un*hooking. We need to consider organizing factors other than dissociation to account for what Bromberg terms "a mental structure that begins and continues as a multiplicity of self-states that maturationally attain a feeling of coherence which overrides the awareness of discontinuity," and preserves "the necessary illusion of being 'one self'" (p. 521). I believe that these basic organizing influences on the structure of the self, other than dissociation, can be conceptualized as general features of complex dynamic systems, or deterministic chaos. Bromberg implies this conceptual framework as well when he invokes Putnam (1988) to support his "nonunitary" model of the psyche. Bromberg notes Putnam's assertion that "states appear to be the fundamental unit of organization of consciousness and are detectable from the first moments following birth" (p. 522)—hence, prior to the mind's deployment of dissociation. Putnam's model of psychological states, and state-shifts, is essentially a complex dynamic system of "self-organizing and self-stabilizing structures" that manifest discrete and discontinuous properties, yet allow for nonlinear state changes. Putnam depicts states as cohesive clusterings of multiple variables; specifically, affect, state-dependent memory, attention and cognition, regulatory physiology, and a sense of self. Each state "acts to impose a quantitatively and qualitatively different structure on the variables that define the state of consciousness" (p. 522). Yet transitions in states of consciousness do occur, most often heralded by changes in affect and mood; and each new state structure "acts to reorganize behavior and resist changes to other states" (p. 522).

CHAOS THEORY AND STATE SHIFTS

Chaos theory, or the theory of complex dynamic systems, supports, with notably close correspondence, the paradigm of nonlinear, discontinuous self-states that exercise a conservative inertial drag on change, yet allow for shifts and access to intersystemic bridging. The sophisticated computer imaging available to support modern mathematical and mechanical sciences (see Figure 1) may help us to picture graphically Putnam's model of states. In the terms of deterministic chaos theory, each state would be depicted geometrically as a swirl of multiple variables forming a stablizing orbital pattern, or *basin*, around a hypothetical *attractor* core. Each attractor basin tends to hold its organizational pattern, preserving the integrity of that cohesive state. Yet, true to the complex reciprocal influences intrinsic to multivariable dynamic systems, small changes in the quantitative or qualitative properties of any element in the system may set in motion bifurcating, ramifying, recursive, feedback, and ultimately

Figure 1. Example of a fractal generated by Mandelbrot set.

profound effects, prompting the transition in dynamic organization from one attractor cluster, across a *separatrix*, to another
attractor. Such transitions may be subtle or gradual shifts, or relatively abrupt switches. By way of illustration, it may help to picture a horse's gait: walking, trotting, cantering, or galloping. Each
gait has its own discrete pattern organizing the total coordinated
movement of the horse's legs; each gait is an attractor. The single
variable of speed, as it accelerates or decelerates, approaches the
point of transition, or switching, from one gait to another: walk,
trot, gallop. Nonlinear state-shifts, as in Putnam's psychological
model, vary in their smoothness or abruptness of transition, in the
degree to which they are reversible or absolute; hence, bridgeable
or unbridgeable. The *distributed* multiple self represents a model
of relatively bridgeable nonlinear state-shifts between contradictory attractors, perhaps along a gradient of interpenetration, overlap, and reversibility; whereas the *dissociated* multiple self
represents a model of virtually unbridgeable gaps between attractors.

   To further develop this discussion of distributed and dissociated multiplicity, and the bridging of paradoxical states, I introduce, from dynamic systems theory, the distinction between chaos
and *dischaos*, and the notion of *fractals*. Fractal geometry presents us with the dilemma of "The Sandy Beach," in the form of
this question: "How long is the coast of Britain?" Of course, we
could refer to a standard, two-dimensional map, read its legend of
scale, and derive the coastline in miles. Or we could look up in an
encyclopedia the length of Britain's coast. Imagine flying over the
coast of Britain with a camera that shows a coast looking much the
same as our two-dimensional map. But now zoom in with your
camera lens, and you will begin to see very small islands, even
pebbles, in a densely packed structure (Abraham, 1995). Try
something else now. Picture yourself on vacation; get off the plane
and simply stand on the beach along the coast of Britain. Take a
good wide stance at the water's edge and look down between your
feet. Now, how long is that part of the coastline between your feet?
And what about the froth, the swirls of surf foam, the grains of wet
sand frothing up, the sucking in of holes, the pebbles interspersed
in the water, and the water penetrating the land? Now do we measure in a straight line? How long, then, *is* the coast of Britain?
   Abraham (1995) has written:

All this is the coast: It has a fractal dimension. . . . Not only is the coast a fractal, with a dimension more than one but less than two, but it is a fractal region: the coastal zone. The ocean and land are not divided by the coast in a binary fashion; they interpenetrate in a fractal geometry. The fractals of chaos theory—attractors, separatrices . . . —are all of the sandy beach variety [p. 163].

Abraham, a mathematician, uses the sandy beach model to consider psychological systems. Within the person, he argues, "the sandy beach concept applies to the boundary between two different behavioral regions" (p. 163). Now bear in mind Putnam's (1988) model of "nonlinear state changes" applied to the relatively healthy person as well as the person, described by Bromberg (1994), who has deployed intrasubjective dissociation in the face of "drastically incompatible emotions or perceptions," as I quote Abraham's (1995) description of "the dischaotic personality":

We now assume a . . . dynamical model for self or life space of an individual. Different aspects of the personality, depending critically on the individual, are represented in this model by groups of basins of attraction. These may be slowly changing in time under the effects of learning, adaptation, stimuli, and so on. Now that chaos theory and fractal geometry have emerged, we expect that fractal boundaries of these psychological regions are the rule, rather than the exception. Following the lead of chaos theoretical models in medical physiology, we may expect that chaotic attractors and fractal separatrices are important for health. Specifically, we may suggest that thick fractal separatrices in the psyche have an integrating effect. For under the effect of random or chaotic stimuli, the trajectory of the . . . model jumps about in small discontinuities, landing in different basins because of the fractal boundaries. This has the effect of integrating the different behaviors of the different attractors into a strongly associated . . . personality. On the other hand, when the boundaries have become (perhaps in a pathological situation) too ordered, or *dischaotic*, or if the fractal dimension is too small, there would be a tendency to manifest one attractor for some time, until an exceptional stimulus pushes the trajectory over the edge into the basin of another aspect of the self and there is a dramatic change in behavior [p. 164].

Thus, the shifts in self-state in Putnam's paradigm become more absolute, and less bridgeable, as the boundaries between nonlinear states become less fractal. Dissociations, or other "splitting" mechanisms that reduce communication between subsystem attractor basins, establish "dischaotic" dynamic systems, where the separatrices (the potential spaces) between attractor basins become categorical divider lines and the trajectories of self-experience (affect, image, memory, cognition, physiological adjustment, and self-representation) tend not to cross over, or bridge, into other basins. Consistent with Putnam's model, discrete self-states exercising their structuralizing influence on the trajectories of variables, resist changes to other states with a varying range of inertial force correlated with the "thickness" of fractal boundaries. Here we can picture again, in metaphoric terms, a basic model of the self distributed into multiple islands (basins) of states, each clustering around affect-laden meanings ascribed to memory, thought, fantasy, percept, and body sense and variously interconnected by bridges that allow for heavy commute or infrequent traffic; and those particular basins that are formed traumatically remain islands cut off from interstate commerce, their fractal bridges sabotaged by defensive dissociation (repelling the approach of trajectories that might strengthen interstate connections). Or, in Bromberg's (1995) terms, we encounter "a dissociative gap, by virtue of which the experience of original trauma is relegated to the part of the self that is unlinked to that part of the self preserved as a relatively intact 'me'" (p. 183). Since, as Bromberg (1994) posits (consistent with Putnam), "the psyche does not start as an integrated whole, but is nonunitary in origin" (p. 521), it is always a matter of degree.

Perhaps it is a matter of the degree of paradox, wherein tolerable paradox is bridged, and cataclysmically discrepant paradoxical experience that strains the elasticity of mind beyond its capacity to span a fractal separatrix coerces a dischaotic splitting to sustain basic survival. We might further picture the chaotic metamodel of self, with its relatively more or less fractal boundaries between states allowing for varying facility for integration, state-shift, or the "inter-state" sharing of resources, according to Edelman's (1992) neurophysiological model of the self. Perhaps the bridges between states represent neuronal pathways preferentially selected, or deselected, for salience according to their advantageous efficacy at linking clusters of memorial systems with currently arriving percepts in the interest of preserving the continuity of the self. Boundaries between discrete self-states that are more bridgeable, more fractal, are neuronal networks that are selectively more available, or more utilized, during ongoing "reen-trant signaling"—Edelman's term for the neuronal process that correlates stored memory and current perception—and the adaptive and creative processes by which we negotiate meaning. Trauma kills the unity and continuity of the self by necessitating a defensive "dischaos" that interrupts the neurophysiological, and psychic, integrity of *freely associative recategorization*.

In the life of each of us, our particular internal template of meaning and affect categories, or "value-laden memories" in Edelman's model, that dynamically determine retranscriptions, may be regarded as the legacy of all object-relational experiences. Indeed, "the shadow of the object fell upon the ego" (Freud, 1917) and the resultant imprints within the psyche, whatever might be the neurophysiological interface, define those "shades of meaning" available to the person for each moment of recategorization. As Sullivan (1953) observed, the person has the sign. Herein lies the individual's unique potential for creativity; the negotiation of fresh acts of meaning (Bruner, 1990). And, since all object experiences are not only conflictual but variously paradoxical (mother feeds/mother frustrates; mother soothes feelings/mother hurts feelings; father protects/father pounces—and, at the cataclysmic level of paradox, someone familiar violates the self), the internal memorial structure that defines the identity and coherence of the self must consist of multiple nuclei of relational affect categories—multiple attractor basins—whose thick fractal boundaries (or lack thereof) describe the self's internal universe of potential recategorizations. *The capacity to tolerate and bridge paradoxical relational experiences and their associated self-states, stored memorially within the psyche as value-laden attractor basins, is thus a vital evolutionary and ontogenetic achievement.* Without the bridging of paradox, reentrant signaling of new perceptions may find only curtailed pathways toward a stunted recategorization. Without freely associated recategorization, the links between the unconscious (value-laden memory) and the conscious (current perceptual awareness) will be diminished. Consciousness arising with diminished memory trace reduces retranscription (*Nachträglichkeit*) and thereby dwarfs the self as an agent of meaning. The person feels "empty," unanchored in personal subjectivity; poorly equipped to negotiate with the tidal surge of environmental impingements, or to select response options other than those repetitive patterns governed by a posttraumatically gerry-mandered reentrant signaling network. The tolerance for paradox that makes possible the bridging of multiplicity within the self is essential for the intactness of consciousness. To return now to Bromberg's statement about dissociation that I considered earlier, whereas the process of dissociation may be "central to the *stability*" of personality, as Bromberg asserts, I believe that it is the inherent capacity to tolerate and bridge paradox that is central to the development and *growth* of personality.

Our conception of the mind's capacity to tolerate paradox gains useful dimension when viewed in the terms of chaos theory. Take the paradox: "I run to mother when someone hurts my feelings. Mother is the person who hurt my feelings." We could picture the child's internal mapping of this paradoxical relational configuration as two attractor basins, roughly labeled "mother soothes feelings" and "mother hurts feelings." The affect trajectories ("mother soothes" and "mother hurts") at the theoretical center of these attractor basins do indeed mutually negate each other—and strain the child's logic to maintain their coexistence in mental representation. Numerous (countless?) trajectories of percept, affect, memory, sensation, and identity, however, do continuously arc across the fractal boundaries separating these value-laden islands of potential meaning. Hence, the thick fractal thoroughfares between these discrepantly valent experiences with mother indeed cross over as bridging tendencies (perhaps mother's smell of cinnamon, or the light of recognition in her eyes, or the sense-memory of her embrace), belonging on both islands of experience, both self-states, while the attractor cores of these states remain an unreconciled paradox. The psyche's tolerance for paradox relies on the free passage of variables that congregate naturally together and thereby maintain relatively fractal boundaries between mutually negating cores of meaning, around each of which these variables yet remain complexly orbited. In this way, bridges extend between islands that could not exist from the perspective of each other's core. I propose that this model describes the human mind in health, to the degree that intolerably paradoxical attractor cores have not been traumatically introduced, necessitating a dischaotic prohibition on the free interplay of evocative trajectories between the distinct islands of internal space.

Now let us recall to mind mother-the-clown, the conductor who facilitates passage from one state to another. I suggest that the caregiver's transformational-object function makes a necessary contribution to the child's development of the capacity to tolerate paradox. The mother whose affect "matching" and tactfully adroit conducting conveys her child from one state to another is communicating to the child a message that can be internalized: "the discrepancy that divides these two states is *OK*; you can go with it, ride the wave, move on with it." And, importantly, it is not only significant that the caregiver facilitates the shift from one state to another; *the child experiences in these moments the very process of bridging itself*. The transition, or transformational process, between discrete, nonlinear, affect-laden states is, in and of itself, a critical experience in development!

The development of our capacity to bear, hold simultaneously, and feel the unforced reconciliation of paradoxical, multiple states is facilitated by our integration of—and practice with our mother's (and others') convoying us across—countless nonlinear switches. For example, the transition from "mastery of walking" to "tumbling downward," and onward to "up and at it," has been accompanied by parental ego-coverage that helped to hold the moment together and negotiated a tolerable mediation of unthinkable anxiety at the brink of "going into pieces" or "falling forever." The mother whose anger startled her child, and who then aided the child's return to an affective relaxation, has provided more than the experience of a trustworthily repeated sequence of relational and internal states, because the child has experienced not only the daily repetitions of sequence, but the repetitions of the *transitions between sequences*. Thus paradoxical relational states come to be tolerated not only through the repetition of their juxtaposition, or sequence, but through the affectively meaningful experience of transitions sponsored within a relational context: *the experience of bridging*. We construct value-laden memories of the negotiation of affective bridges that serve as the affective experience and regulatory mechanism accomplishing shifts in state. We come to trust the experience of getting from here to there without yet knowing how. Hence, by internalizing the affective experience of state transitions, we form the basis for our ability to bridge, to straddle, paradox without a disruption of our sense of self, although we may be cognitively or affectively strained. The feeling that unsolved paradox is OK is tantamount to what Bollas (1995) describes as a

sense of humor, a spirit of enjoyment in the sense of self amidst
its multiplicity.

It is also obvious, then, that when a state-shift is *instigated*
(rather than facilitated or mutually regulated) by a mother (other)
who is herself in a relatively dissociated state, we find the context
for traumatic impingement and the likelihood of intolerable paradox. When the personality interacting with a child is not relatively
integrated, with fractally separated subsystems at play, then state-
shifts will tend to be abrupt cleavages, interruptions of going-on-
being. The child who has experienced state switches induced by
nonnegotiated, or dischaotic, impingement, will face life propor-
tionately less equipped with the competence to tolerate and bridge
paradoxical realities.

THE ANALYST'S ROLE IN THE BUILDING OF BRIDGES

Eventually, this child, now grown up, may enter a psychoanalysis.
I have elsewhere (Pizer, 1992; Chapter 1, this volume) described
the psychoanalytic process as an ongoing negotiation of paradox,
in which the patient's capacity to participate in the intersubjective creation of meaning is cultivated within the analytic duet. I
have also considered elsewhere (Pizer, 1996a; Chapter 2, this volume) specific elements of technique—play, metaphor, and the subjunctive—that enhance available analytic potential space for the
uses of negotiation. Here I focus on a particular dimension of therapeutic action and the role of the analyst, in the light of this exam-
ination of multiple self-states, dischaotic and fractal boundaries,
switches and transitions, and the building and repair of bridges
between paradoxically associated, or dissociated, islands within
the self's value-laden memorial system. I will outline my ideas
through a dialogue with selected statements of Bromberg's.

Bromberg (1994) writes:

> It is in the process of "knowing" one's patient through direct related-
> ness, as distinguished from frustrating, gratifying, containing,
> empathizing, or even understanding him, that those aspects of self
> which cannot "speak" will ever find a voice and exist as a felt pres-
> ence owned by the patient rather than as a "not-me" state that pos-
> sesses him [p. 537].

Here Bromberg is advocating the analyst's awareness of those moments when analytic technique itself may impose too dischaotic a hold on the intersubjective attunement of the analyst to the relationally enacted multiplicities of the patient. Thus Bromberg cautions the analyst to remain open to shifting his own responsive posture as an act of recognition that might meet the spontaneous gesture from a remote trajectory within the patient. Celebrating the wonder of parapraxes, Bromberg affirms their value thus:

> Not because they provide a window into what a patient "really" believes but because they allow opposing realities held by different self-states to coexist, and mutuality can increase simultaneous access to a fuller range of self through the analytic relationship [p. 531].

Here Bromberg emphasizes the value of those moments of surprise heralded by parapraxes, wherein "opposing realities" in the patient's mind may be juxtaposed and given a recognition in the analytic dialogue that sponsors their acceptable coexistence. Thus, we might regard a parapraxis as not only a "slip" but a "bridge." When we stumble on a parapraxis, we discover a potentially meaning-laden trajectory across a gap within the patient's internal world, separating the attractor basins of "different self-states." I fully agree with Bromberg but would add that such moments deliver access not only to a "fuller range of self," but also to the conscious experience and potentially augmented use of bridges that may connect states. Perhaps, in Edelman's (1992) terms, the neuronal mappings of bridges themselves may become more salient reentrant loops as "opposing realities" find linkages cultivated within the analytic relationship.

Bromberg encourages the analyst to join in duet with those affective notes issued from multiple self-states within the patient. As participant/observer, the analyst offers the structuralizing efficacy of linguistic symbolization (interpretation) along with the transformational influence of his authentic-yet-disciplined presence. The analyst's responsively adjusting self goes out to meet the multiplicity within the patient's self and, like the good-enough mother, holds the moment together by the grace of "ego-relatedness." Bromberg (1995) has written:

> It is this "room for relatedness" that turns static, frozen space into "potential space" and allows the creative encounter between a

patient's multiple realities and those of his analyst to form something new—a negotiated enhancement of the patient's perceptual capacity and an increased surrender of the dissociative structure of his personality organization [p. 185].

Perhaps Bromberg uses the word "surrender" because he offers this statement in a paper on resistance. Nonetheless, I want to emphasize that we can recognize in the "surrender of the dissociative structure" a dialogical practice of bridge-building that potentiates ego development within the patient (and analyst!); and the enhanced "perceptual capacity" that may result is, in essence, the capacity for recategorization, retranscription, freely associative state-shifts during reentrant signaling, and the working through of transferences. We might playfully describe the therapeutic action of the psychoanalytic relationship in these terms: where dischaotic boundaries were, there shall fractal boundaries be!

How does the analyst straddle the paradox between maintaining the necessary analytic frame and maintaining the necessary "room for relatedness"? Bromberg (1994) acknowledges:

> Over the years I've come to believe that it may be the *limitation* in my flexibility—the fact that I do implicitly draw a line in the sand— that has the most impact because it emanates from relational authenticity. If I do ultimately move the line, *the process through which that happens is at least as important as the accommodation itself*. It carries the fact that what I'm doing is not a technique but a personal effort I am willing to make as long as it does not exceed the limits of what I establish as my personal boundaries and is thus part of a genuine relational negotiation [p. 544].

Bromberg, grappling internally with the conservatism inherent in his own value-laden memories as analyst, *negotiates* fresh meanings with his patient in the immediacy of the analytic encounter. Here we have the "Sandy Beach": what begins as the analyst's line in the sand becomes a fractal zone, an area of overlap, during the intersubjective dialogue. Thus, a negotiated shift may occur reciprocally (see Aron, 1996). As I conceptualize such moments, the analyst joins the ranks of mothers, comics, and conductors who offer their own precariously maintained comfort with the discomforts of paradox as an intersubjective bridge for the linking of discontinuous worlds and the regulation of harmonies, through a process of reciprocal influences.

When analysts are receptive to the multiplicity within their patients, they serve as transformational objects, sponsoring their patients' tolerance for paradoxical self-states by holding them within the unity of a single negotiated relationship. In this way patients may bear "the spaces between realities" and maintain an enriched unity of self-experience. When "the spaces between realities" are named by interpretations, or straddled by transitions, arrived at together by therapist and patient, realities are not lost because the person now stands "in the spaces" on a bridge that spans paradoxical realities.

Winnicott (1967) began his paper on "The Location of Personal Experience" with an epigram from Tagore: "On the seashore of endless worlds, children play." Of course, Winnicott had not encountered an as-yet-uninvented Chaos Theory. But he implicitly understood the "Sandy Beach" dilemma. He recognized that potential space, the area of overlap and transition, is a fractal region. As he commented, "The quotation from Tagore has always intrigued me. In my adolescence I had no idea what it could mean, but it found a place in me, and its imprint has not faded" (p. 95).

With Winnicott's gift for creative recategorization, he knew the seashore to be a thick fractal boundary, an endlessly paradoxical potential space in which children, playing, construct their bridges between a multitude of internal and external worlds.

5

Facing the Nonnegotiable

Folks, I'm telling you,

birthing is hard

and dying is mean—

so get yourself

a little loving

in between.

—Langston Hughes, "Advice,"

from *Montage of a Dream Deferred*

THE FLAVOR OF THE NONNEGOTIABLE: EVERETT

I faced the nonnegotiable several years ago in my work with Everett. A 38-year-old director of a small charitable trust, Everett was referred to me by his wife's therapist because of marital conflicts that had persisted in angry stalemate, delaying a decision about having children. The referring therapist described Everett as "probably hard to work with, maybe even hard to like." I was predisposed to do my best to work with him because this referral was my first from a highly respected former supervisor. Thus, I was motivated to take Everett into treatment and look for what was likable and workable.

Everett at first impression was appealing enough. He stated a need to resolve his own conflicts over fully committing to his marriage of five years. Despite a lifelong prejudice against psychotherapy, he indicated some psychological mindedness. He said, for example, that he remained uncertain whether his nagging feeling of his wife's insufficiency reflected a true mismatch or the emotional residue of his own childhood background. Everett clearly was intelligent, and he seemed to have ideals for himself: to be a successful, contributing, solid citizen. His presentation also seemed subtly, and oddly, fragmentary. He interrupted himself frequently, anticipated my questions, expressed self-doubt, even accused himself of speaking "for effect." At moments arrogant, referring to colleagues, employees, or his wife, with a facile disdain, he would shift abruptly to self-deprecation and embarrassment. So, as he began his story, he seemed to me like a kitten all snarled in his own yarn. And so his therapy began, twice weekly.

Soon, however, Everett began to snarl at me. In his third week of therapy, Everett voiced doubts about working with me. So far, he had felt that I was attentive, caring, and smart. And I had come very highly recommended. The referring therapist, however, had mentioned to Everett's wife that he knew my work through years of supervision. Everett acknowledged that his mind formed a ready hierarchy and that he assumed there was an echelon of supervisors who were at the top level. And he wanted to be sure that his therapist belonged to the top level. Also, his father-in-law happened to be a senior training analyst and, however conflictual was Everett's regard for his wife, he was aware that he idealized his father-in-law, sought to be close to him, and identified him as the standard for the analytic field. So, was he compromising himself by seeing me? I told him that this seemed to be a serious doubt to have to carry along, perhaps akin to doubting he had made the right marital choice. I reassured him (or was I reassuring myself, or defensively parrying?) that while, indeed, I had been a supervisee, I had also been, for years, a supervisor. I told him that we should nevertheless take his doubts seriously, discuss what they could mean, and also remain open to his considering another therapist. "Oh, no!" he immediately exclaimed. "My wife said if I blow this with you, that's it. I don't want to raise any more doubts with her. So, I guess we're stuck with each other."

Bristling inside at this, I said, "I don't know that anyone would be served if your choice of therapist was a manipulation of your wife, yourself, or me." Everett said he liked my honest answer and that he hoped I would still work with him. I said, "Let's see what develops"; and, indeed, I began to wonder what would or could develop. Everett began presenting to me some of his painful memories of childhood.

Everett was the family's third child, considerably younger than his two sisters. His family culture and climate seemed succinctly evident in his description of a "typical dinner." His sisters, always in competition with each other, would unite in teasing him—their taunts seemed to him to escalate, as if the girls were trying to outdo each other. Everett's parents allowed this scenario to go on; but, if he began to pout, protest or, on occasion, cry, his father would quickly snap, "Everett, for God's sake, stop whining!" Everett's mother took little part in dinner conversation. She cooked and served, often conveying to Everett that she was giving him special portions or his favorite foods. Mother's conversation was much more active when she was alone with Everett. Preoccupied by unresolved struggles with her own family of origin, Everett's mother continually talked with Everett about her own mother and sisters, how much they always hurt her feelings and how he had to shine and do her proud at the frequent extended family gatherings. Everett reported that he took solace, and sought refuge, in his mother's pride and allowed himself to be thus groomed as her champion in the family hierarchy. Everett's relationship with his father seemed to him shadowed by his father's volatile temper and a form of humor that struck Everett as "sadistic and undermining." For example, often Everett's father, rather than offering a direct response to a statement or question of Everett's, would instead produce puns and other non sequitors: "he'd show off his cleverness at my expense!"

And Everett wondered if there could be particular significance in those occasions when his sisters undressed him, tied him up, and showed his genitals to their friends. I asked Everett if his parents knew of this. He replied that he remembered telling his mother and believed she had said something like, "Oh, Everett, they're playing! That's playing doctor." Everett said he assumed that meant it was ok, and he felt embarrassed to be a poor sport. He also vaguely recalled, but wondered if he was just making it up, that once his mother had been in the room during this so-called play. Everett glanced at me sideways when he said, "That's not abuse, is it?" I said, "It's not clear whether you'd prefer me to say yes or no." "Well," Everett continued, "*I* don't think it was abuse." I responded, "What you think is an important part of what it was. I wonder if we can leave it to further reflection, what it was or was not. But, at the moment, I'm particularly struck by how your statement of feelings was handled in the family." Everett said he appreciated my empathic statement. Then he quickly followed with, "I bet you just said that because you're supposed to. Maybe you're even self-satisfied; like, boy, *you* just said the therapeutic thing! You're probably showing off how good you are. Is that how you make people admire you?"

Taken aback by this sudden snarling, I asked Everett where he thought this feeling came from. He ridiculed my "typical shrinky" question. And then he reverted to questioning whether he had a good enough therapist. Maybe someone more senior would not ask such a shrinky question, would know something better to do. His father-in-law, even just hanging around at a family visit, could be counted on to make wise and insightful statements. I felt myself silently hating his goddam father-in-law. I asked Everett if he would think about how his mind turned once again to comparisons and competitions, and asked him if he were placing me with him back in the family. Everett replied, "Why do you have to interpret? Are you competing with my father-in-law now? Why can't you just empathize with my need to feel satisfied that I'm in the right therapy? My father-in-law says the most important thing you're supposed to do is empathize."

Now *I* felt tied. And maybe somewhat naked too. What I said to Everett was: "Here's the dilemma I think we're in. You say you need empathy. And I believe you do. I really believe that. But, when I empathize with your feelings, it's often hard for you to accept. That in itself would not be too much of a dilemma. Because I can accept, and respect, how you might have trouble receiving empathy. But when the very thing you are expressing is contempt for me, or denigration of me, then *at that moment* I can't help but close off. So, you miss the empathy you need, and I can't give it. I can bear your hostility and try to understand it, but I can't, at that moment, empathize. And I wonder how we will negotiate this." Everett received these remarks in silence, paused, and then went on to talk about something else. I silently assumed he needed some time and space to digest my words.

During the weeks that followed, Everett would come in and talk about his parents, triggered by an unsettling phone conversation or visit with them; or he would recapitulate his quandary about whether he could ever be satisfied with his wife, whose attentiveness and family money did not compensate for her lack of "beauty," which, he feared, was a necessity for him; or he returned to questioning whether or not I was a senior enough therapist for him. I found my own feelings toward Everett fluctuating between sympathy for how helpless he was, how hurt and defeated, in the face of his parents' perpetual intransigence; and then unsympathetic, or annoyed, with his obsessing about his marriage, oscillating between his entitlement to a dazzling partner and his self-recrimination at his acknowledged "criticalness and superficiality"; and, of course, I felt challenged to tolerate his recurrent devaluings of me. I noted, in particular, how Everett would introduce each of these issues in relative isolation from the others and without conveying a sense of thematic continuity or cumulative insight. He seemed to jump back and forth from one state or island of personal concern to another, without an evident line of progression. Often he would begin a session in prolonged silence; he looked as if he were holding discourse with himself in my presence. From time to time, he would say, "I'm not sure what to say today," or "I don't know if it will do any good to tell you what I'm thinking." At times, I would ask Everett if he was aware of what made it hard to speak with me at the moment or what might make it easier. I never ceased to be startled when he would snap, "Now I feel pressured by you," or "You've just interrupted my thoughts." When I asked Everett if we could consider the way our sessions and their content seemed to recur but not link up, and the function this might serve, he replied, "I thought I had the right here to tell you what was on my mind, and you were supposed to listen. You're just making me self-conscious now. I feel like you're not really willing to listen to me." Indeed, I was thrown back on my own uncertainties: Was I trying too quickly or too intensely to influence him to change, to become an easier and more gratifying patient? Did I have too urgent an agenda to help him become a

mensch? Was I too soured by his repeated attacks on my competence? Was I giving him enough time, unpressured, to develop a
relationship with me? Was I giving him too much room and not
enough guidance? Was I trying to prove my value to him? Were
we, indeed, mismatched, and who else could do this work with
him? Was a productive therapy taking shape between us, unbe-
knownst to me? I comforted myself that his occasional fleeting,
hapless smile implied a budding attachment and the hope of something more substantial ahead. So, I committed myself to wait and
try to contain this process with Everett.

Soon afterwards, Everett brought in a surprise. He told me, hes-
itantly, that he had been having an affair with his secretary, a strikingly attractive young woman. He said he would never marry such
a woman, but that being with her sexually told him what he was
missing with his wife. On the other hand, he thought maybe this
was the best arrangement for him; maybe he could stay married,
even choose to have children, and benefit from the financial security, respectability, and family life his wife provided, but continue
with this affair so that he could also enjoy the excitement he
needed. He said he assumed I would judge him to be a cad and
that maybe he was. Or, maybe I was just uptight and incapable of
adventuring like him. Maybe I would even envy his ability to
improvise and add color to his life; and, instead of examining my
own humdrum existence, I would try to reform him. I received this
challenge in silence. I did not know what I could say to this setup
and wondered what would follow.

After a pause, Everett said, "My secretary and I have been arguing lately. I know this arrangement is hard for her, and I was thinking of bringing her in here with me one day. Would you mind?" I
found myself replying, "Yes, I would mind. In fact, I wouldn't see
you together." Everett flushed. I added that he could certainly talk
with me as much as he needed to sort out and understand this
relationship, and its place in his life, but to see his secretary along
with him was a boundary crossing that made me uncomfortable.
Everett insisted that my position typified the very uptightness,
rigidity, and narrowness he suspected of me. He said that here was
where a more senior therapist would have the security and
resourcefulness to take on his request. I stuck to my guns. I
thought about his family history of boundary crossings—his sisters' invasive play, his mother's recruiting him into her own family

scenarios—and how his own attempts to define boundaries had not been taken seriously. I reflected that this man, so enacted on and enacting, might need to experience my enactment of boundaries and limits before he could think effectively about them for himself. I hesitated to say this to Everett, as I had already anticipated that he would accuse me of hiding my rigidities behind psychological rationalizations. And I asked myself, was I indeed justifying to myself a therapeutic usefulness in my own refusal of his wish? To my surprise, Everett said, "I won't argue it with you. You've got the power. I need this therapy too much to get bogged down."

In the weeks that followed, Everett focused on his relationship with his secretary and his relationship with his wife. He compared and contrasted them, at moments concretely and at other moments wondering what each relationship meant to him. He acknowledged that he structured each relationship to control the distance. As usual, he would interrupt himself, saying, "Where does this talk get me?" or "Maybe I should just accept that I've got it pretty good, and just see how I can keep it going." Everett also began to express frustration at his job. He thought perhaps his position at the foundation was a mismatch, a dead-end for his ambitions, too small an organization to showcase his talents. Everett's jabs at me subsided but did not disappear. For example, he entered one session saying, "I saw your last person leave the office smiling. I figured, you've got your favorites. They probably act really nice. You probably train them to make nice. And you all keep up this conventional niceness. No room for real stuff." Hearing what I surmised to be Everett's envy, as well as shame and longing, I marveled at how I felt that there was no room to say any of this to him. Not now, at least. How could I respond openly as I felt his forays close me down? All I could say was, "I suppose you wonder what our relationship could be and how you need to act." Everett nodded, paused, and changed the subject.

A few weeks later, his therapy reached a brink. Everett informed me that he and his secretary had come up with a way to skim money from the foundation without its showing up on the books. He felt proud of his cleverness. This kind of adventuring could really be a thrill. He told me that, of course, he could see that it was wrong, even "despicable," to embezzle a charitable foundation. But, then again, they don't pay him enough for what he does. And, even though the amounts wouldn't be large, the excitement *would* be.

I asked myself, Why is Everett telling me this? What does he want? What does he need? Do I inquire? Do I back off and allow us both the time to see what develops? Do I use silence, or the interrogative, or the imperative? I felt shocked. Should I keep this raw reaction to myself? Would a statement of my feeling of shock constitute reality testing or rejection? Did he need me to set limits? Did *I* need to set limits? I felt impelled to act.

"Everett," I said, "I'm shocked." He looked up abruptly. "Oh," he groaned, "Now you're gonna step in and be righteous. And how am I supposed to explore this?" I replied, "Everett, I do hope we can explore this. But I am shocked." I went on, "I know you don't want me to be judgmental, and you think sometimes I'm out to clean up your act, and you need to be free to say whatever it is you have to say. But right now I feel a responsibility to say to you that I think you're putting yourself in harm's way. I hope you don't do it. This is just too destructive. And too risky. And maybe I just can't sit with it. But, please, don't do it!" "Jesus!" exclaimed Everett. "Are *you* being controlling!" "Perhaps," I responded. "Let's look at it. But let's have time to look at it."

But Everett now questioned whether time looking at things with me would really lead anywhere. "You really lost it," he declared. And then I received what felt like a torrent of rebuke. Everett asked what kind of therapist I was, swooping in, ending discussion with my pronouncements, trying to turn him into just another one of my bland, obliging little "nice" patients. He'd been right all along. He needed a therapist more like his father-in-law, able to stay quietly and calmly in his seat. I should keep my opinions to myself and try to understand him! How could he tell me his thoughts? We weren't here to talk about me, but about *him*; and I was indulging myself in announcing I was "shocked." As I listened to Everett, I felt my gorge rising inside.

"Look," I finally said, "I understand you're angry with me. And I accept it. You didn't welcome what I said. You've been angry with me before, and I can accept a certain amount of it, hoping it will lead us somewhere. But there are limits. This feels like a barrage, without any process of exploring or understanding. Enough already. I'll accept your anger, but I won't take shit."

"Wow," said Everett, 'You've really lost control. This isn't therapy anymore. You're just being angry with me. You're so righteous. But, admit, you're really out of line." "I do admit I'm angry," I said, aware that I was working to contain my feelings while expressing them. I felt a powerfully implosive force in the room and in my own head. "I do admit I'm angry," I repeated. "But I don't think I'm out of line." "How could you not be out of line?!" Everett insisted. "Are you supposed to tell me you won't take shit from me? Is that what you think I'm saying: shit? Am I crazy? Or are you really out of control? Boy, admit what you did was wrong!" I felt amazed at the lightning speed with which my comment about his doing something wrong had done a 180, and I felt the heat of a klieg light on me now. I said, "Everett, I don't believe I'm wrong to tell you my limits. It's how I protect myself, and your therapy. Yes, I got angry. I am angry. But I'm still trying to do my work with you." "Oh, right," Everett retorted. "Now you're back up on your therapist seat, putting me down. It's all my doing. I'm the sick one. You're just doing your work." For today, we were out of time. I told Everett I assumed we would take this up further. Indeed, for two weeks this was all we did talk about. Everett came to my office four more times, saying the only thing he would talk about was my loss of self-control. He was thinking he could not go on with me until I admitted I'd been unprofessional. He would not humiliate himself by giving in to me, accepting what he took to be my self-defensive accusation that his behavior was to blame for my loss of control. He said it came down to deciding either that he was crazy and impossible or that I had mistreated him and now was trying to pin it on him by pathologizing him. I told Everett again that I admitted my own anger, and that certainly we *both* had to be involved in what had happened. I asked if we could both explore it together. Everett received my message as my further attempt to play shrink and not admit my serious loss of control. I asked if there was no alternative to one of us being humiliated. He said he'd like to find out. And we went around and around. I felt as if we were spinning round and round.

The situation felt to me nonnegotiable. Everett's pain and desperation were clear. In whatever ways this eruption had followed our exchange about his notion to skim funds at work, it seemed beyond the two of us at the moment to explore that issue and its short circuit. Everett seemed fixed on his dread of humiliation and hell-bent to humiliate me. I have never felt such a concerted effort mounted to dismantle me as a therapist. I sensed that Everett was attached to me, though fighting it. I felt like kicking him out; yet, for that very reason, I also felt loath to inflict harm by unilaterally declaring finality. But it was also clear to me that Everett and I both needed to be protected from this unproductive and scorching intensity. So I recommended a consultation in the hope that such a step might open up some room for us to move with each other. Everett accepted this idea. I thought of Elkind's (1992) work, providing consultations to resolve impasses in therapy. This was an impasse if ever I saw one. I offered a few names of possible consultants. But Everett preferred to ask his father-in-law for a referral. During the consultation that Everett had, he decided to suspend therapy and to consider at some future time whether or not to pursue the process with me or with someone else. Everett has not returned. As I look back on the time I spent as his therapist, I feel as if I was facing the nonnegotiable.

IT GOES BOTH WAYS: WILLIAM

William, a psychiatry resident in his early 30s, came to me for a consultation. Already in an intensive analytic therapy of several years' duration, he had begun to doubt the therapeutic process with his analyst. In the course of several visits in which he described his treatment relationship with a well-regarded analyst whom he loved and respected, he portrayed his analyst as using interpretive gems that he had gradually come to feel left him vaguely unreached and unrecognized. As we came to see it, the analyst would offer quite beautiful or pithy statements, many of them impressive quotes from literary sources or—as later came to light—imitations of his own former analyst, supervisors, or teachers; he was passing along the "canned" canon of analytic quotable quotes. It seemed to me that the analyst's self-idealization had been met with William's complementary transference idealization; and the patient, receptive to his analyst's inducements, was awed. This admiration of his analyst continued, while William remained unaware of its connection to a parallel feeling of missed recognition at his own core. This feeling could not be spoken because of several intolerable factors: the analyst would be exposed, like "the emperor's new clothes," and William apprehended how much was riding on the analyst's never having to face his own narcissistic "house of cards"; William could not bear to be disillusioned, to face another in a history of fallen heroes; and, finally, William seemed not yet capable of crystalizing his tacit sense of unease into a focal articulated affect that would be complete and vivid enough to counterweigh his own defensive measures of splitting and ideal-ization. Nor, it seemed, was William's analyst motivated to inter-vene in the service of boosting the necessary intrapsychic, affect-organizing process. Into this foreclosed analytic space, William delivered to himself the following dream, which, inex-plicably, had prompted him to seek a consultation:

> I was in a crowded airport, walking quickly down a long corri-dor, trying to reach my departure gate. Suddenly, I'm aware of a blind man on roller skates, coming very fast in the opposite direction. At first, I'm impressed that he's skating so well in all that crowd. Then, suddenly I realize he's aiming straight at me, and he's about to run right into me. He can't see me. Now, over the airport loudspeaker, I hear an announcer's voice—like he was announcing flights, but more like the over-dubbing of an announcer's voice in a movie preview—and he's saying, "'Blind.' The next installment in the series, 'Death in Traffic'." I know that when the blind man collides with me it will kill me, and I wake up in a nightmare panic.

Together, we came to understand that this dream was a fortu-nate gift from his own unconscious. He was able to receive it as a warning that his analyst was hidden behind his own unadmitted personal agendas and, while performing a marvelous act of fancy footwork, remained essentially blind to William's being. Reflecting on his dream, William associated to his early childhood history of profound loneliness and isolation in the face of pervasive parental misrecognitions. As his dream's announcer warned, this was a mat-ter of psychic life and death. William was now able to voice his recognition of why his dream's anxiety had signaled him to seek a consultation on his continuing treatment. As he put it, using the imagery of his dream, "I need to be in traffic where the other dri-ver can see beyond his own windshield." I suggested that William address this frustration directly with his analyst. Two months later, William contacted me for follow-up. He had indeed confronted his analyst, who did acknowledge the reality basis of William's upset. The analyst, however, had gone on to say, "That's me. I'm not about to change who I am. If you want another style, I suggest you see someone else!" William had taken the two months to leave that treatment.

Everett and William both illustrate forms of the nonnegotiable. A therapist may face the nonnegotiable in a patient. A patient may face the nonnegotiable in the therapist. Ultimately, the nonnegotiable is a *relational* property, determined by the convergence of qualities, and limitations, in both members of the dyad. In a relational model of psychoanalysis or psychotherapy, where it clearly takes two to tango, either partner can make it impossible to take a step, or can reduce the dance to hollow gestures or kill the music. Of course, since the analytic process unfolds as an ongoing, or recurrent, or evolving negotiation, we would expect the growing edge of the dialogical exchange always to be reaching the limiting points of each partner's expectations, capacities, boundaries, understandings, or wishes. At any moment of urgency, conflict, or surprise in the course of the analytic relationship, we may feel the strain and uncertainty of negotiation. The relational process of negotiation may, from time to time, feel frustrating, intense, blocked, hurtful, tedious, confusing, or scary to analysand or analyst alike; but all of that is a far cry from the nonnegotiable. The nonnegotiable enters analytic space like a deadness, or deadliness, eliminating space, time, or process. How are we to understand the nonnegotiable in analysis? When does "a meeting of minds" (Aron, 1996) default to a stand-off of minds? And where is the hope for the nonnegotiable in any particular analytic dyad to yield to the reciprocal negotiations of an analytic process?

A THEORY OF THE NONNEGOTIABLE

Perhaps each of us has faced the nonnegotiable in one, or more than one, patient, or in an analyst, parent, or lover. Maybe the nonnegotiable is an inescapable part of our contact with institutions. Quite likely, the choice to become analysts ourselves bears the imprint of our relationships with the nonnegotiable and the relief we have found or searched for.

THE ANALYST

The nonnegotiable in the analyst receives our attention first. Our commitment, as analysts, to a responsible self-analytic practice should be the assumed grounding for our participation in each therapeutic dyad; we must ever ask ourselves how our own growing, aching, and aging characters may be foreclosing the potential in analytic space. Aspects of the analyst's professional attitude, framework, and technique may, in themselves, impose a deadening effect on therapeutic interaction and negotiation.

As I examine how the analyst's technical or ideological framework may impose the nonnegotiable on the patient and on the treatment process, I must emphasize the distinction between the nonnegotiable, as I define it, and the givens of the analytic frame, which might, in some people's view, appear to constitute elements of the nonnegotiable. I refer here to such factors as the existence of a schedule, the length of a session, a fee, an office to which the patient travels. While the details of schedule, fee, and so on may themselves be negotiated between the two parties (perhaps defining a third, or middle, region of "frame negotiation" between the givens and the field of relational negotiations contained within the analytic frame), the irreducible given of a professional contractual relationship, with its terms, limits, and economics, forms the ground on which the analytic relationship is built. When the analyst exercises responsibility to be explicit and consistent about such givens, I do not regard this action to entail, necessarily, the nonnegotiable. Indeed, the respectful (toward self and other) maintenance of consensually contracted arrangements represents an aspect of the analyst's function of containment: protecting and preserving the holding space of the therapeutic relationship.

Further, I believe that in therapy or analysis there are some things that must rightly, and necessarily, remain nonnegotiable. Among them are the analyst's responsibility to hold at the highest priority a commitment to contribute therapeutically to the patient's interests, well being, and treatment goals. I do not mean a *furor sanandi*; but I do mean that the analyst, by contract, owes responsibilities to the patient. Aron (1996) might say that what is nonnegotiable here is the asymmetry of the analytic relationship. The analyst owes it to the patient to work at understanding, acceptance, self-examination, and negotiation. The analyst also owes the patient a primary responsibility to honor boundaries—although these also may be subject to a process of negotiation or renegotiation. It is a given, a necessary nonnegotiable, that the analyst remains respectful of boundaries, sexual or otherwise. The analyst who refuses the temptation—internal or external—to make love to a patient is not being nonnegotiable in the recalcitrant or peremptory sense, but, rather, is preserving the givens, the necessary nonnegotiables, of a specific professional relationship.

And, finally, it is a given—and, hence, ultimately nonnegotiable—that analyst and patient do not join each other as life partners. They join one another as analytic partners. While schedule, fee, office location, vacation separations, and so on serve their own particular purposes and evoke their various problematics, they are also intrinsic elements of the given that the actual, everyday life of the analysand and analyst are not joined. However intimate the pair may be, however loving (or hating) in the course of their journey together, or however poignant and vital their shared experiences in an intersubjectively created analytic space, they face together, all along their way, the nonnegotiable fact that all their negotiations will ultimately shape an end between them. Sometimes explicitly, but always implicitly, analyst and patient join in approaching their eventual separation and mutual loss. All these given features of the analytic frame belong to the realm of the necessary nonnegotiable, the container of all the rest that is negotiated between the partners to a process. And the analyst who is being explicit, or standing firm, regarding the givens, should not be regarded as enacting the nonnegotiable in the sense I am discussing.

Myerson (1990) has emphasized how the analyst who proffers interpretations prior to negotiating the relational foundations for offering them into dialogue will likely be experienced by the patient as seductive or critical. Premature, automatic, or relentless interpretation may impose the nonnegotiable on a patient. Similarly, peremptory interpretation that declares the certainty of analytic authority may defeat the purpose of analytic negotiation, particularly when the patient tends to be compliant, passive, or awed (perhaps an especially common susceptibility of analytic candidates). To the extent that the analyst claims a tacitly complacent, arrogant, or defensive prerogative to name psychic reality, this unexamined position delivers the nonnegotiable. Mitchell

(1993) has argued that even the analyst's hopes for a patient's growth and healing may have little to do with the patient's hopes. And Aron (1996) has described, thoroughly and eloquently, the importance of the analyst's sensibility, humility, and discipline in recognizing and honoring the essential mutuality and asymmetry of the analytic relationship. The analyst who cannot navigate the waters of mutual influence, exposure, risk, and complicity, or who remains naive, obtuse, or disingenuous about the asymmetry of power and responsibility, will participate in the process in ways that remain nonnegotiable.

I would add that the analyst who cannot apologize, even when convinced that the patient, wounded in the analytic exchange, has transferentially placed his or her own sword in the hands of the analyst, dead-ends the potential for a crisis or injury to move on to therapeutic negotiation and transformation. As Russell (unpublished)[1] wrote of the therapist's engagement with transference repetitions,

> the patient focuses on those aspects of us that in fact do recapture the past, real parts of ourselves that do, to some degree, prove their point. However odious, this aspect needs to be located in us, and for us to try to disown or disavow it, to ascribe it all to 'transference,' is to sever the patient's emotional connection with us. *The only thing that works is negotiation, namely a negotiation around whether things have to happen the same way this time* [p. 10, italics added].

Central to this discussion of the nonnegotiable is *misrecognition*: its unfortunate occurrence in development; its damaging effects on the formation of a person and on the person's capacity to house an inner affective life or accommodate relational negotiation. Patients bring their history of misrecognitions into analysis as their "unthought known" (Bollas, 1987), redundantly structuring their deformations of desire, stunting their subjectivity, fogging over their self-reflections, and foreclosing relational potential space. The discussion to follow focuses more particularly on how

---

[1] Paul Russell's life work examined, with wisdom, compassion, and generosity, the power of the repetition compulsion, its antecedents in relational trauma to the capacity to feel, its power to disrupt or destroy the therapeutic relationship along familiar recursive fault lines, and the precarious and delicate process of locating genuine negotiations between patient and therapist that may transform the inexorability of repetition and rage into the paradoxical hope of affective competence and love.

we work with the patient's nonnegotiable as it recapitulates the residue of misrecognitions. The contributions of Ogden and McDougall enrich this exploration. Ogden (1988) has cogently described how the analyst's misrecognition of the patient, brought about through various influences, may mimic the patient's earlier encounters with the nonnegotiable and further reinforce the patient's defensively warding off of inner awareness of how the self has been annihilated through the blindness of the "other." Ogden writes:

> The analyst may unwittingly be induced (as unconscious participant in the patient's projective identification) to enact the role of . . . an authoritarian internal-object-mother. . . . Under such circumstances the analyst may find himself interpreting more "actively" and "deeply" than is his usual practice. He may come to view the analysis as bogged down and feel despairing that the patient will ever arrive at meaningful insight. The analyst may rationalize that the patient needs a more didactic approach in order to demonstrate to him what it means "to think reflectively and in depth." Alternatively, the analyst may feel moved to pursue a line of analytic thinking espoused by his "school of psychoanalysis" or an idea about which he has recently read. Reliance upon analytic ideology represents a common method of warding off the analyst's anxiety of not knowing. . . . The patient's internal version of an early object relationship is in this way being replicated in the analytic setting and, unless analyzed in the countertransference and in the transference, will reinforce the patient's unconscious conviction that it is necessary to utilize omnipotent substitute formations in the face of confusion about what he is experiencing and who he is [p. 652].

Thus, the clinician may be deploying the canonical formulas of Analytic Technique as similar "omnipotent substitute formations in the face of confusion about what he is experiencing and who he is." Ogden focuses particularly on analytic candidates who "frequently utilize this type of unconscious identification with an omnipotent internal object (e.g., an idealized version of one's own analyst). This identification serves as a defense against the anxiety that the candidate does not feel like an analyst when with his patients" (p. 652).

The analyst's authentic recognition of the patient's subjectivity (Benjamin, Aron, Bromberg), uncontaminated by Procrustean and objectifying explanations, is a prerequisite for any good-enough analysis. But, in the face of the nonnegotiable that emanates from a patient, the analyst's only constructive recourse is a combination of containment, acceptance, and recognition. As we now turn our attention more fully toward the patient, we shall see that the analyst's *containment*, *acceptance*, and *recognition* are all that stand between the patient's version of the nonnegotiable and the prospects of awakening hope, and thereby opening between analyst and patient a dialogical space for the potential negotiation of transferences. Only through such a process may the "dis-affected" patient, defending against the agonies of "nonexistence," or the traumatized patient, shattered into pieces by a desperately deployed dissociation, have a chance to come into a relational and personal existence. In the service of this hope, the analyst, facing the nonnegotiable in the patient, must continue to ask: Can I contain intolerable affect between this patient and myself? Can I accept and live with this rendering of despair, destructiveness, heaviness, helplessness, emptiness, or hopelessness? Can I accept this patient's efforts to deaden me? Can I keep alive my own sense of process, paradox, and potential? Can I be quiet and present (and do I remain free to speak)? Can I be here waiting?

Mitchell (1993) has put it beautifully:

> An important feature in the emergence from stalemates is the analyst's ability to regain her equanimity despite the collapse of understanding, her ability to survive the destructiveness of the patient's dread and despair without withdrawing. Sometimes, when language itself has proved treacherous and corrupt, the analyst can say nothing; affirmation through continued presence is the only solution [p. 214].

THE PATIENT

As suggested earlier, the nonnegotiable inheres to the repetition compulsion, at least, as it surfaces and challenges a particular analytic pair at a particular time. Since transference is ubiquitous, and since it constitutes the sum total of each patient's repetitions delivered into the analytic relationship, we might assume that each analysis of transference is transacted at the leading edge of the specifically nonnegotiable. Deep analytic work lives at the brink of the nonnegotiable. We repeat just those relational patterns that we could not negotiate originally; whether we do it to convey the history of our relational plights, or because it is all we know to do with what we feel, or because we seek delayed mastery, or because we remain marooned on those dissociated islands of subjective experience that we were cast upon by traumatic shipwreck. As Russell (1973) wrote, "The only way new territory is gained is by exploring the outer limits of old vulnerabilities." I will explore in some detail the vertiginous steps taken by the patient to bridge the grounds of "old" and "new" object experiences in the working through of transference–countertransference constructions. I will examine how the internalization of these inherently paradoxical experiences in the treatment relationship transforms familiar repetitions into novel renegotiations of being and relating. And I will consider extreme conditions of the nonnegotiable in those transference enactments of abused, misrecognized, and "dis-affected" patients whose inner emptiness, deadness, rage, or near-disintegration precedes the desperate hope embodied in the "rendering" of repetitions into the potential space of an analytic relationship (Russell, unpublished).

Years ago, I was helped to visualize a vital aspect of the repetition compulsion—its function as storytelling—by my Bernese Mountain Dog, Johann. When Johann was left in his rather large pen for any length of time, he would ignore the expanse of playground we had provided for him. He tended to remain in one spot, sitting or dozing directly behind the gate of his pen, where we had just left him and where he knew we would eventually fetch him. When I unlocked and opened the gate, Johann habitually did something quite remarkable: he would run out to me, leaping around with joy; then he would run back inside the pen, and run out again, and run around me, and then, once again, run back inside the pen, and then out again through the gate, repeating this sequence several times. It seemed to me (or to my imagination) that, without the benefit of words, Johann was telling me his story: first he was locked in his pen, alone and unhappy; then I came and got him, and let him out. Running back and forth, in and out of the pen, as he did, I believe Johann's resourcefully enacted narrative served several purposes: it discharged his excited affect; it informed me as witness to his sequence of states, from lonely abandonment to rejoicing reunion; it carried his protest ("Hey, I was in there a long time!"); and it held me there to receive his message until he was through. I would think, here is how you tell a story without words—thing-presentation prior to word-presentation; here is enactive memory, conveyed in the only way possible for enactment, through repetition!

With language, one's story could be told with less reliance on repetition, once the feeling is correlated with a communicative symbol or metaphor. Yet our experience with transference repetition tells us how regularly a person will enact, rather than communicate the story of painful experience. It is as if trauma has corrupted the symbolic utility of words or disrupted the bridging process necessary between internal feeling state and that representational element garnered from the outside to describe experience in metaphoric terms. The patient who lacks, or cannot bear to keep open, an internal metaphoric space, or who lacks the basis for trusting in a communicative relational process, will enact the story of "who I am and what I feel" in a concrete mode that forecloses the negotiation of meaning and relationship. The patient for whom linguistic narrative has failed or has ceased to be a trustworthy tool for representing personal interests and negotiating "acts of meaning" (Bruner, 1990) in a relational dialogue, presents the analyst with the most severe and recalcitrant forms of the nonnegotiable. This person enters treatment in a state of hopelessness that cannot yet even be named because internal psychic space remains either imploded by "action" defenses that obscure meaning-and-affect, or exploded by dissociative defenses that unlink and disperse meaning-and-affect.

The "action" defenses that implode internal psychic, or potential, space include compulsions, addictions, perverse constructions, externalizations, somatizations, and, as Benjamin (1988) might add, relational submissions. All of these very real struggles, sufferings, and symptoms persist in such a way as to dominate the life and attention of the patient and fill the time spent in therapy. These enactive automatisms are nonnegotiable because they are essentially nonrelational, and they serve the purpose of insulating the patient from exposure to meaningful communication with self or other. Action defenses differ from Johann's enactive narrative of despair and release. They are intrasubjective and intersubjective imploders.

McDougall (1992) employs the term dis-affected to refer to persons who are separated from their own affect and emotion and, thus, suffer the loss of their own psychic life. More specifically, these persons rapidly deploy "action" defenses to dispel affect upon arrival. They empty themselves of feeling (I assume, through dissociation) and maintain action techniques (the addictions, compulsions, perversions, externalizations) to mask their inner void and hold at bay near-psychotic anxieties (such as Winnicott, 1962b, described as "going to pieces"). In the developmental histories of these persons were parents whose own preoccupations precluded their availability for the containment and guidance of libidinal wishes or narcissistic demands. These individuals grew up in a theater of the "Impossible" (another word for nonnegotiable?) in which fundamental issues of existence and identity—like the challenges of separation, intersubjectivity, gender, aging, and death—were faced by the child in the absence of meaning-making in relational dialogue. McDougall observed that their mothers, in particular, were not only "out of touch" with their emotional needs—chronically misrecognizing and misnaming them—but also tied their children closely to their own urgent emotional orbit, often controlling the meaning of the child's thoughts, feelings, or spontaneous gestures. Everett's mother, in the earlier vignette, appropriated her son into her own narcissistically driven family competitions. Another patient of mine told me, "My mother always took me shopping, even into adulthood. She picked out all my clothes, and, until recently, I believed I was two sizes larger!" Another patient said, "As soon as you disagreed with my father, the conversation stopped. He could never be wrong—he wouldn't hear of it! I mean, I'd *know* the author of a book, and he'd say, 'No; you're wrong!' And, if it was something more personal—forget it! He was unreachable, unpetitionable. Words were useless. I'd struggle to get through, and feel my energy just drain away. It was like spitting up blood." In treatment, according to McDougall, these patients don't change; they don't hold on to insights; the analysis goes nowhere, and the analyst feels bored, tired, or guilty of uselessness. McDougall reports experiencing in these treatments a recurring assault on the analytic process itself, and on the analyst herself, as they threaten the patient with connection and affect arousal. In these attempts by the patient to destroy her very capacity for concern (as, I believe, I faced with Everett), McDougall discerns primitive communication, a decree "that communication is useless and that the desire for a live affective relationship is *hopeless*" (p. 263, italics added). This assault on communication in potential space is actually a very potent direct communication that forecloses the space between the analytic pair and the psychic space within each party (hence, the analyst's boredom or drowsiness). If the analyst is able to recognize, and not merely succumb to, this conveyance of "the maternal law"—which is, "Don't be alive: at least not beyond my omnipotence!"—this awareness "allows him or her to feel, sometimes poignantly, the double-bind messages and forgotten pain and distress of the small infant who had to learn to render inner liveliness inert in order to survive" (p. 257). Or, as one patient, looking back on his emotional life, said to me, "There was a special literal meaning for me in the phrase 'Void where Prohibited'."

Ogden (1988) considers McDougall's "affect-dispersing action" techniques as defenses against the profound anxiety of not knowing what one feels, wishes, or needs; in short, not knowing "who, if anyone, I am." The inability to elaborate the raw material of internal experience derives from one's developmental history of severe misrecognition and misnamings of one's inner affective or appetitive states, rendering the child confused and exposed to the primitive agony of mounting needs, or expectations, that remain unidentified. Ogden's developmental model thus resonates with McDougall's, and uses Winnicott's observations of how the mother's adaption to her baby's state, when it is "good enough," correctly "names" the state. (As Sullivan, 1953, put it, needs become identified by the infant through appropriate actions taken by the mother in the service of the need, guided by her own inner tension of tenderness and an interpersonal empathic linkage.) Because it is anguish to the mother not to know her child's needs, if she is blocked in her own receptiveness to affect or urgency in the "other," she will substitute her own authorial "knowing" of her child. She might obsessionally impose her schedule, her regime, as her defense against not knowing what her baby requires. She might resort to stereotyped explanations, while remaining blind to her child's true subjectivity. This "mother knows best" rigidity was described by Alice Miller (1981) and R. D. Laing (1969); and it seems apparent in Everett's mother's reply to his upset after his sisters had tied him, naked: "Oh, Everett, they're playing!" And, as Ogden (1988) pointed out, it can be recapitulated in treatment by "analytic authority" presuming to name the patient's psychic reality (as did William's therapist, by formulaic statements that had been handed down through generations of authoritative analytic misrecognition). The child who grows up in an environment in which the meaning of her internal states (of feeling, need, wish) has not been negotiated in a relational context, remains vulnerable to "the anxiety of not knowing one's internal state." A patient told me, "I can be driving my car and not know if I'm cold and need the heater, or hot and need the air conditioner." Fearing breakdown—or, as Winnicott (1974) explained, the realization of a breakdown that has already occurred—whenever powerful affect arises in the context of a relationship that does not "hold" the state, the person must defend, at all cost, against affect, wish, and relationship. Instead, the "action" defenses serve as a substitute, or false, self, perpetuating the internal mother's misrecognition of true inner state, while insulating the person against the apprehension of psychic nonexistence. One reason such defenses are nonnegotiable, so resistantly entrenched, is that the patient dreads the certainty that underneath there is *nothing* (as, outside, there is *no one*); no internal space exists for holding personal experience where no external Other has been present to hold relational experience. Thus, profoundly alienated from an internal affective life, one is hard pressed indeed to relinquish in therapy those repetitions and automatisms that are one's only known existence!

Ironically, the patient who maintains this form of nonnegotiable position, defending against the hopelessness of ever owning a reliable personal existence, of ever knowing "who, if anyone, I am," persists in occluding the very hope of bringing an internal life into being by perpetuating those "action" techniques that fill "the potential space in which feeling states (that are experienced as one's own) might arise" (Ogden, 1988, p. 665). These affect-dispelling defenses perpetuate the nonnegotiable at the severest level of hopelessness. (I believe that Everett diverted his own attention from a recognition of inner emptiness and fragmentation—the residue of severe misrecognitions and mistreatments—by resorting compulsively to such "action" defenses: his externalizing, projectively identifying, excitement-seeking, crisis-generating, and paranoid foreclosings.)

On the other hand, in contrast to the "action" defenses, repetitions rendered explicitly within the transference relationship raise the nonnegotiable to the level of despair. Indeed, the sign that a space for hope has begun to open within the patient is that he or she now delivers the repetition of despair into the transference, coercing (and, paradoxically, permitting) a relational dilemma, or "crunch." We might say that McDougall's "dis-affected" patients repeat in analysis the deadness that derives from early trauma to their capacity to feel (Russell, unpublished), but they will not yet repeat the wishes that preceded traumatic disappointment, nullification, or shock. Indeed, as McDougall (1992) described experiencing assaults on her capacity for concern, I believe the gravely disaffected patient may intend to deaden the aliveness in the analyst, or others; to extract the inner life, to evacuate the space for wish, desire, or hope, to kill the innocence that attaches and loves; in a kind of psychic vampirization that memorializes a history of "soul murder" by concrete, direct action narrative—telling by doing. Sitting with Everett, at times, I experienced such a blood-draining. In retrospect, I recognize the difference between Everett's telling me by doing, while disavowing narrative linkages, and Johann's greeting me by his enactive narrative of despair and release. A relational story in the enactive mode is different from an enactive story in the nonrelational mode!

Whereas the hopelessness of the disaffected patient defends against the primitive anxiety of nonexistence, or *annihilation*, in relationship, despair rendered through transference repetitions defends against the anxiety of surprise and change, or *potential*, in relationship. We might call this *the continuum of the nonnegotiable*. If the patient does not deliver repetition into the transference, the treatment relationship is at an impasse; and if the patient does deliver repetition into the transference, the treatment relationship is at risk. The patient's transference repetition of a familiar pattern of despair about relatedness, like the "antisocial gesture" described by Winnicott, carries the paradoxical hope that the destructiveness in the gesture will be met by some environmental adjustment that could name the protest and the tacit wish, the disappointed hope, in the patient's expression of rage and hate. Thus recognized, accepted, and contained, the patient may hazard the transformation of an old and orienting despair into a new and disorienting hope, which becomes the negotiation, or working-through, of the transference.

Of course, there are also those—unfortunately, too numerous—cases in which the working-through of the transference entails a particularly harrowing form of the nonnegotiable. These are the treatments in which the narrative that must become speakable is the story of profound, invasive, sexual, violating, and violent abuse at the hands of familiar, formative loved ones. As Davies and Frawley (1994) have vividly and valuably detailed, the nonnegotiable quality of these treatment dilemmas involves a massive degree of dissociation within the survivors of such abuse; the extent to which, not simply affect, but entire subsystems of the self, attached to the jarringly contradictory dimensions of their abusive relationships, remain dissociatively out of communication—and, hence, beyond intrapsychic negotiation—within the mind of the patient. For patients afflicted by such serious postabuse dissociative disorders, the treatment process becomes a special case of prolonged containment of multiple self–other relational configurations—involving "abuser," "victim," "witness," "rescuer"—that must inescapably be enacted, and reenacted, in shifting transference–countertransference entanglements, until gradually a coherent narrative and an intrapsychic bridging of contradiction may become negotiable; and split-off, compartmentalized subselves may begin to coexist in paradoxical relationship.

Before attempting to describe the process through which the nonnegotiable may enter into negotiation, I want to remind us that any therapy relationship involves two very human persons with limitations and limits. Each therapist brings to the dialogue whatever remains nonnegotiable for him in the way of character, context, concepts, and technique. Each analyst, however well analyzed and assiduously self-analyzed, is host to an idiosyncratic assortment of blindspots and dim spots (McLaughlin, 1995) and will, at some times or under particular conditions, misrecognize and misname either self or other. Perhaps I failed Everett in just such a way. And, conversely, as Shabad (1993) has pointed out, "There may be the occasions when such patients are so filled with bitterness and venomous spite that they do not want even to be understood. Such understanding may be viewed as a coercive attempt to appease their spite, the dignity of which they would like respected" (p. 487).

From this perspective, as I have searched within for an understanding of the particular nonnegotiable stalemate enacted between Everett and me, I have wondered whether his pursuit of revenge and recompense, his absence of hope for relationships of good will and good intentions, and his dread of interpersonal or intrapsychic connectedness left him little space to allow for therapeutic goals other than what McDougall (1992) calls "settling accounts." As McDougall further asserts, we therapists "wait for the birth of a true desire in the other" (p. 270), even as the patient continually nips an inchoate desire for relationship in the bud. But profound therapeutic dependencies do hold their terrors, and their humiliations, and their anguish. I wonder if, in the face of these risks, the hopelessness in Everett said, "Who cares? What's the use?"

I hope it is clear by now that what made my work with Everett seem nonnegotiable was not simply a matter of his unrelenting aggressive onslaught. While intense aggression, rage, and hostility in the transference may rattle, daunt, or strain the analyst, they do not necessarily define, or remain, nonnegotiable. The nonnegotiable is determined by the conjunction of a multitude of subtle and particular intrapsychic and relational factors matched, or mismatched, in each therapeutic partnership. Linda's therapy is an example. A divorced high school principal in her mid-30s, Linda entered therapy in an intensely distressed state. Three years earlier, her husband's infidelities had been exposed shortly after she had suffered a miscarriage. Linda was abandoned by her therapist in the midst of that crisis. Prior to that, as the details of her story made clear to me, her first therapist had failed her, and a second therapist had mistreated her. Now she was driven to enter yet another therapy when her current boyfriend "ditched" her and took up with a mutual friend. Linda felt raw, scorched by betrayal, and embittered to her core. She told me forthrightly that she felt little grounds for trusting any man (beginning with her philandering father, who had left her to grow up alone with a depressed and clinging mother). She told me that I had better not fail her, that she would not spare me, and that I'd better not accuse her of being difficult. Her cheeks flushed with rage readily and often. She declared, "Everyone who was supposed to take care of me failed me. I took care of my mother—I still do. I'm taking care of teachers and kids all day long at the school. Meanwhile, I'm getting screwed." Linda's one relationship that she counted on never to let her down was with her dog, large, loyal, and protective.

Linda required my total, unwavering attention. Whether she was telling me about how her husband had wrecked her life, or about her infantile and enmeshing mother, or her father who refused to acknowledge he'd abandoned her—or detailing her daily routine of work duties, or listing the dog's endearing features, or choosing a new paint color for her kitchen—I was expected not to shift in my seat or interrupt with questions. At times, I did ask questions, and they were usually tolerated and considered but rarely without a warning look that told me I was at the verge of going too far. I found myself sitting very still in my chair, working to quiet my usual fidgets. I felt riveted to the edge of my seat in a state of hyperalert stillness.

Often Linda let me know when I unwittingly made a move. For example, if I tilted a stiff neck, I might receive Linda's reflexive objection, "You're not listening!" Once, when I made the mistake of saying, "I *am* listening," Linda growled at me, "I want to tear the skin from your face!" Sometimes, when she left, she slammed the outside door with such a force that I braced myself, expecting the pane of glass to shatter. A few months into her therapy, I developed a symptom, a harsh pain deep in my stomach that would start in the middle of her session—my last appointment in the day—and continue through my dinner. I found myself dreading her appointments, afraid of making my next false move, and relieved when the end of the hour reassured me of survival. At the same time, I felt an intense aliveness in the atmosphere between us; and I knew that I cared deeply about Linda and her suffering and that I was rooting for her to find satisfaction in life. At the once-a-week pace of our sessions, all the time and money she could afford, I wondered whether our time together could sufficiently provide either the insight or the nurturing I sensed she needed. Yet I also recognized that Linda's sessions acutely strained me, and I wondered how I would handle a greater frequency. I felt sad and frustrated that I could not offer Linda more than a disciplined stillness in my seat; I was aware that, while I was not allowed for a moment to move back from Linda, I did not feel safe enough to move closer.

I also sensed that, even when Linda was telling me the new color of her kitchen, she was doing something she needed to do with me. Once she brought her dog in the car and asked me to leave the office and come out to see her beloved companion. Without question, I went with her to her car. She let the dog out and, despite its impressive majesty, I greeted it with the playful affection one naturally opens toward an animal but that I could not so freely or simply extend to Linda. I conjectured that Linda must have seen me with my own dog, Johann; and, while this possibility was left unspoken, I imagined that she may have made some positive use of picturing me with him. This tenuous attachment process between Linda and me was, however, paralleled by the continual recurrence of her rage episodes. Sometimes, shocked by the sudden and carbolic quality of Linda's attack, I would ask, "What stirred this up? I know my attention drifted, but can you consider what lies behind the strength of your reaction?" And Linda would retort (in retrospect, understandably), "That's your chickenshit defensiveness, asking me questions. You're trying to put it on *me* now. But you're the one who wasn't listening. You're asking me questions to cover up your anger." Generally I would say, and usually it seemed to make a difference when I did, "Linda, I'm sorry my attention drifted" or "I'm sorry I forgot something you wanted me to remember." Less frequently, I would say something like, "Yes, Linda, I am angry. I feel forced into a corner, where it's hard for me to move, or even think. I'm doing the best I can to manage my anger. Sometimes these moments give me stomach pains. And I'm trying to find what therapeutic use we can make of them." While I did feel overwhelmed, even lacerated, at times with Linda, the severity of these experiences did not feel nonnegotiable in quite the way I felt with Everett. For one thing, I felt that I could accept the real pain of Linda's sessions. Perhaps this was supported by my contact with multiple dimensions of Linda, like the love for her dog that she had allowed me to see.

What I consider critical is that our relationship was able to contain both my experience of Linda's raw rage and her experience of my struggle to live with it. I believe this ability was helped by my implicit awareness of an ongoing relational process—unexplained and largely unarticulated—that gave me a sense of meaning in between the moments I strained to keep, or relocate, my balance. I further believe that, for all the harshness of Linda's aggression toward me, Linda was herself engaged in a precarious and subtle collaboration to keep our therapy alive and make it work for her. Looking back at my beleaguered moments, I think Linda was exquisitely attuned to my limits of tolerance, so that, even as she excoriated me, she gave me time to take in her message or catch my breath. She also gave me room to move with her.

If I acknowledged my anger, or apologized, or shared my awareness of the effort to bear pain, Linda could indicate to me that I had reached her with some meaningful communication. At the very least, she would back off; in this, I sensed her tacit wish for my survival as her therapist, and I was grateful. Here I contrast Linda with Everett, who, at our most nonnegotiable moments, would receive whatever efforts I made at reflection or reparation with a malevolent shift of frame that would recast each of my statements as startlingly, categorically, and inexorably "wrong." Everett collapsed the paradoxes necessary to keep a relational potential space open for progressive negotiation. In the face of Everett's stalemate endgame, I felt hopelessly defeated. *With the room that Linda gave me to move, I sensed the uncertain hope that attends the repetition of despair in a more relational space.* Such relational space remains open to the extent that destruction and survival (subjectivization and recognition) are sustained in a paradoxically coexistent tension. Linda's therapy did not abort; instead, it took surprising turns.

Sadly, one turn suddenly occurred when Linda's dog was hit by a car and was killed. Week after week, Linda came and cried with me. Eventually, Linda, who could not bear to get another dog, began to wonder how to fill the emptiness she felt in her apartment. Six months later, as she was telling me the details of her renewed interest in athletic exercise, I was distracted by the distant ringing of the telephone in my house. On that day, I had been awaiting a call from Johann's vet to inform me whether a tumor, from which he would soon die, was operable. As I wrestled internally with the conflict of whether or not to interrupt the session and run to the phone, I totally lost track of what Linda was saying. She caught me: "You're not there! You've stopped listening!" Too vulnerable to reassemble my therapist ego, I simply said, "I'm sorry. I heard the phone and I've been expecting a call from the vet. My dog is very sick." Linda flushed and then, with her voice rising, said, "I'm not interested in your problems. Don't give me your excuses. This is *my* time!" I silently accepted Linda's reproach. She paused and then returned to talking about exercise.

This turned out to be the last time Linda raged at me. She never asked about my dog, and I did not tell her when Johann died. But, shortly thereafter, Linda reported to me her first dream. In it, Linda entered a palace, climbing wide and bejeweled stairs to a second floor (I have a second-floor office), where she encountered a king, or sultan, sitting on a throne surrounded by an entourage that seemed very colorful, like a circus. I did not interpret this dream but privately noted its positive, bright, and idealized quality. I wondered to myself whether Linda had first needed to establish that it was safe enough to hate before she could venture to explore with me whether it was safe enough to love. Linda's dream seemed to me possibly to herald a more idealizing transference.

But we negotiate what we can, as we can; and Linda and I would not have the opportunity to work through this aspect of the transference. Within a month of her dream, Linda reported meeting a man and falling suddenly in love. This man, Sam, appealed to her intensely, and she felt passionately for him, but she also recognized many problems and incompatibilities they would need to surmount. Suddenly, I found myself to be a kind of "Dear Abby," as Linda filled her therapy sessions with questions about how to negotiate her new relationship. Several months later, she asked me if she could bring her boyfriend with her for couple therapy. She said that she really wanted her relationship with Sam to work, and this was the best way I could help her. I struggled inside with questions of whether I would be abetting her in a flight (through "love") from transference, juxtaposed in my mind with questions of how to benefit her within the constraints of a weekly therapy, and also what risk of harm to her might lie in my placing my own therapeutic agenda above her consciously avowed needs. Realizing that either way lay an enactment with risks, I consented.

For three months, Linda came for sessions with Sam. Indeed, between these two volatile people, there was much to sort out. I tried to help them focus on basic communication skills, to consider how they listened to one another and made room for their differences. Whatever we did, or did not, accomplish in the couple sessions, I sensed that Linda wanted me to meet her boyfriend and, in some way, sponsor their growing courtship. Soon Linda announced she would stop our sessions and give her new relationship a chance to develop on its own. And so she did.

I was left to wonder whether Linda had bolted from the risks of transference love; whether she had taken flight into a problematic relationship that would again repeat the familiar pattern of disappointment and despair. Could we not further pursue the analytic work augured by her dream and address the idealized, magical, and promising world where she felt like a visitor and an outsider? Could Linda and I manage to open for exploration the implicit question of whether this exotic cameo world could also be hers, a richer relational world that she might more fully own, inhabit, articulate, and negotiate? Or had we done whatever work we could? Would Linda now carry her idealized "Circus King" like a relic, a miniature bright "world" under glass, held inside without shaking, without change, without challenge? I wondered if she would return to therapy, again in distress. She never did.

In a final surprising turn, I met Linda six years later in a supermarket. Actually, she spotted me, ran up to me, and threw her arms around me in a warm and wholehearted hug. Bubbling over with pleasure, she told me that she and Sam had married and were very happy together. They had a home and a dog and a good life. Linda told me she was grateful for all we had done, and we wished each other well. She left me feeling as though I had just been given a gift or a blessing.

THE PROCESS

In therapy, or analysis, we do what we can. Negotiations are ongoing and incomplete. Some issues may remain nonnegotiable, even in a "successful" process. In the extreme, the establishment of a treatment relationship itself remains nonnegotiable. Russell (unpublished) called the repetition compulsion "the scar tissue of the trauma to the capacity to feel." Some scar tissue remains forever untouched by the negotiations that occur in a therapeutic relationship. Sometimes what seems utterly nonnegotiable, a state of hopelessness, awaits the accretions of relationship or the passage of time for the patient to open to engagement with his or her despair.

Rebecca, one of my first patients, phoned me 13 years after ending her treatment to ask if she could come for a visit. I happily agreed. Rebecca had entered therapy with me when she was in her early 20s. Although a creatively gifted person, she had finished her senior year of college by the skin of her teeth, having engaged in heavy drug use, reckless driving, and destructive relationships. She lived an urchinlike existence, abhorred aloneness, and sought out bars so that she could "stand in the crowd between two people and feel like I exist." Rebecca stayed for eight sessions and then left to attend her out-of-state college graduation. Our plan was for her to return to Boston, and to her therapy, in a month. Instead, she disappeared. After four months of whereabouts unknown, Rebecca resurfaced at my office door. She had been on a binge of drugs and various forms of high speed ("One night," she said, "I danced barefoot on beer bottles and ended up with a staph infection"). Seeing Rebecca's state and fearing that she might soon end up dead in a ditch, I hospitalized her that day, mobilized her extraordinarily ungiving family, and undertook a therapy that lasted nine years. In the course of this treatment, I felt devoted to offering her a sponsoring and sheltering provision in therapy. She became highly dependent on a sustaining relationship with me, which included phone calls between sessions. She also withheld information, manipulated me by either exaggerating or underplaying her states of danger, and evoked in me acute feelings of worry, helplessness, and exasperation. At times I felt like a mother whose infant will not eat; at other times I felt ridiculed for loving her. Rebecca would only haphazardly talk about fragments of her life history, requiring us to focus on the chaotic surface of her current daily life. In those early days of clinical practice, I brought to the work my inexperience and earnest naivete. At that time, I did not have the benefit of more recent work on the treatment of childhood abuse survivors to confirm my suspicion that her alcoholic father had sexually abused her. While Rebecca readily reported that when she reached adolescence he would make raunchy remarks to her, she recalled no further boundary crossings. Although she and I neither accumulated our insights into a thoroughly coherent narrative reconstruction nor worked through the sadomasochistic features of transference–countertransference patterns, Rebecca eventually ceased her drug use, stabilized practices of self-care and self-soothing, developed a solid career, and, just before abruptly quitting treatment, married a successful professional.

I felt pleased and expectant as the two of us, now middle-aged, sat opposite each other in my office after 13 years. Rebecca told me she had come for three specific reasons: to apologize to me, to inform me, and to thank me. Her apology was succinct and astoundingly incisive. She said, "I could not bear to be so dependent on you. At the same time, I was furious that you wouldn't just fix my life for me. So, I set out to destroy you. I had to make you suffer. I'm sorry." Rebecca also had a second apology: She had quit therapy abruptly because she and her new husband had begun a pattern of heavy alcohol dependence, which she feared she could not continue to keep from me. At that time, her secret alcohol abuse had been nonnegotiable. The information she wanted me to have was that, during a subsequent time when she had been try-ing to get pregnant and had joined AA and ceased her drinking, she had recovered memories of extensive sexual abuse by her father. She had then entered another therapy to address these memories more thoroughly. Finally, she said she wanted to thank me. She said, "We couldn't address my alcoholism together. Or the abuse. I wasn't ready yet. But you did everything right. You stood by me. I felt loved and sheltered. You made it possible for me to stay alive long enough until I was ready to really face the work I had to do. You gave me the hope that I held on to even when things got worse. Until I could find it in myself to make them better."

Rebecca's visit, and her message, exemplified for me how even an incomplete therapy, one that fails to negotiate significant symp-tomatic or transference conditions, may still serve a vital purpose. In the course of our work together, Rebecca's abuse history and her own substance abuse remained nonnegotiable issues. Yet her message anticipated how I would summarize the process of ther-apeutic work in the face of the nonnegotiable. Indeed, although Rebecca and I did not accomplish a comprehensive therapy together, her message highlights how, before the nonnegotiable can begin to enter into substantial therapeutic negotiation, the patient's entrenched hopelessness must move toward hope, which is the prerequisite for a healing dialogue. And the first sign of hope may be when a patient's self-isolating defensive techniques give way to a rendering directly into the treatment relationship of her repetitions of despair. For Rebecca, it may have been essential that I hold her feelings of futility and hopelessness, so that she could begin to entertain hope without feeling unrecognized.

As Rebecca's own words suggest, the therapist, facing the non-negotiable in the forms of enactive foreclosures or dissociations may still offer the patient three elemental features of his presence: containment, acceptance, and recognition. *Containment* implies boundaries, and a space within. The therapist's containment of the patient's nonnegotiable relates to Winnicott's notion of the "holding environment." Simply by being there and remaining the (through silence or speech), sustaining the potential for a relationship over time, the therapist gives the patient a chance to precipitate a multiplicity of feelings into the continuity of one abiding relationship. By surviving intact, even if rattled, exposure to the patient's plethora of moods, affects, and manipulations over time, the therapist conveys that "I contain multitudes"; that is, personal integrity may survive the containment of contradiction and paradox (for example, futility *and* hope).

By *acceptance*, I mean to emphasize the therapist's open, willing, and disciplined receptiveness to the patient's feelings, as well as the feelings evoked by the patient within the therapist. The tenacity or perseverence with which the therapist struggles within himself to tolerate, and remain open to, the patient's rage, hopelessness, dread, or anguish, conveys a fundamental human respect: the therapist thereby communicates to the patient, "I am willing to take your pain deep inside myself; I am willing to be confused, disconcerted, and unsettled; I am even willing, up to a point, to be hurt by you. I will struggle inside myself, and not expect the process to be easy or convenient or suited to my own self-interest. I will be as patient, undemanding, nonjudgmental, and noninvasive as I can be. I will work at our negotiations." I believe that any patient who has been faced throughout life with nonnegotiable, unpetitionable, categorical stances—without effective appeal—in relationship to parents or other figures feels, somewhere inside, the glimmerings of gratitude if she experiences a therapist authentically struggling inside with his or her own personal limits of acceptance and tolerance. Here acceptance and containment are overlapping features of the basic relational process of negotiating boundaries and mutual survival (as when the therapist says, "I will accept this much strain, or hurt, but only up to this personal limit; or in the service of this mutual effort").

The third, also overlapping, feature of therapeutic process in the face of the nonnegotiable is *recognition*. Clearly a counterbalance to a patient's history of misrecognitions, the therapist's recognition in the presence of the nonnegotiable is not conveyed through interpretations or explanations, but only in the form of authentic enactments. Sometimes the only form of recognition is a silence, a quiet that states wordlessly the tacit awareness that words at that moment would be coercive, intrusive, confusing, corrupting or trivializing (as if to tidy up an ineffable vastness), or a quixotic exercise in futility. The therapist's recognition of the patient can, of course, also include words, a naming of state, or feeling, or relational impasse. The fundamental quality of therapeutic recognition—whether conveyed in verbal, gestural, or tonal form—is that the therapist is making an internal adjustment to the patient; the therapist is registering the imprint of that patient's state even while striving to preserve personal integrity and equilibrium. In these primal modes of containment, acceptance, and recognition, the therapist faces the nonnegotiable stance of the patient and implicitly says, "I am with you." Inevitably, if this is not a self-idealizing, narcissistic-masochistic, or deceptive (Slavin and Kriegman, 1998) position of the therapist's, he or she is also saying, "This is hard for me; I am in conflict; I will not fall into your hopelessness if I can help it; I am trying to keep both of us from being hurt; I don't know how this will turn out between us; and, I continue to hope."

As Rebecca reported, and as I believe began to occur with Linda, the prolonged process of containment, acceptance, and recognition in the face of the nonnegotiable may lead to the opening, within the patient, of a space for hope and, hence, for transference repetitions. Once the emergence of hope (even in its paradoxical appearance as despair of hope) opens a potential, or metaphorical, space for dialogue between patient and analyst, the intractably nonnegotiable may begin to enter a more vital, if uncertain, relational process of negotiation.

THE NEGOTIATION OF PARADOX

Russell (unpublished), in his unique, nonlinear style, made a brilliant leap of connection. He juxtaposed the repetition compulsion, the powerful impact of paradox, and the structure of scientific revolutions. Connotative, impressionistic, and imaginative as it was of Russell to assemble these pieces on the table, I believe that, as he gathered these elements, they crystalized a powerful recognition of how analyst and patient may negotiate transferences once the nonnegotiable enters a relational space. As Russell observed, each patient must deliver a particular "crunch" into the treatment relationship, coercing (and opening) a relational crisis; and the "way out for the patient is *by identifying with the struggle that emerges*" (italics added). This is essentially what I mean by the process of containment, acceptance, and recognition; but it also announces the threshold of a more openly and explicitly relational transference–countertransference opportunity, as the containing and recognizing processes, taken inside by the patient, become the basis for the patient's ability to contain, accept, and recognize conflict, multiplicity, contradiction, and paradox.

Here, then, is how the negotiation of paradox in the transference works. Let us assemble the pieces provided by Russell:

The first piece is the repetition compulsion. As Russell consistently argued, "We find ourselves repeating that which, so far as we know, we would far rather not repeat." The repetition compulsion is our nemesis, our patterned relational ineptitude, our "education-resistant" formula for making each new relational opportunity default to the same old feeling. Russell asserted, "Trauma *is* that which gets compulsively repeated." It is as if trauma folds our soul's pristine sheet of paper; and, try as we might to smooth it out, we always return to the places we were creased (in Balint's, 1968, term, our "basic fault"). Thus, we prejudicially negotiate each new relationship in the direction of our most nonnegotiably established paradigms. Outlook forces outcome. In analysis, the recalcitrant force of the patient's relational paradigms always renders uncertain the possibility of the fresh negotiations that may herald change and growth. This is why Freud (1915a) saw transference as both foe and ally of the analyst's task and used as a metaphor the anecdote of the clergyman who visited the atheist insurance agent at his deathbed and came away, not with a converted soul, but with an additional insurance policy. While despairing of ever finding comfort, competence, or intimacy, the patient adamantly recapitulates as transference those familiar— self-defeating and self-orienting—paradigms that ensure the perpetuation of despair.

Ogden (1988) has noted, "As a result, no encounter is experienced as new. Transference provides the illusion that one has already been there before. Without this illusion, we would feel intolerably naked and unprepared in the face of experience with a new person" (p. 655). Yet, according to Russell, "In some peculiar way, the enterprise of life requires that one both remain the same and change, all at the same time" (p. 61). Here is where the analytic pair may activate the potential inherent in the paradoxical nature of transference–countertransference repetitions.

Paradox is the second piece in Russell's juxtaposition. He observed that "the capacity to tolerate paradox is a measure of ego strength" (p. 68). We might say that this capacity both permits analytic negotiation and grows in the practice of analytic negotiation. About how the mind works with paradox, Russell stated: "Insofar as we understand anything, we attempt to make our understanding *consistent* (that is, without contradiction) and *complete* (because what we leave out might be the most important). But paradox shatters the attempt to be both consistent and complete. We cannot live with it" (p. 68). Yet Russell emphasized that, if we can bear to tolerate paradox, we can learn from it. He goes on to consider the impact of paradox on any philosophical, scientific, logical, or personal system of thought; and, to this end, he invoked Gödel's proof:

> For *any* system, it is impossible to be both logically consistent and complete, that is, without paradox. A simple *contradiction* is something that can be discovered, sooner, or later, to be either true or not true, without expense to the rest of the system. A *paradox* is something which the *coherency and consistency of the entire rest of the system requires to be both true and not true; a contradiction from which there is no escape without the destruction of the system* [p. 69].

Russell's third piece of juxtaposition was an episode from the history of science, used by Kuhn (1962) to illustrate *The Structure of Scientific Revolutions*, in which the old Ptolemaic cosmology gave way to the Copernican model of the solar system. Briefly, the Ptolemaic system was a geocentric paradigm that assumed the sun and other planets revolved around the earth (the center of God's interest). Astronomical readings, made by available instrumentation, that were inconsistent with the Ptolemaic model (that is, a planet appeared in a spot unpredicted by its hypothetical orbit in the Ptolemaic paradigm) were reconciled with the insistent geocentric worldview by the elaborate construction of complex hypothetical suborbits—a kind of curlicued planetary path—that were called "epicycles." Eventually, the massive scale of complex epicycle-juggling necessitated by actual readings that contradicted the Ptolemaic system attained a level of cumbersomeness that forced the reluctant scientific, and ecclesiastical, world to yield to the

Copernican paradigm shift: the heliocentric system we believe in today without the necessity of built-in epicycles to manage contradictory evidence.

Putting together these three pieces—repetition compulsion, paradox, and the process of paradigm shifts—Russell helps us understand the working-through of transference repetitions through the negotiation of paradox. You can't escape paradox. You can't preserve a relational frame (a transference paradigm) *and* experience all the relational exchanges in the mutual and reciprocal enactments of patient and analyst. Starting with an insistent, nonnegotiable, and despairing relational paradigm (a personal cosmology) superimposed on the analytic relationship, the patient may seek to remain *consistent* by refusing to be *complete*. That is, the patient may resist, repudiate, eject, expel, or otherwise nullify insights or enactments that contradict their closely held worldview and the internal object loyalties that bind them. The patients described by Ogden and McDougall, or those who undo "Penelope's Loom," as described by Mitchell (1988), come to mind here. Eventually, over time, however, the very repetition of the transference paradigm will expose the patient, within its frame, to moments of startle in which the "old" object does not obey "the laws" of internal object relationships—and the contradiction cannot be thrown out as bum data. The patient, having first implicitly established the adequate safety of analytic containment, places the entire relationship at dire risk by venturing repetitive enactments of the internal laws of despair (see Greenberg, 1986); and, hope lies in the analyst's ability, sometimes, to come through with acts of recognition that contradict his expected position in orbit. Sometimes, inevitably, the analyst will fail to negotiate the paradoxical potential in these repetitions. Sometimes the analyst will look truly Ptolemaic! But, by slow accretions, relational negotiations will perturb the patient's sealed psychic universe. And the analysand's nonnegotiable outlook, or paradigmatic system, proliferating relational epicycles to account for contradictory readings in the course of transference–countertransference enactments, will begin to fall of its own cumbersome weight. Thus, the patient's self-system comes to accommodate and straddle relational paradox; to stay the same while changing (Russell, unpublished; Bromberg, 1995). I believe that this process approaches what Loewald (1980) meant by the new discovery of object relationships and by his statement that "the passive reproduction of experience does present the opportunity for arriving at re-creative repetition, depending on a variety of internal and external conditions" (p. 91). Or, as Hoffman (1996) has written, "The relationship between repetition of pathological aspects of the past and relatively new experience is usually highly complex and paradoxical. In fact, it is generally useful to view their relationship as dialectical, that is, each not only serves as ground for the other but is actually on the brink of evolving into the other" (p. 126).

Thus, I believe that Linda's repetition of relationships with men whose attentions had wandered (her philandering father, her husband, her earlier therapists, her boyfriend) were enacted relationally between us until she could experience me as struggling within myself to remain steadfast on her behalf. Despair and hope, old and new, coexist in transference–countertransference repetition. When a full transference regression concentrates the patient's paradigms of despair into the treatment relationship and analyst and patient are able to negotiate mutual survival of its destructive force, there is a potential for anomalous, contradictory relational moments to perturb the system and, as dynamic systems theory has taught us, nudge a systemic shift with enormous ramifying consequences. Like Russell, I suggest that, just as cosmological paradigm shifts can change the way we *think* about celestial objects, psychological paradigm shifts can change the way we *feel* about our relational objects, when the nonnegotiable has been engaged in an analytic, dialogical negotiation of paradox, when the analyst's presence for the patient represents an absence that, finally, can be addressed.

CODA

In Sarajevo, in a pedestrian plaza, a grenade was thrown into a crowd of people standing in line at 4 PM to purchase bread at the bakery. Twenty-two people, of all ages, were killed. Following this event, each day for 22 days, Vedran Smailovic[2] (of the former

---

[2] I thank Yo-Yo Ma and his gracious office staff for providing me with program notes written by David Wilde to introduce his elegiac piece, "The Cellist of Sarajevo," a mournful solo cello rondo dedicated "in admiration" to Vedran Smailovic, whose story Wilde conveys.

Sarajevo Opera) dressed himself in his tuxedo and carried his cello and a chair into that plaza. At precisely 4 PM every day, for 22 days, Smailovic played the cello, solo, in the plaza, regardless of machine gun fire, mortar from the surrounding hills, and the risk of further grenade attacks. His repetition, like Johann's run in and out of the pen, told a story and emphasized an event. Like Linda's repetition of despair in my office, it bore witness to trauma and declared the reality of heartbreak. Unlike Everett's duplications of trauma, which blasted the life space between himself and me, unlike even Johann's literal dance of liberation, the cellist of Sarajevo, with the metaphoric strength and potential of his music, rendered his daily repetition of lament in the plaza for himself and for all who could hear and for all who could not hear. His act of despair was his act of hope, sending his message out to the surrounding hills in the strains of his music.

Part II

Paradox and Negotiation in Wider Contexts: Genders, Species, Nations

A Wider Context ... and a Critique of "Tribal" Gender Categories

When the tension between complementarity and mutuality breaks down—individually or culturally—the absence of a real other creates a kind of paranoid free fall. The cycle of destroying the reality of the other and filling the void with the fantasy of a feared and denigrated object, one who must be controlled for fear of retaliation, characterizes all relations of domination [Benjamin, 1995, p. 94].

"One's-Self I sing, a simple separate person,

Yet utter the word Democratic, the word En-Masse."

—Walt Whitman ("Inscriptions")

In Part II, I explore conditions of paradox and processes of negotiation pertaining to, and addressed in the disciplines and discourses of, intergroup conflict resolution, evolutionary biology, and matters of sex, sexuality, and gender identity. My aim is to pursue a usefully coherent unity—of theme, idea, dynamic, and perspective—while including the multiplicity of these conceptual domains regarding genders, species, and nations. Unity of theme is commonly advised, and advisable, in exposition or dramatics, just as—psychologically, socially, and adaptively—a unity of identity is convenient. But postmodernist thinking has reminded us that such conveniences are costly, as they are inherently distorting, deforming, and alienating by the exclusion of multiplicity, nuance, and the freedom of options. So, into the conceiving and writing of this chapter, and the two that follow, I carry the very problem of straddling unity and multiplicity that is the object of my study. I am asking how paradox and negotiation, as I have been developing these terms as tools in psychoanalytic thinking, apply to the wider contexts in which negotiation, evolutionary adaptation, and gender discrimination are studied; and, reciprocally, how these distinctly articulated fields may contribute dimensions of meaning, metaphor, and method to my notions of paradox and negotiation in the analytic process. We will be revisiting the Winnicottian paradoxes of ruthlessness and concern, privacy and connectedness, separateness and interrelatedness, dependency and provision, destructiveness and creativity. We will see this particular linguistic rendering of essential paradoxes refracted through such legal and diplomatic concepts as "positional" and "principled" negotiation (power versus mutual gain); and in the individualistic (selfish) versus mutualistic (altruistic) interests built into the ancestral hard-wiring that has become our universal evolutionary inheritance; and in the counterposition of intrapsychic and intersubjective, exclusionary and inclusionary, morphological and metaphorical, unitary and multiple versions of gender definition in contemporary, feminist informed, psychoanalytic debate. Thus, common to these disparate realms we encounter the paradox of our selves necessarily existing both as one and as many and the challenge of bridging this paradox through ceaselessly ongoing interior and "interentity" negotiations.

Sullivan (1953) described, in his way, how the "self-system" functions as an "envelope of experience," a relatively enduring (although transformable) pattern of inclusions and exclusions of identity and awareness ("me" and "not me") maintained by our vulnerability to gradient anxiety. A case in point: When I was roughly six years old, I accompanied my parents to a large New York department store. While they pursued some shopping errand, I stood alone nearby at a table that displayed piles of baseball-emblem T-shirts. My eyes were drawn to a pile of "Jackie Robinson" T-shirts, with a large-size portrait of one of my baseball heroes. I recall standing alone, picking up one of these T-shirts,

and wanting my parents to buy me one. Then I had an interven-
ing thought: "I can't wear this T-shirt. I can admire Jackie
Robinson. But I can't *be* him [on the identificatory stage of my
own imagination]. We're different colors." I put back the T-shirt
and stood there. I felt thwarted by an impossibility that I had no
way to comprehend or explain, either in its power, its meaning, or
its derivation. I just knew I was the wrong color for *being* Jackie
Robinson. My parents took their time completing their transaction. I remained for the time caught in conflict and anxiety and
frustrated desire. When they returned, I did ask them to buy me
this Jackie Robinson T-shirt, but I believe I was by then so disconcerted that I had entered a state of semidissociation.

What could I be while being me? What could I not be? And
why? While this moment of personal experience relates most
prominently to racial dichotomies, I believe it cuts across general
problematics relating to gene, genus, gender, and genocide. I refer
in this context to Benjamin's (1995) eloquent statement, which
begins this chapter.

I believe that the tension between complementarity (subject–object relations) and mutuality (subject-subject relations)—
that is, between the "doer-done to" of power exchanges and the
reciprocal identifications of symmetrical exchanges—is sustained
through the exercise of our capacity to negotiate paradox. As we
saw in Chapter 4, the capacity to tolerate paradox is a developmental, ontogenetic achievement. In a similar vein, Slavin and
Kriegman (1992) point out that "in the evolutionary narrative,
the innate mutuality and relatedness—the evolved, universal tendency to incorporate in one's self and to promote the interests
of others—remains in constant, essentially unresolvable, tension
with individuals' efforts to shape relationships toward their own
biased, subjective perspective"[1] (p. 122). Seen from this framework, the ability to tolerate paradox can be regarded as a phylo-
genetic achievement, an evolved adaptive competence for each
individual's negotiating with others the irreducible coexistence

---

[1] This model assumes a quality of singularity to the individual's "biased, subjective
perspective," a notion contested by postmodernist thinking. Nonetheless, even
granting a multiplicity within subjectivity, the individual's most singularly selfish evolutionary bias is to survive and preferentially supply germplasm to the
gene pool.

of utterly selfish and intrinsically overlapping survival interests.

But let us not assume that our ancestrally hard-wired deep structure has already fully evolved and that we live our present lives enjoying the benefits of evolutionary completeness. We have not left the evolutionary chain, and one sign of our incomplete evolution may be our limited competence at bearing and bridging the paradoxes of our nature. Whether our limitations can be attributed to the hardware constraints of biological structure or to the software constraints of evolved cultural practice, we have already noted how painful it can be to encounter, to represent, and to contain paradoxes in our intrapsychic and relational existence. Paradox perturbs the mind and coerces mental work. And the work of juxtaposing contradictions, encompassing multiplicity, and straddling reciprocal negations—while accomplished with the nimbleness of primary process in our dream world—continually threatens the stable footing of our conscious minds. That is why even Winnicott (1971a), who so incisively recognized our potential for creatively *playing* with irresolvable paradoxes, noted how precariously close the play state is to the brink of "unthinkable anxiety": flying into pieces (the uncontained baby? the uncohered multiplicity?) and falling forever (the unheld baby? the "paranoid free fall"?).

When we cannot bear to preserve paradox, to dwell at the fractal seashore of potential space where "children play" with the manifold possibilities of reality and fantasy—when we cannot tolerate the affect attending the "chaotic" quality of our complex dynamic (self) system—we default to the foreclosure of paradox and the segregating-out of dischaotic, rigidly bounded, more dissociatively isolated mental constructions. In short, to escape the tensions of holding paradox we tend to categorize reductively, to reify and dichotomize. We jettison "both/and" for the immediate relief (and ultimate costs) of the simpler "either/or."

What are the consequences of our relative inability—as individual, family, tribe, nation, race, gender, or species—to straddle the paradoxes of our nature? Here are my speculations. Prime casualty of the failure to sustain the tensions of paradox is our capacity to access subjectively the rich multiplicity that relational theorists (see Dimen, 1991; Harris, 1991, 1996; Mitchell, 1993; Bromberg, 1996; Davies, 1996; Flax, 1996; Slavin and Kriegman, 1998) have recognized to exist within the organization of the self in health. I described in Chapter 4 (see also Pizer, 1996b) the conditions under which a healthily *distributed*[2] multiplicity of self yields to a predominantly *dissociated* multiplicity of self. To recapitulate, in health the self is distributively structured among multiple memorial islands of relational experience, but held integrally by the mind's capacity to bridge paradox. This distributed self is maintained to the extent that one is adept in straddling paradox, bridging from one associated cluster to another. One factor may be constitutional, hard wiring. Another factor may be the degree of shock obtaining in discrepant experiences, or the severity of paradox. At severe levels of shock and discrepancy (related to either constitutional or contextual factors, or their combination), paradox becomes unbridgeable, and one deploys the default mechanism of dissociation. Here we recognize the essence of trauma: the disruption of continuity of being (the "illusion of being one self"). The difference between a distributed multiple self (decentered) and a dissociated multiple self (fragmented) lies in the severity of paradox and the degree to which the self's facility for bridging paradox has become overburdened by shockingly

---

[2] As I sat writing in 1996, developing the concept of "a distributed self" for Chapter 4 of this book and using this concept to introduce a Symposium on "The Multiplicity of Self and Analytic Technique" in *Contemporary Psychoanalysis* (Pizer, 1996b, pp. 504–505), I was not consciously aware of how Jerome Bruner (1990) already had used the terms "distributive" and "distributed." I appreciate Mary-Joan Gerson's pointing this out to me. Bruner wrote, "In the distributive sense, . . . the Self can be seen as a product of the situations in which it operates, the 'swarms of its participations,' as Perkins puts it" [pp. 108–109]. Later, Bruner considered how a "cultural psychology" might pose "the problem of the Self":

> It seems to me that a cultural psychology impose two closely related requirements on the study of Self. One of them is that such studies must focus upon the *meanings* in terms of which Self is defined *both* by the individual *and* by the culture in which he or she participates. But this does not suffice if we are to understand how a "Self" is negotiated, for Self is not simply the resultant of contemplative reflection. The second requirement, then, is to attend to the *practices* in which "the meanings of Self" are achieved and put to use. These, in effect, provide us with a more "distributed" view of Self [p. 116].

When Gerson, responding to my article in *Contemporary Psychoanalysis*, referred me to Bruner's book—which I had indeed read in 1995—I was startled to find these passages of Bruner's. Although my own use of "distributed" is as different from as it is also similar to Bruner's, I am indeed indebted to Bruner and glad to make this acknowledgment here.

discrepant relational juxtapositions (including the juxtaposition
of true-self prompting and cultural/linguistic/conceptual disal-
lowal). Might not dissociation enter the picture in a gradient, as
the capacity to bear and negotiate paradox is increasingly strained
toward the breaking point (and dissociations, disavowals, splits,
and banishments increase and intensify)? Thus the woman with
multiple personality who told me that paradox is a nonexistent
concept for her: she could not locate inside herself a subjective
position from which to hold in view the underlying processes (see
Ghent, 1992) or the superordinate matrices that would allow her
contradictory self-states to conserve a sense of each other's imma-
nent (potential) presence and thus maintain the tension of internal
paradox. The distribution of the self into multiple islands of memory, affect, meaning, awareness, intention, and passion may be a
condition of health, whereas the dissociation of the self into multiple subselves marooned on unbridgeable islands would be the
condition of a compromised self.

Dimen (1991) uses metaphorical terms similar to mine when
she writes, "If life is a sea, then gender is an island. Sometimes
people drown in the sea, sometimes they are stranded on land. I
am arguing that we need the sea as much as we need the land,
and, to push this Winnicottian metaphor further, we also need the
seashore, where land and water merge" (p. 350). Thus Dimen
requires (assumes and calls for) a human capacity for (intrasubjective and intersubjective) fractal boundaries—which, like the
place where sea and shore meet in sandy seafoam, renders both
separation and overlap in a fluidly interpenetrating area of "potential space," where distinction and deconstruction continue to ebb
and flow. As I see it, this capacity for a complex, chaotic self organization—one in which contradictory islands are bridged and not
cut off from "interstate commerce"—is indeed a precarious space
in which to play. When the tension of paradox can be held with
respect to gender, then, as Dimen suggests, "Alternatingly definitive and liminal, gender identity also permits us to find in ourselves the overinclusiveness we have had to renounce so that we
can also recognize it in the other, of whatever gender" (p. 350).

But, as is so often the case, when the tension of paradox cannot be held and mechanisms of splitting, dissociation, repudiation,
and projection collapse potential space, we are left indeed
marooned on islands, in states of reciprocal remoteness instead of

mutual recognition (see Benjamin, 1995) with respect to gender identities, or racial identities (as in my encounter with the Jackie Robinson T-shirt), or any other instances in which sameness and difference are given discrimination.

Goldner (1991), in a deconstructionist critique of cultural, and psychoanalytic, categories of gender, challenges "the assumption that an internally consistent gender identity is possible or even desirable" (p. 249). She argues that "gender is fundamentally and paradoxically indeterminant, both as a psychological experience and as a cultural category" (p. 250) and that the "normal" process of gender sorting entraps each person in double binds, that is, paradoxes that are inescapable as well as unnameable and non-negotiable. Such unbridgeable paradoxes coerce mental foreclosures and dissociative recourses; so that, far from being "natural," the presupposed cultural (or psychoanalytic) requirement of conforming developmentally to a singular gender role identity carries the universal problematic of the collapsed subjective paradox of a coexistent psychic unity *and* multiplicity, and is indeed pathogenic. As Goldner asserts, "consolidating a stable gender identity is a developmental accomplishment that *requires* the activation of pathological processes, insofar as any gender-incongruent thought, act, impulse, mood, or trait would have to be disowned, displaced, (mis)placed (as in projective identification), split off, or, as Dimen suggests, . . . renamed via symbolic slippage" (p. 258).

We might say, invoking a Kleinian framework, that the inherent tyranny of "essentialist" dichotomies (of gender, and so on) operates by forcing the breakdown of *essential paradoxes* within each self, pushing each of us back from a depressive position to a prejudicially favored paranoid-schizoid position. This "paranoid-schizoid tilt" skews the dialectical interplay of nonlinear mental states (Ogden, 1994), closing out potential spaces wherein paradoxical subjective juxtapositions may be tolerated and negotiated. Winnicott's thinking, devolved as it was from Kleinianism, recognized that paradox, potential space, and play assume the developmental attainment (and lifelong accessible relocation) of the depressive position, wherein the person is capable of housing internal multiplicity—love and hate, envy and guilt, destruction and reparation, and so on. As I elaborated in Chapter 1, the advent of the depressive position heralds the two- or three-year-old's emergent capacity to manage the paradox of destroying and using the (surviving) object. Thus, with the arrival of a guilt sense and an organization of internality, the child begins to negotiate the paradox of equally valued ruthlessness and concern and participate in relationship characterized by "cross-identifications"—that is, the ability to put the self empathically in the object's place, consolidating that intersubjectivity (described by Benjamin, 1995) in which the object (of continued ruthless subjectivization and demand) is also recognized as a separate "subject" with her own requirements (desires, needs, limits, vulnerabilities, and biases). With a "paranoid-schizoid tilt," inside and outside are kept separate but not well interrelated, and "dischaotic" (sharp) boundaries divide the self from the now projectively–introjectively distinguished object (evacuated of a separate subjectivity). From behind the walls (both battlement and tomb) of the paranoid-schizoid position, the shards of self that cannot be held in paradoxical tension are catapulted out toward the object, who is then utterly (mis)recognized as the repository of ejected elements of the self, such as: shame, humiliation, weakness, dependence, inferiority, messiness, nastiness, and aggression; or hate and murderousness; or, inversely, desire, passion, strength, freedom, virtue, resourcefulness, and other idealized polarities. At a group level, such polarizing mechanisms of splitting, disavowal, dissociation, and projection—the reciprocals of sustained paradox—constitute the basis for bigotry, dominance–submission, scapegoating, and the persecutory intensities of what I think of as any form of "tribalism" (including genders or, for that matter, psychoanalytic "schools").

Altman (1995) arrives at a similar argument in his cogent psychoanalytic study of race, class, and culture in the inner city. He describes the defensive and self-definitional psychic functions provided for individuals by their recourse, at a societal level, to Kleinian projective–introjective mechanisms that create categories of "race, social class, gender, and societal orientation." These conceptual group discriminations set up repositories into which "unwanted psychic content"—such as depressive, impoverished, and degraded (as well as idealized) positions—may be discarded and extruded from self-identity, while they are deposited into the definition of the Other, or "not me." Thus, group identity serves the individual group members' self-definition and integrity—what I am inclined to call *the illusion of self-*

simplification—by deployment of primitive mechanisms that provide for its subscribers a psychic excretion of perturbing, contradictory, threatening, burdensome, and otherwise challenging personal qualities. As Altman also points out, these self-streamlining social group categories come with a price: "Projective identification and other defense mechanisms that seek to disown aspects of self inevitably impoverish or distort the person and his psychic life" (p. 60). Altman invokes a postmodern perspective to argue the sinister absurdity of such arbitrary, essentialist categorical groupings as race or gender: "something created within a discourse, thus contingent, that is, not inevitable or fully given by an 'objective' reality" (p. 69). Such categories, defensively promulgated and institutionally maintained by power, remain potent place-holders for each individual's construction of self. For Altman, hope lies in the individual's negotiation of meaning even while being inducted into the hegemonic framework of dominant societal discourse categories. In the "transitional space" afforded by the individual's negotiation of the meaning of received tribal identity categories lies whatever potential exists for freedom from the tyranny of group definition. All members of all groups pay for our defensively circumscribed, reciprocal self-definitions. As a counterbalance, Altman suggests the value of "dialogue, finding some balance between recognizing the otherness of one's 'opponent's' point of view and recognizing, in Hegelian fashion, the ways in which these seeming opposites create, negate, and preserve each other" (p. 73). In his own terms, Altman thus promotes the value of sustaining a paradoxical tension through ongoing negotiation, rather than a default to rigid, bipolar, exclusionary, and defensively heirarchical categories for "constituting and maintaining a self and a disowned other" (p. 73).

On the basis of years of extensive research on small Bionian self-analytic groups at Harvard, Bales (1970) developed a model of personality and interpersonal behavior in group process. He devised a detailed methodology whereby each group member could identify the interaction patterns of all other group members, and the analytic compilation of all ratings could be used to locate each person in "interpersonal space." Bales's three-dimensional model of the interpersonal space of a group was formed by three intersecting axes: upward–downward, positive–negative, and forward–backward. The polarities defining each axis refer to patterns of interpersonal acts that are upward (dominant/assertive) or downward (submissive/passive), positive (liking/likeable) or negative (disliking/dislikeable), and forward (instrumental/progressive) or backward (expressive/regressive). Year after year, Harvard undergraduates of all personality types would constitute new groups and, participating in the group dynamics in the course of a semester, scatter through interpersonal space to fill out the elegantly repeating, almost architectual, structure of reciprocally defining role relationships. Mary or Sue or John or George, each with a complexly developed self, would enter a group, and each would migrate in group space to that place where she or he would settle into a (circumscribed, recurrent, definable, predictable) group role identity: for example "Upward-Positive-Forward" (an actively assertive, but friendly and affirmative, task leader), or "Upward-Negative-Forward" (a dominating, critical, or hostile taskmaster), or "Upward-Positive-Backward" (an enthusiastically assertive advocate of freely expressed intimacy and affect), or "Downward-Backward" (quiet, and perhaps exhibiting neediness, vulnerability, or moodiness while not seeking attention), or "Downward-Negative-Backward" (the person who, by innuendo, gets others to take obstructive or destructive action—a Iago-like role). With striking regularity, each new group, unsystematically assembled, would evolve its own social and cultural microcosm in which complexly constituted young adults would come to be recognized reductively as they filled their niche in "interpersonal space," like ball bearings that had rolled into the holes in which they would tend to remain identified through the life of the group.

What need, wish, or susceptibility leads individuals to exchange their own distributive dimensionality for a pigeonhole? What quality of the group as an entity militates toward the distribution of individual complexity into the recognized reductive roles of its population? What sense do we make of the stunning regularity with which each new "microcosm," in the space of an undergraduate semester, recapitulates the "regulatory practices of culture" (Foucault, quoted in Goldner, 1991)? Is it necessarily the price of group membership that each person remains seated in a form of "false-self" position?[3] Are we observing conservative group con-

---

[3] Freud's (1921) suggestion holds up that group membership reduces people to their "lowest common denominators"; an irony—or paradox—for Freud, given

straints that operate through the influence of those group members who gravitated "Upward," assuming and consolidating power positions? Are we observing group constraints that reflect the limitations in mutual recognition as an evolved and sophisticated human competence, and the attendant reification of the separate, unitary "identities" of participants? Are we observing the unwitting relief individual members seek, and find, in surrendering their internal complexity, conflict, and contradiction to the group structure and thereby collusively escaping the tensions of containing intrasubjective paradox? Is there a superordinate adaptive function served by the group's tacit assignment of complementary, designated role specializations?

Interestingly, we may note that Bales's categorical dichotomies closely parallel the traits commonly recognized as sorted in Western culture along gender lines: the "masculine" *upward*, aggressive/assertive, dominant, instrumental, autonomous, logical; and the "feminine" *downward*, passive, submissive, expressive, dependent, and irrational (see Benjamin, 1988; Goldner, 1991). While Bales's researchers regularly observed male group members in a "downward-backward" position and females in an "upward-forward" position (and, occasionally, individual group members protest their pigeonholes and fight to be recognized as more multifaceted, spontaneously variable, and contradictory), the very definition of Bales's categories prompts the question of how these particular polarized dimensions continue to crop up as observable behavioral clusters, or as the analytic constructs that stencil repeated observations of interpersonal behavior patterns; and why our larger culture and psychoanalytic tradition have accepted these trait clusters as the "givens" of "gender identity." On this issue, Goldner (1991) quotes Rubin: "The idea that men and women are mutually exclusive categories must arise out of something other than a nonexistent "natural" opposition. Far from being an expression of natural differences, exclusive gender identity is *suppression of natural similarities*" (p. 254, italics added by Goldner).

Rubin's perspective reflects her argument against an "essentialist" justification of hegemonic heterosexuality. Ironically, an

---

his fundamental assumption that culture curbs impulse, sublimating the bestial in the individual (somehow, for Freud, group culture makes us *both* more civilized *and* more primitive).

answer to Rubin's question may come from evolutionary biology, but not in the traditionally biologizing analytic sense of "anatomy is destiny" or "sex naturally equals gender." Slavin and Kriegman (1992), building on the evolutionary-biological thinking of Trivers (1974, 1985), elaborated a conception of the "adaptive design of the human psyche." While I examine their work in more detail in Chapter 7, it is relevant here to consider the implications of the superordinate factor that organizes modern "evolutionary" theory: from the "gene's eye view," requiring preferential reintroduction into the reproductive pool, it is equally advantageous for the (skin-bounded) individual to survive in order to reproduce *or* for others of closely related genotype to survive to introduce their own similar genetic material into the gene pool. Thus, the "survival of the fittest" is redefined to mean not "every man for himself," but each individual both for the self *and* for the closely related (kin or reciprocally implicated) group—even, at times, at sacrifice to the (somatoplasmic) self. Hence, each person is equipped with an ancestrally evolved deep structure to promote both individual fitness (to survive) and "inclusive fitness" (the survival of "like" genes). Consequently, each person has been designed adaptively, through countless evolutionary generations, to pursue *both selfish and altruistic interests*. As Slavin and Kriegman (1992) emphasize, our evolutionary "deep structure" prepares us to negotiate our way through the intrinsic coexistence of overlapping and conflicting interests that are an irreducible condition of each and every relational context, including the most intimately related group context of family kinship; and to practice deceptions, self-deceptions, and the detection of deceptions practiced by others as they exercise their own biased interests.

The copresence of individualistic and mutualistic interests returns us to the Winnicottian paradoxes of ruthlessness and concern, human isolatedness and interrelatedness (Winnicott himself was influenced by his reading of Darwin; see Phillips, 1988). From the evolutionary-adaptive perspective, the human mind must have acquired the ability to tolerate and negotiate the elemental and irresolvable paradox of the contradictory biological imperatives to be both selfish and altruistic (see Chapter 4). And, although evolution may have outfitted us elegantly to negotiate parent–offspring conflicts (child wants attention, while sibling needs feeding, or mother needs rest), might we still—as I suggested earlier—require further evolution of our ability to bear, encompass, and negotiate the *paradoxes* of our nature? Paradox perplexes and provokes, and it strains the mind. Severe paradox overwhelms the mind, prompting recourse to foreclosures, splits, and dissociations. Paradox, collapsed, defaults to dichotomy. Might the evolutionary-adaptive challenge to the mind be related to the "suppression of natural similarities" and the assortment of the human group into arbitrary "genders"? I would conjecture that the paradox of concurrent (fundamental and urgent) selfish and mutualistic interests, which each individual self must accommodate in mind, strikingly parallels the contradictions within the self that break down into the dichotomous "gender" categories critiqued by feminist and postmodernist writers. "Selfish" sorts closely with dominant, autonomous, active, aggressive, penetrating, and "subject–object"; "mutualistic" sorts closely with submissive, interdependent, passive, nurturent, receptive, and "subject-subject." Might it be that the human group, latching on to the obviously apparent anatomical differences of the sexes (both genital and otherwise morphological), has assigned "role" specializations that distribute predominant patterns of responsibility for individualistic and mutualistic survival functions to the male and female of the species? The benefit of this arbitrarily designated pattern of role assignments is that each (male and female) individual reduces the tension of internal paradox, of straddling ruthlessness and concern, self-interest and "inclusive" interest. The cost of this arrangement is that each (male and female) individual thereby reduces the option of harnessing, articulating, expressing, and enjoying his or her wholeness. The price of our retreat from the strain of negotiating paradox—and, perhaps, the evidence of our limited fitness as a species—may be found in the human group's recurrent recourse to reductionistic, split-off, (self and other) alienating, polarizing, dichotomous, oppositional, and exclusionary, categorical "identities."

NEGOTIATING PARADOXICAL CATEGORIES: THE CASE OF GENDER IDENTITY

Benjamin (1996) notes that the psychoanalytic "art of uncertainty"—which accounts for its embrace as a compatriot of postmodernist and deconstructionist thought—stands in "paradoxical relationship" to its own history of presuming to be a "natural" science "that offers definitive answers, a method with definitive rules, a body of technique with prescribed do's and don'ts" (p. 28, see also Goldner, 1991). Historically, beginning with Freud's "anatomy is destiny," classical psychoanalysis has presumed to know and prescribe the regulation (hetero)sexuality, which grafted gender on to biological sexual dimorphism along with a "phallisy" fallacy that the more conspicuous male genital is *the* positive pole in a sexual dichotomy that alots the negative to the female (what you see is what you got), leaving woman in the *position* of the one who "hasn't got" and awaits the male for her completion. Benjamin (1996) asserts:

> The rethinking of gender categories in psychoanalysis is necessarily associated with the shift from a subject–object to a subject–subject perspective. This shift, as I have suggested elsewhere (Benjamin 1988, 1995), is crucial in order to critique the heretofore unquestioned heterosexual gender model in which the male subject (male implicit) requires the *position* of woman as his object. Such a shift in perspective is congruent with, and virtually requires, subjecting psychoanalytic categories to a critique of essentialism [p. 28, italics added].

As negotiation theory informs us, "positional" thinking is bad negotiation technique. Fisher and Ury (1981; see also Chapter 8, this volume) distinguished between "positional" and "principled" negotiation in terms that have been generally accepted and widely applied in the international field of negotiation theory and practice. In brief, "positional" negotiation is governed by individualism (or tribalism), rigidity, territoriality, power, tradition, categorical absolutes, and asymmetrical "win–lose" strategies; whereas "principled" negotiation is guided by reciprocal communication of the underlying "interests" behind the "positions" of the various parties to any negotiation. Hence, "principled" negotiators seek to recognize each other's desires, needs, fears, and constraints, voice their own particular "interests," and join in generating increased options for mutual gain. Critical reading of Freud's (1905) "Dora" case (Moi, 1990; Rose, 1990) elucidates how Freud's technique failed to negotiate an analysis with Dora particularly because of the patriarchal, phallocentric "position" he took; it does not seem to have occurred to Freud to inquire beyond Dora's "position" (e.g., masculinity complex) to the "interests" that lay beneath. No one in the case appears to have been interested in what Dora wanted (also a dramatic failure of parental "kin altruism" or psychoanalytic balancing of biased "self-interest"). With sober whimsy, I repunctuate Freud's famous tribal exclamation: "What?! Does woman *want*?"

As I speculated earlier, perhaps the structuring of thought—including thought about identity, the recognition of self or other—in terms of dichotomous ("either/or") categories (and their inescapable stratification into hierarchies) reflects the limited competence of our evolved, deep psychic structure (and our evolved cultural applications of psychic structure) to tolerate and straddle paradox ("both/and"). I am not intending here to elevate paradoxical ("both/and") thinking over conflictual ("either/or") thinking. I fully affirm the existence and importance of conflicts, oppositions, and divergent pulls, which must be resolved through choice, compromise, or action—including, at necessary times, the assertion of relational, political, or military power. I am, however, arguing here against our *substitution* of conflict for paradox in our thinking! Because paradox bedevils the mind, we tend to default to thinking about paradox as if it were conflict. Paradox that is not foreclosed (collapsed into "conflict") describes a provocative space for inclusion, play, and ongoing negotiation (see also Chapter 4). Thus, while institutionalized hegemonic identity categories may constitute a tyranny (in the Foucaultian, 1980, sense), they may also reflect a sadomasochistic collusion, in the sense of Benjamin (1988), to ease each individual's mind by allocating to it recognizable "positions," or, in the sense of Ogden (1988; see also Chapter Five on the nonnegotiable and the dread of "misrecognition"), "omnipotent substitute formations in the face of confusion about what he is experiencing and who he is" (p. 652). In particular, I offer the conjecture that gender role identity sorting relieves the mind of the profound tensions of paradox, the anxieties engendered at the times one finds oneself in the "sea" that Dimen (1991) advocates—but feeling at sea without any buoys (or girls).

And might it also be that, if our most elementally challenging paradox is the evolutionary contradiction of individualistic (selfish) and mutualistic (altruistic) survival interests, we have tended to default to cultural constructions that collapse (and relieve) internal paradox. These constructions latch on to (practically) universally obvious sexual dimorphism and "create" gender specialists that hold, in opposition, the repertoire and range (which we also make into polarities) of subject–object, active–passive, will–doubt, autonomous–dependent, want–need, fertilizing–fertile, ruthless–concerned, or (in Benjamin's terms) assertion-recognition. Thus, I conjecture that the tendency to sort persons into "masculine" or "feminine" gender "tribes" has arisen and persisted as a flight from the acute challenge faced by each individual to house and negotiate the paradoxes of concurrent selfish and altruistic intentions. As Bales (1970) observed, we tend to migrate toward relatively circumscribing roles in group life, and groups in turn conserve and institutionalize complementary, reciprocally defining roles, preserving ease of (mis)recognition. But, while germplasm and sexual dimorphism render their evolutionary-biological imperatives, it is a fallacy for psychoanalysis to attribute constructed gender roles to a process of "natural" selection: after all, it is the male penguin who hatches the egg while the female puts out to sea to replenish herself. Let us bear in mind that our somatoplasm has evolved a deep psychic structure capable of generating metaphor, imagination, and paradox along with adaptive strategies for surviving as an intact individual. In the infinite time of its evolutionary life, our germplasm remains categorically (sexually) sorted. In the finite time of our mortal life, our psychosomatic potential holds infinite identity options—to the degree that we are able to bear and negotiate paradox.

Benjamin (1996) comments on the issue of psychoanalytic gender categories (or "tribal" identities):

> Should identity be abrogated altogether, or, more modestly, be seen as balanced by multiplicity (Aron, 1995)? If it does not refer to fixed identities or oppositions, to what does gender refer? Is it meaningful to keep gender as a singular, defining category that refers to one central division? Approaching these questions without prematurely offering simple answers requires us to accept a paradoxical view [p. 29].

Indeed, gender fluidity, the straddling of singularity and multiplicity, relies on the human capacity to negotiate paradox.

How do we manage to "contain multitudes"—to "feel like one self while being many" (Bromberg, 1996)— maintaining the practice of individual self-interest amidst our own bewildering multiplicity of (contradictory) self-interests? How do we experience a

"core" identity—an adaptive achievement of *e pluribus unum*—
without foreclosing gender paradox? Layton (1998) reflects:

> Indeed, clinicians find that those who do not have a conviction of
> being either male or female do not usually enjoy the fluid identity that
> postmodernists hold out as ideal but rather often hate themselves and
> are riddled with shame. A fluid identity is a desirable outcome, but
> clinical work suggests that fluidity is an accomplishment, not a
> given—and achieving it may presuppose the experience of a "core"
> gender identity [p. 24].

Layton proceeds to consider the controversial status of "core"
gender identity. She writes:

> Postmodernists charge that notions of a "core" are essentialist, that
> they fix identity in a way that denies cultural construction and eman-
> cipatory practices. But feminist relational theorists' conception of
> "core" does not in fact assume the kind of unity postmodernists
> abhor, the kind that silences otherness. In the relational paradigm,
> "core" does not mean innate; nor does it imply a true self. And it is
> not incompatible with cultural construction. . . . But "core" does
> imply something internal that recognizably persists even while it may
> continuously and sublty alter. . . . I maintain that "the subject" is both
> a position in discourse (sub-jected to the multiple and contradictory
> discourses of culture, including family) and a multiple and contra-
> dictory being whose negotiation of early relationships will shape the
> meaning that these discourses take on and so shape the discourses
> themselves [pp. 25–26].

I believe that in the development of gender identity, through its
overinclusive (Fast, 1984) and exclusionary phases and dimensions—where "multiple selves, singular self" (Mitchell, 1993) coexist—we must assume a child's innate and emergent capacity to
tolerate and negotiate paradox and that, to theorize about the contradictions of multiple and singular gender identity, we must conceptualize a psychic capacity to negotiate paradox. Benjamin
(1996) addresses the developmental contradiction whereby each
child renounces particular opposite-sex identifications (yielding
them to become aspects of the heteroerotically appealing object)
while also sustaining cross-sex identifications that perpetuate the
person's mental capacity for genderless or opposite-gendered self-
representations. She recognizes that this coexistent, contradictory
aggregating of relinquished *and* maintained gender identity features

"presumes that we can tolerate highly different self-representa-
tions if continuity of nominal gender identity is maintained" (p. 33).
Benjamin continues:

> Even high degrees of ambiguity are not the same as dedifferentiation
> or psychosis, for core gender identification provides a frame for *con-
> flicting* and discordant lines. This contradiction could be solved by
> further differentiating between sexual and nonsexual representations,
> as if to say only sexual identifications with the other were being relin-
> quished, however that solution would be based on a narrow and over-
> simplified picture of sexuality, contrary to the whole spirit of
> psychoanalysis. It might be more useful to postulate that this contra-
> diction between renouncing and maintaining identifications reflects
> an important aspect of psychic reality [p. 33, italics added].

I suggest that this "important aspect of psychic reality" is our
evolved capacity to organize the mind as a distributed multiplicity bridged by our capacity to hold the tension of paradox. Thus,
I would word Benjamin's statement about core gender identification in terms of "a frame for *paradoxical* [rather than "conflicting"] and discordant lines." Elaborating on this "important aspect
of psychic reality," Benjamin (1996) continues:

> Aron (1995) has elucidated this point by suggesting that we think not
> of phases that supersede one another, but positions that coexist.
> Rather than postulate that the overinclusive phase is fully superseded
> by the oedipal phase, it oscillates with it, Aron says, as the depressive
> and paranoid-schizoid positions oscillate. Thus we could say that in
> one position, we attribute certain elements to the other, in another
> position, we consider them to be free-floating attributes of self and
> other. While these positions develop phase-specifically, they become
> coexistent. The unconscious capacity to tolerate *conflict*, and indeed
> the capacity to split the ego and take up antithetical positions, may
> be potentially creative in certain conditions, as well as a more com-
> mon feature of sexual enjoyment than is usually supposed [p. 33, ital-
> ics added].

Again, I would substitute *paradox* where Benjamin writes *conflict*, in the spirit of her own recognition that "conflict" connotes
dichotomous (what I am calling "tribal") opposition and implicitly
establishes a hierarchy with a privileged pole, a presumptively predominant position. Aron's (postmodern, postoedipal) model of
oscillating oedipal (exclusionary) and preoedipal (overinclusive)

positions has the quality of a "chaotically" organized complex dynamic system, a fractal seashore. Benjamin continues: "In fact, it can be argued that without access to the overinclusive identifications, the oedipal renunciation inevitably elides into repudiation. . . . For the other's qualities not to be threatening, identification must be tolerated" (p. 33). To my mind, Benjamin's notions of cross-identifications and recognitions squares well with the notion of "sustained dialogue," in negotiation theory (see Chapter 8), that holds open the potential for reducing splits and repudiations (and rigidified "positions") between "tribal groups"— including *masculine* and *feminine* "tribes"—and optimizes their discerning appreciation of overlapping "interests" along with an ongoing respect for irreducible distinctions of "interest."

Layton (1998), building on Butler's (1990) ideas about "the narcissistic binds of gender identity," clearly states the individual's dilemma of shaping a gendered self-representation in the context of prevailing dichotomized, tribalized, cultural prescriptions and proscriptions. She writes:

> An internal sense of masculinity or feminity is an effect of constant citings and re-citings of the normative gender practices of one's culture, practices that include how one speaks, how one plays, how one dresses. Gender is brought into being in the performance of a gender identity. Performativity is not a voluntaristic activity; gender norms dictate what performances are possible and how they are to be performed. Citings of the norm include what gender one is allowed to identify with and what gender one is allowed to love. In our particular culture, assuming a sex and gender identity involves not only identifications that are allowed within the cultural norm, but also repudiations of those that lie outside the cultural norm. Thus, identity is based as much on disidentifications as on identifications. What is repudiated, disavowed, however, always returns to threaten the boundaries of the subject [p. 50].

Seen from this light, might the perversion of the cross-dresser lie, not in the practice of dress, but in the compulsive requirement to make categorical shifts in "position"—leaps across dissociative gaps, splits in self-states—because the person's underlying distributed multiplicity of "interests" could not be accessed and bridged by a sustained tension of internally symbolized and externally recognized paradox, an oscillation between psychological positions of overinclusiveness and selective "core" identity? Or, take the following jarring case reported in *Newsweek* (March 24, 1997): "John," at eight months of age (in the late 1960s), underwent a surgical procedure to repair some fused foreskin. The surgeon botched the operation, mistakenly removing most of John's penis. As *Newsweek* reports:

> Concerned that he could never become a well-adjusted male, the doctors persuaded John's parents to raise him as a girl. They bought him dresses, gave him dolls and taught him how to put on lipstick. Surgeons created a vagina from his remaining male genitalia. At 12, John—now called Joan—received estrogen treatments to grow breasts. Medical reports said that he had "easily and fully" accepted his life as a woman. The case became an often cited example of the power of nurture over nature in developing gender roles [p. 66].

"Joan's" development, however, did not proceed as seamlessly as the experts had assumed. Despite his "feminized" body and the determined upbringing of him as "Joan," John remained alienated and perplexed by his manifest gender. He is quoted now as saying, "I thought I was a freak or something." John recalls tearing off his dresses, dreaming of becoming a mechanic, and trying to urinate standing up. It was not until John was 14 that someone leveled with him about his tampered history. John reacted profoundly to the missing information then provided by a doctor; he felt, "For the first time, everything made sense." Indeed, John then acted on his own behalf, pursuing further surgery to remove his breasts and rebuild his penis. Eventually, John married a woman and adopted children. The *Newsweek* article ends with this assertion: "John's case shows that, regardless of a child's upbringing and anatomy, some boys will always be boys." That's quite an essentialist punchline! I am left wondering to what extent genotype or fundamental morphology demanded to be declared in John's ultimately lived gender identity. But I mostly wonder about John's family and the surrounding circle of doctors, and their uncannily anxious scrutiny for any dreaded sign of "masculine" gender performances in "Joan." I wonder about the severe influences of deception, biased parental and medical self-interest, prohibitions, mystifications, and misrecognitions that may have mandated in "Joan" profound dissociations of those elements of internal multiplicity (overinclusiveness, cross-sex identifications) necessary for a sense of unalienated wholeness—perhaps even, ironically, foreclosing the potential in gender paradox that might have allowed "Joan" to negotiate a tenable female self. Goldner (1991), sensitive to the powerful injunctive workings of "the communicative matrix of family relations" (as conceptualized by such pioneers as Laing, Bateson, and Haley), has observed:

> Just as gender dichotomies dictate that one psychic state cannot include the other, gender categories also "lend themselves" to divisive family processes that dictate that one kind of love must preclude another. As a consequence, relationships come to be defined as mutually exclusive, so that complex attachments must be renounced for a Hobson's choice of loyalties organized in terms of gender [p. 266].

Relationships "negotiated" in "the communicative matrix of family relations" along coerced, nonfractal, mutually disidentificatory, and oppositional lines of oedipal gender complementarity strike me as reflecting the face-off of tribalized "positions." Relationships "negotiated" with access to a more postoedipal (Benjamin, 1996) complementarity—sustaining the complexity of concurrent mutual identifications and disidentifications, and holding multiplicity and contradiction as a competent repertoire for joining in play—strike me as reflecting the paradoxical tension of exclusive and overlapping "interests," the recognition of copresent separateness and kindredness (isolation and interrelatedness), the dialectics of assertion (subject-object relations) and recognition (subject-subject relations).

The story of "John/Joan" highlights the failure of a family to negotiate gender paradox, a failure of both kin altruism and intersubjectivity that perpetrates tragic misrecognitions. The politics of perception in "the communicative matrix of family relations" denies "John/Joan" the birthright of a personal identity, a biological and relational recognition of self. The failure of any family to provide for each child's negotiation of biological and relational recognition—the knowledge of "who I am and how I may relate to others"—recasts the Oedipus myth[4] in contemporary terms. Much challenged and critiqued in current psychoanalytic and feminist

---

[4] Benjamin (1988) revisited oedipal theory (see her Chapter 5, "The Oedipal Riddle") for the purpose of critiquing the tendency in psychoanalytic thinking to equate the mother with irrationality/regression /fantasy/ego ideal/narcissism, and the father with rationality/autonomy/reality/superego/guilt. In her reading of

thinking, the classical oedipal metaphor has come to stand for the discipline's phobic flight from considering the dependent needs and affects of the powerful mother–infant developmental moments; phallocentricity, polarity, and ungrieved renunciations; the Lacanian paternal rescue of the subject from the otherwise inescapable presymbolic maternal island of Circe; presumptive "regulation" heterosexuality; and reductionistic gender "tribal" complementarity. I propose that we resuscitate the Oedipus myth as the central psychoanalytic metaphor, but interpret it as a story that conveys these particular meanings: the failure of a family to maintain the paradoxical tension of self-interest and kin altruism and the failure of intersubjectivity. That is, we should evaluate the oedipal myth as a story in Bruner's (1990) sense: not the inscribing of the canonical (as in Freudian essentialism) but as the cautionary narrative of a deviation from the canonical. With respect to an evolutionary-adaptive paradigm, the oedipal story describes a failure of inclusive fitness, a collapse in the precarious parent–offspring balance of individualistic and mutualistic interests. With respect to intersubjectivity theory, the Oedipus myth relates the implications and consequences of failures of recognition: Laius and Oedipus fail to recognize each other at the crossroads, and Jocasta and Oedipus fail to recognize who they are and how they may (and may not) be related. Thus, Oedipus' blindness can be understood not only as his punishment for incestuous scopophilia, but also as an emblem of his failure to find within himself the basis for recognizing the identity—the separate Subject status—of the object of aggression and the object of desire. The oedipal story carries the tragic implications of a failure in the family to negotiate

---

Oedipus, Benjamin questions the canonical theory of the oedipus complex and its resolution. She argues that the suppression of recognizing the preoedipal intersubjective mother (in all her mentoring functions that foster differentiation, recognition, and competence) and the preoedipal archaic father (in all his devouring savagery that instills dread and hate) serves to defend an entrenched repudiation and subordination of femininity, a "loss of balance" that promotes gender polarity. While my own reframing of the oedipal myth here is consonant with Benjamin's explications of autonomy and relatedness, difference and likeness, destruction and recognition, I highlight these very issues by viewing Oedipus through a different interpretive lens (my particular emphasis on the "loss of balance" in terms of the central paradoxes of evolutionary and negotiation theory as well as intersubjectivity).

the multiple, contradictory, and paradoxical promptings experienced at the core of each individual's participation in group life.

In summary, the negotiation of gender paradox in the family matrix elementally embodies those dilemmas that we face at every level of human experience where existential paradoxes are collapsed and concretized into "tribalized" conflicts; where splitting mechanisms and discriminatory arrangements remove the disquieting internal tensions incumbent in each individual's concurrent promptings both to separate from and to join with the Other, to be all and have it all and to be recognized as one among one's fellows. The struggle of feminists and psychoanalysts to conceive of gender definitions that serve to bridge conflictual and paradoxical oppositions—to find divisions that join and unions that divide—locates the heart of the problem of human intersubjectivity, and the use of objects (Winnicott, 1969), requiring the practice of ceaselessly skillful negotiations.

7

Paradox and Negotiation in a Wider Context
Species

Slavin and Kriegman's (1992) carefully detailed treatise on contemporary evolutionary biological theory and its implications for
a psychoanalytic understanding of human nature, psychic structure, and psychotherapeutic change locates the capacity for the
negotiation of individualistic and mutualistic interests within the
ancestrally evolved deep structure of the mind. They observe that
each infant's evolutionarily hard-wired psychic apparatus—
equipped for perception, discrimination, learning, and adaptive
regulations—is both capable of, and required to, take shape developmentally through the "software" installed during a prolonged
period of dependence on caregivers and programmatic socializa-
tion patterns imposed by parents (in a family kin and cultural context). From this premise, they argue that each individual is
challenged to establish a personal identity and preserve an adequate measure of self-interested autonomy, while remaining subject to the formative influences of caregivers. Those caregivers,

while elementally motivated to nurture, empathize, and sponsor their offspring's survival and well-being, are equally elementally motivated to maintain their own biased agendas, to juggle the competitive interests of other dependents, to revert to their own fundamental self-interests when pressed, and to deploy deceptive communications that would obscure from the child the degree to which it has been coopted, or subsumed, within a family system that is not 100% adapted to its needs.

According to Slavin and Kriegman, who base their thinking on the work of evolutionary theorists, particularly Trivers (1985), the master plan that shapes the behavior of parents toward their offspring—with its mix of giving and withholding, sponsoring and competing, empathizing and deceiving—is governed by the genetic imperative to survive preferentially in order to replicate its material "identity"—its unique genetic program—in the gene pool. I would put it metaphorically—at the risk of conjuring science fiction fantasies of our being taken over by aliens (then again, where do these fantasies come from?)—that the germplasm (genetic material) uses the somatoplasm (embodied phenotypic individual life) to serve its program of advantaging self-perpetuation; and the design of the human psyche, as well as the kinship and social arrangements conceived by the human mind, must carry the mission of adaptation, survival, and—ultimately of prime value—reproduction that replicates the commandant gene.

The evolutionary law governing this basic biology is not the simplistic "survival of the fittest" or "every man for himself," the popular Darwinian notion of rampant individualism. Rather, according to Trivers (1985), the principle of "every *gene* for itself" may actually be best served, as mathematical modelling supports, by an optimized combination of individual survival *and* the survival of kin, or others, with similar enough genetic "fingerprints" to sustain the genotypic species group and its longstanding adaptive features. From the "gene's eye view," survival is assured by a mixture of individualistic and collectivist adaptations. As Slavin and Kriegman (1992) explain:

> The evolutionists W. D. Hamilton (1964) and R. L. Trivers (1971, 1976b) began to recognize how, from a *genetic* point of view, the selfish pursuit of self-interest and mutualistic cooperation with others, though genuinely clashing aims, were not, in the long run, necessarily

antithetical. When the vast range of data was examined, it turned out that extreme versions of individually costly behavior that were helpful to others were virtually always found to exist in the relational context of *kinship*. Such altruism, it turned out, actually benefited one's *genetic* self-interest because of the high degree of overlap between one's own genes and those of closely related others. This meant that what appeared (phenotypically) to represent a foregoing of self-interest by some individuals actually represented a net benefit to them (or, more accurately, to their genes) through related others who carried copies of their genes. In other cases, among unrelated individuals, "altruism" could predictably bring benefits to the "altruist" if complex, internal mechanisms (e.g., friendship, the affective and cognitive elements of a moral system, etc.) existed to facilitate and regulate longer-term, sometimes indirect reciprocal "repayments" and exchange (Trivers, 1971). These evolutionary advances ("kin altruism" and "reciprocal altruism") enabled evolutionists to explain how natural selection, operating, as always, to favor the most reproductively favorable genotypes, could have produced inner designs that could work in both selfishly individualistic and other-directed, altruistic ways [pp. 85–86].

Here we note the genetic basis for Winnicott's observation of the human paradoxes of isolation and interrelatedness, ruthlessness and concern. Slavin and Kriegman elaborate:

Since our genotype is, literally, shared with kin, the phenotypic (or overt, observable) behavior that is actually most advantageous to our genes will necessarily include the welfare of these other individuals, albeit always in somewhat "discounted" form relative to one's own interests. The fact that inclusive fitness does not refer to the *individual's* fitness per se, but rather to the survival and successful reproduction of the *genetic material* carried by the individual, simply means that inclusive fitness ultimately is a measure of one's net contribution to the success or one's relatives, especially offspring [p. 87].

In a summary statement of "paramount evolutionary truth," Slavin and Kriegman declare, "Personal survival and well-being are necessary for any effective action, purpose, or goal. Yet, the goal of all evolved life forms, all motivations, must be part of a system that *in the end* enhances the fitness of *others!*" (p. 95).

This genetic paradox, as I understand it, becomes a feature of life introduced with the advent of sexual differentiation and sexual reproduction. In contrast with asexual reproduction—simple

cell division or parthenogenesis, for example—in which the pro-
toplasm of the individual organism lives on (divided, distributed
fractionally, and replenished in the growth of subsequent generations), the somatoplasm of the sexually reproducing (phenotypic)
individual constitutes a husk that holds the germplasm and that,
eventually after supplying its genetic material for replication
through sexual combinations, will inevitably die. We might say
that, in evolutionary biological terms, the arrival of sex was the
arrival of death.[1] Winnicott recognized the larger life force that
operates within each of us at a phenotypic level when he posited
a superordinate human drive—the drive toward development. In
Chapter One, I described this as the paradox of our being both
consumers and providers, basking in environmental provision during the span of our dependency yet innately maturing toward our
destiny of becoming ourselves a facilitating environment; and ever
carrying within ourselves the irresolvable paradox of our isolation
and interconnection, our irreducibly coexistent ruthlessness and
concern.

Slavin and Kriegman suggest the phenotypic manifestations of
the individualistic-mutualistic genetic paradox in family life, which
shape the reciprocities and conflictual tensions of parent–offspring
relationships, and they discuss the implications for the evolved
deep structure of the psyche. As they conjecture:

> What are the broader implications of the universality of this intrinsic
> juxtaposition of shared and distinct identities, mutual and conflicting
> interests, and deception within the family matrix? The evolutionar-
> ily successful parent, that is, the parental design that was likely to
> replicate its own genes more effectively than did its evolutionary
> rivals, had to be inclined to invest heavily in his or her child and the
> child's success, and simultaneously, thoroughly inclined to invest in
> the maximization of the parent's own fitness. This meant that, at the
> level of evolved deep structure, parental motives were designed to
> enhance their own interests in all of the ways that these interests *may
> differ from* and at times *literally compete with* those of their child.
> Investing or preparing to potentially invest in other offspring is a
> major expression of these competing interests. . . .
>
> The design of the child's psyche has been fashioned, in part, by
> hundreds of thousands of generations of such alliance and conflict.

[1] I am indebted to George Wald for this juxtaposition of sex and death in his lec-
tures on biology at Harvard in 1965.

The modern child must be one whose ancestors had a relatively more effective deep structural design for coping with a relational world that shares some of the child's interests while being biased toward its own (often competing) interests. He or she comes into the world with a unique genetic identity, and, ipso facto, a distinct, intrinsic self-interest: a novel creation of nature with a host of innate features, dispositions, capacities, etc. The evolutionarily successful child must have been prepared to organize its subjective experience of reality in a fashion that best represented and promoted its own unique, genetic interests. The universal features of the modern child's evolved, psychological deep structure "anticipates" such a relational world and is prepared for it [pp. 115–116].

Slavin and Kriegman enumerate particular features of each individual's "evolved, psychological deep structure" that equip the child to negotiate a separate identity as a dependent and developmentally influenced member of an inherently biased (and mystifyingly deceptive) nurturent group while defending against "having one's interests usurped by others" (p. 144). Among the dimensions of our evolved, deep structure are endogenous "drives"; the capacity to recognize other individuals related by kinship or "reciprocal altruism"; the capacity to detect deception and, in turn, to practice deception; the capacity for psychic defenses, such as repression; and the capacity to probe relationships for the parameters of one's inclusive fitness, which Slavin and Kriegman relate to the capacity to form regressive transferences. These innate properties and capacities "prepare" the self *to record, monitor, and promote a dialectical process in which the ambiguous, deception-filled web of competing and overlapping interests in the relational world is continuously negotiated and renegotiated"* (p. 12). The scope and focus of this chapter allow me to consider and comment on just a few elements of the evolutionary-biological model.

PARADOX

While paradox is a prominently used term in Slavin and Kriegman's thesis, I believe their conceptualization of paradox is subtly, but significantly, different from mine. They tend to use "paradox" more as a descriptive term than as a structural term, even though the paradoxical copresence of universally selfish and mutualistic interests constitutes the basic existential dilemma that shapes "the adaptive design of the human psyche." As I understand Slavin and Kriegman's (1992) reference to "the paradox of human relatedness," their emphasis is on the child's need to develop an individual identity (a private self in the Winnicottian sense) within the "socializing" matrix of an ambiguously—and deceptively ("For your own good, dear")—biased, and often competitively motivated, formative family environment. I believe that Slavin and Kreigman indeed grasp a significant paradox, intrinsic to prolonged childhood dependence, which exposes us to accommodating the hidden agendas of those powerful figures who feed and guide us. But I would emphasize a different central definitional paradox in Slavin and Kriegman's evolutionary paradigm: the inherently contradictory presence of selfishness and altruism *in each individual's*—each parent's and child's—inner nature. With this subtle shift of emphasis, we can recognize that each child's central challenge is not the negotiation of conflict in the parent–offspring relationship (important as this truly is), but the negotiation of *paradox* in the self and in each conflictual-interdependent relationship. Had Slavin and Kriegman crystalized as *definitional* the very paradox that is their first evolutionary postulate—the genetic paradox of "inclusive fitness"—they likely would have included among the elements of our "evolved psychological deep structure" the innate capacity to achieve in development a tolerance for paradox, a competence to hold its tensions and bridge its contradictions (see Chapter 4, this volume). Instead, even as Slavin and Kriegman repeatedly stress the paradox of selfish and overlapping interests, of individualistic and mutualistic tendencies, their exposition recurrently collapses paradox into conflict—and they frame their concepts in terms of the negotiation of parent–offspring conflict or, in the psychotherapeutic setting (Slavin and Kriegman, 1998), the negotiation of "the inherently *diverging interests* (identities and needs) of analyst and patient" (p. 248). As we have seen, negotiation theories consistently stress that parties begin to engage in negotiation, not when they are aware of conflict (diverging interests), but when they are aware of the coexistence of conflict and interdependence (overlapping interests). Clearly Slavin and Kriegman (1992) know this phenomenon quite well— they describe it at the very heart of their theory. Yet they tend to name the underlying paradox in terms of conflict, as in the following example:

> An evolutionarily based "metapsychology" thus depicts us as innately individualistic and innately social; as endowed with inherently selfish, aggressively self-promoting aims, as well as an equally primary altruistic disposition toward those whose interests we share. We are, in short, never destined to attain the kind of highly autonomous individuality enshrined in the classical tradition, nor are we the "social animal" of the relational vision. *We are essentially "semisocial" beings whose nature, or self structure and motivational system, is inherently divided between eternally conflicting aims* [p. 281].

Here Slavin and Kriegman summarize a profound truth of human nature—indeed, the nucleus of their contribution to psychoanalytic theorizing. Yet I believe the central meaning of their thesis is better served by a statement that depicts our nature as "inherently divided between eternally *paradoxical* aims." What would be the implications of substituting "paradox" as the structural term, rather than "conflict?"

First, I want to affirm that Slavin and Kriegman have raised our consciousness to the *conflicts* inherent to all relationships, including both the "parent–offspring conflicts" of the "average-expectable" family environment and the perspectival conflicts of the analytic partnership. Thus, they deflate the idealized myths that have been made of Winnicott's notions of the "ordinary devoted mother," or "good-enough" parenting, as well as the myths of an exquisitely attuned, self-erasing, and empathically virtuoso analyst. They remind us of the "undertow" of conflicting interests (needs, desires, aims, identities, values, perspectives, ideologies) sucking at the self-possession of each person engaged in even the most nurturent and facilitative human relationships. I believe in the validity of this view of conflict, as manifested interpersonally and intrapsychically. (And I also wonder whether there are constraints on the psychoanalytic writer that derive from the hegemonic psychoanalytic language of *conflict*.)

But, by adhering to an explicit emphasis on the *paradox* that parent–offspring and analyst–patient interests are *inherently both diverging and converging*, I believe that an essential tension, and truth, could be held in mind. Once we conceptualize in terms of conflict, we have organized our thought and discourse in dichotomous categories. Dichotomy establishes a polarity that pulls toward the privileging (and reciprocal suppression or exclusion) of one or the other pole; or, as Flax (1990) put it, "binary oppositions are inseparable from implicit or explicit hierarchies" (p. 101). On the other hand, paradox sustains the ongoing tension of juxtaposed elements that remain counterpoised while contradicting each other. As I argued earlier, conflict connotes the "either/or" opposition of categories that obtain when the "both/and" tension of paradox has collapsed. As Benjamin (1995) has elegantly stated:

> To decenter theory is to move away from explanatory positions that postulate one central hub, one motivating principle (or two conflicting, interlocking ones), propelling one dynamic system, which thus can be seamlessly explained. It means reflecting on the perspective of our knowledge and accepting the paradoxes that can arise from an ability to identify with more than one perspective. To accept paradox is to contain rather than resolve contradictions, to sustain tension between elements heretofore defined as antithetical [p. 10].

To illustrate a contrast between "conflict" and "paradox" (see also Chapter Four, this volume), let us consider the "semisocial" individual from the perspective of Benjamin's (1995) model of intersubjectivity. Faced with "conflict" between individualistic and altruistic motives, the semisocial individual might *resolve* the conflict by alternating positions, akin to the reversible complementary roles (of "doer" and "done to") that characterize the child of the early rapprochement phase, prior to the advent of a fully developed intersubjectivity. Thus, child and parent could take turns having their way, being the "boss." Clearly such negotiations of conflict occur typically in each parent–child dyad, and are appropriate to the age of "preintersubjective" complementarity. Clearly also such negotiations of conflict remain a position (in Ogden's, 1994, sense of alternative functional self-states) to which each person will resort throughout the course of a relational lifespan. Yet, in its extreme, such reversible complementarity reduces to exchanges of power "positions" (as in negotiation theory) and sadomasochistic calcifications of domination and submission; the turn-taking of "win–lose" scenarios that characterize many problematic adult partnerships (including, particularly, partnerships sorted into rigidified role positions based on "gender"). By contrast, when Slavin and Kriegman's "semisocial" individual manages to accommodate, sustain, and negotiate *paradox*, the extremes of reversible complementarity (taking turns being "selfish"; or the predominating status quo of the designated "giver" and "receiver," the "subject" and "object" of desire) yield to a more fluidly available multiplicity—at least *of consciousness*—of the coexistence of "self-promoting" and "altruistic" aims in both parties.

This is what Benjamin (1995) means by a mutual recognition of being "like subjects" while being "love objects"; that is, a sustained identification with the other even while the subjective interests (needs, desires, affects) of the other stand in conflict with the subjective interests of the self. Negotiation is necessary and vital specifically because we are always both identifying and disidentifying with the other: recognizing both competing and overlapping interests, divergent and convergent (affect and need) states, individualistic and mutualistic aims—held, when we are able, in the tension of paradoxical juxtaposition. Benjamin and I concur in regarding Winnicott's concept of the "use" of the object (who survives our destruction)—recognized as a subjective other, beyond one's own ruthlessly subjectivizing omnipotence—in these terms. As Benjamin (1995) writes: "From the standpoint of intersubjective theory, the ideal 'resolution' of the paradox of recognition is that it continue as a *constant tension* between recognizing the other and asserting the self" (p. 38). Thus, "divided between eternally *paradoxical* aims," the "semisocial" individual oscillates between a *reversible complementarity*, of trading reciprocally selfish and altruistic roles, and an available *intersubjectivity*, of holding the inner tension—straddling the multiplicity—of perpetual selfish–altruistic internal contradiction. I agree with Benjamin (1995), and Ghent (1992), that psychoanalytic thinking needs to be conceived more in terms of paradox.

LANGUAGE AND DECEPTION

Slavin and Kriegman (1992) consider as part of the evolved biological design of our mind the "hard-wired" program that "is required for the immense amount of cognitive processing needed to master languages even though each language is, patently, a culturally constructed product" (Chomsky, cited on p. 4). They relate this mental "deep structure" to the human adaptive strategy of complex information-gathering during the tutelage years of our prolonged childhood. As they assert, "The highly dependent, slow to develop, but highly flexible, symbol-using child of today was favored by natural selection." Slavin and Kriegman then proceed to articulate some implications of this adaptive program:

> In the course of human development that follows from such a design, most intersubjective transactions are mediated by language and other forms of symbolic communication. Much that is communicated and learned about reality (including crucial realities about the self) is not rooted in direct observation but, rather, comes transmitted through a complex system of signifiers—signs, symbols, and icons (Langer, 1942). What is communicated is a highly encoded version of reality, one that is inevitably infused with a great deal of "extra information," or meta-communication (Bateson, 1972) added by the sender. Through language and other forms of symbolic communication, the human child is able to efficiently construct a map of the world that far exceeds (and differs in quality from) anything that could be created from his or her direct experience (Konner, 1982). At the same time, this unique feature of human symbolic communication—its liberation from the need for direct observation—greatly amplifies or potentiates the power of the parental generation, as well as the child, to create *biased* versions of reality and to communicate them in strategic ways in the course of development [pp. 138–139].

These propositions juxtapose interestingly with some ideas of Bruner's (1990) on a "cultural psychology," as he develops an argument for the human capacity to construct meaning. Bruner writes:

> *Symbolic* meaning . . . depends in some critical fashion upon the human capacity to internalize . . . a language [that "contains an ordered or rule-governed system of signs"] and to use its *system* of signs as an interpretant in this "standing for" relationship. The only way in which one might conceive of a biology of meaning, on this view, is by reference to some sort of precursor system that readies the prelinguistic organism to traffic in language, some sort of protolinguistic system. To so conceive the matter would be to invoke innateness, to claim that we have an innate gift for language [p. 69].

Bruner questions Chomsky's postulated "language acquisition device" as an innate deep structure for accepting language syntactically in a way that has "nothing to do with the 'meaning' or even with the actual uses of language" (p. 70). Bruner posits three preconditions for language acquisition, "all of which can guide us in our search for a biology of meaning."

The first precondition for acquiring a mother tongue is the interactive process between child and caregiver:

> Language is acquired not in the role of spectator but through use. Being "exposed" to a flow of language is not nearly so important as using it in the midst of "doing." Learning a language, to borrow John Austin's celebrated phrase, is learning "how to do things with words." The child is not simply learning *what* to say but how, where, to whom, and under what circumstances [pp. 70–71].

The second precondition is that "certain communicative functions or intentions" already be "well in place before the child has mastered the formal language for rendering them linguistically." These prerequisite functions include indicating, labeling, requesting, and misleading (deception), along with generalized communication skills such as "joint attention to a putative referent, turn taking, mutual exchange" (p. 71). Bruner conjectures that a child may be partly motivated to master language as a tool for more efficiently fulfilling these preestablished functions. Bruner's third precondition for language acquisition is context, that is, "it progresses far better when the child already grasps in some *prelinguistic* way the significance of what is being talked about or of the situation in which the talk is occurring" (p. 71).

Bruner claims that "a protolinguistic grasp of folk psychology is well in place as a feature of *praxis* before the child is able to express or comprehend the same matters by language" (p. 74). This "folk psychology" includes a kind of "theory of mind," the child's ability to mentalize, as evidenced by a capacity, demonstrated even by two- to three-year-olds, to bias a story—to withhold or falsify information—when motivated to mislead; that is when their "own self interests . . . pitted them against those of another" (p. 75). By this line of reasoning, Bruner is led to propose that the deep structure that precedes language acquisition is a capacity to *narrate*, to tell stories that negotiate the individual's place in the social group. As Bruner declares, "our capacity to render experience in terms of narrative is not just child's play, but an instrument for making meaning that dominates much of life in culture—from soliloquies at bedtime to the weighing of testimony in our legal system" (p. 97). And, he concludes:

> Our sense of the normative is nourished in narrative, but so is our
> sense of breach and of exception. Stories make "reality" a mitigated
> reality. Children, I think, are predisposed naturally and by circum-
> stance to start their narrative careers in that spirit. And we equip
> them with models and procedural tool kits for perfecting those skills.
> Without those skills we could never endure the conflicts and contra-
> dictions that social life generates. We would become unfit for the life
> of culture [p. 97].

Thus, Bruner's thesis comes around to a place closely akin to
Slavin and Kriegman's. While, for Bruner, language is a tool
acquired not so much in the service of installing "software" about
reality as in the service of telling stories, nonetheless the function
of this deep structure—the "biology of meaning"—lies in each individual's need to negotiate self-interest in the context of group life.

Slavin and Kriegman (1992) emphasize the potential uses of
language—by parent or child—for bias and deception. This perspective squares with Bruner's notion of the child's putting a
motivated "spin" on a story. Yet I also sense in Slavin and
Kriegman's developmental narrative a perspective verging toward
the Lacanian (1953) notion that language constitutes the Other
(the biased outside influence of culture) that forever alienates the
in-formed Subject from contact with self-interest. In contrast, I
think of Bruner's perspective (including his Vygotskian, 1992,
sense of the negotiated meaning of language) as capturing the
spirit of Winnicott's notion of language as a form of communication that, by being both "explicit and indirect," serves the individual's interest in revealing while concealing (see Chapter One)
and remaining paradoxically both recognized and "incommunicado," interrelated and private, found and unfound. Layton
(1998)—in an incisive study of gender, postmodern cultural theory, and psychoanalysis—offers a perspective on language, compatible with Bruner's and Winnicott's, that nicely counterpoints
Slavin and Kriegman's emphasis on the parental power to bias
identity formation through the shaping influence of language.
Layton writes:

> Those who produce cultural messages have limited control over how
> these messages will be interpreted for two reasons: (1) language is pol-
> ysemous, that is, the nature of language is such that it generates mul-
> tiple meaning possibilities, and (2) people are made of mulitiple and
> conflicting identity positions, which means that different subcultures

or individuals interpret messages in ways different from how those who produce the messages may have wished them to be interpreted. In this view, culture is always a site of struggle over meaning, where dominant and non-dominant interpretations compete for hegemony. Dominant interpretations may appear to have hegemony, but their hegemony is contingent and always needs to be re-won against competing interpretations. The only certainty is the struggle [p. 55].

I heartily concur.

MULTIPLICITY

According to Slavin and Kriegman (1992), the evolved adaptive design of the human psyche includes the child's protean capacity to adjust to environmental constraints (the existence of substantial competitive interests or proscriptive pressures) by sequestering away aspects of self-interest for future potential actualization, when and if the context allows for their reemergence. This chameleon-like competence to pattern and repattern the self while probing the biases of the environment predisposes self-structure to the kind of multiplicity observed by Mitchell (1993), Bromberg (1996), and Davies (1996) and examined here in Chapters 3 and 4. Thus, the evolutionary-biological perspective offers a plausible ontological basis for the existence of a normatively distributed "multiplicity of self" held in paradoxical relationship to the individual's subjective sense of intactness and personal continuity. As Slavin and Kriegman propose:

> Indeed, if the process of developmental renegotiation is, in fact, rooted in the need to revise and recognize our overall self-structure in accord with continuously shifting interests in the relational world, one can argue that we are quite *unlikely* to have evolved an inner system that fosters a state approaching the true cohesion or integration implied in at least certain metaphors of self. . . . In contrast to a design that included *multiple alternative* versions of the self's relationship to the world—versions that may be necessary for different contemporary social contexts in addition to the renegotiated versions of the self for future contexts —even a flexible version of a unitary self-organization would likely reduce the range of available adaptive self/object schemas.
>
> Although the coexistence of "multiple versions of the self" (Mitchell, 1991) that we observe introspectively and clinically may

thus represent crystallizations of different interactional schemas, this multiplicity may also signal the existence of an inner, functional limit on the process of self-integration. . . . The kind of evolved system we would expect natural selection to have favored is a kind of ongoing tension between multiplicity and unity: a constellation of multiple versions of the self that was set up to be "purposely upsettable" by the kinds of recurrent, ancestral situations that signaled significant potential changes in the complex tapestry of competing and shared interests into which each human life is woven [pp. 204–205].

As I argued in Chapter Five, the degree of self-cohesion experienced by the "negotiated self" is a function of the complex interplay of such factors as the severity of paradox (that is, the starkness of contradiction between conflicting and mutual interests); the degree of clash between subject and culture; a constitutional constraint (aptitude) limiting each individual's capacity to tolerate and bridge paradox; and perhaps the current "state of the art" of our evolved adaptive capacity to straddle identity and multiplicity. These issues have particularly interested feminist, and feminist-sensitive, critics of psychoanalytic constructions of "gender identity."

One final reflection on evolutionary biology and our adaptive design: Slavin and Kriegman do not include in their theory the evolved human mental capacity for metaphorization, symbolic actualization, creative generativity, and play in the area of cultural activity, which I believe constitute in our deep structure alternative forms for meaningful dissemination. It is a notable irony that Winnicott, theorist of the parent–infant relationship, pediatrician, and child analyst, had no children of his own, no genetic offspring. And, yet, while his germplasm did not squiggle its way into the gene pool, his conceptual seeds and personal gestures have populated a potential space, assuring his "inclusive fitness" to supply a surviving legacy in the intergenerational chain. How many of us include Donald Winnicott in our lineage!

8

Paradox and Negotiation in a Wider Context
Nations

The dividing-up of the human group into subgroups that define their "identities" as reciprocally oppositional or antagonistic—the segmentation of community into "tribal" categories such as labor–management, Israel–Arab, "our" side–"your" side—has necessitated the development of a discipline (both academic and applied) variously defined as negotiation, mediation, and conflict resolution. Witness the vicissitudes of the protracted "peace process" in the Middle East and the efforts to negotiate livable settlements of the violence tearing apart Bosnia and Northern Ireland. Negotiations also occur over the sale of a used car, the rent and repair of an apartment, the allocation of scarce resources among inner city constituencies, the custody of children in divorce—or the possiblity of collaborative dialogue among psychoanalytic associations over such issues as credentialing. Diplomats, lawyers, social psychologists, and mediators approach a mission that appears to be different from the mission of a psychoanalyst, and they have developed a specialized field of discourse, discipline, and practice. The Harvard Law School houses a Program on Negotiation, representing a consortium of schools of law, politics, and economics. Programs on negotiation exist now at many universities, often located in schools of law or public policy, or free-standing institutes. According to Kelman (1997):

> In the past two decades or so, the world had witnessed the development and profileration of a variety of new approaches to conflict resolution, which together constitute a new field of theory and practice. . . . Practitioners of conflict resolution work at different levels—ranging from the interpersonal to the international. They operate in different domains, such as the court system, public policy, labor-management relations, interethnic relations, or international diplomacy. They derive their ideas from a variety of sources, such as law, psychotherapy, management theories, group dynamics, peace research, decision theory, the study of conflict resolution in traditional societies, and theoretical models from the entire range of social science disciplines [p. 213].

My purpose here is to investigate how this domain of negotiation might articulate with the processes of negotiation that I have observed at the heart of the psychoanalytic relationship. Do our fields have useful perspectives to offer each other, or are they endeavors too disparate to be mutually conversant? Here I venture to find what ideas might come into play through an inquiring juxtaposition of psychoanalytic and legal/diplomatic views of negotiation. For example, how do statesmen face and address the "nonnegotiable," the entrenched resistances of passionately, or desperately, held aggressive or defensive positions? Or when might psychoanalytic technique constitute "bad" negotiating technique?

While one social psychologist (Rubin, 1988) has asserted "a common set of processes that underlie all forms of conflict and their settlement" (p. 8), a first glance at the specialized literature on the settlement—or resolution—of conflict through negotiation suggests a realm of discourse far afield from psychoanalysis—more practical and pragmatic, more strategic and tactical, more focused on the operational plane of behavior, action, and interactive finesse. Book titles such as *Getting to Yes*, *Getting Past No*, and *Strategies for Mutual Gain* conjure images of businessmen, lawyers, and warring adversaries coming to the table. One career negotiator (Vare, quoted in Ury, 1993) defines diplomacy as "the art of letting someone else have *your* way" (p. 3). Not, at first glance, the art of psychoanalysis! And, yet, consider how Ferenczi (1928), Aron (1996), Mitchell (1993), and others have reflected on the ways in which an analyst's hopes and goals for a treatment may differ markedly from the patient's; or Slavin and Kriegman's (1992, 1998) emphasis on how the therapist must be accountable for his own self-interested hidden agendas. In this regard, Vare's cynically paradoxical aphorism may serve as useful stimulus for an analyst's self-reflection. And consider how a constructivist, perspectivist, or intersubjective view of the analytic process of arriving at intimate meaning (narrative, insight, awareness) entails "a meeting of minds" (Aron, 1996), a getting past the "no" of repetition, or resistance, and a getting to the "yes" of consensual validation or mutual recognition. Or consider the following advice to would-be negotiators, and how readily it adapts as a kind of thumb-nail reminder of challenges to a therapist's maintaining an "analytic attitude" in the face of a patient's resistances, projective identifications, role inductions, negative transference repetitions, and affect surges:

> The essence of the breakthrough strategy is *indirect action*. It requires you to do the opposite of what you naturally feel like doing in difficult situations. When the other side stonewalls or attacks, you may feel like responding in kind. Confronted with hostility, you may argue. Confronted with unreasonable positions, you may reject. Confronted with intransigence, you may push. Confronted with aggression, you may escalate. But this just leaves you frustrated, playing the other side's game by *their* rules. . . .
>
> Breakthrough negotiation is the opposite of imposing your position on the other side. Rather than pounding in a new idea from the outside, you encourage them to reach for it from within. Rather than telling them what to do, you let them figure it out. Rather than pressuring them to change their mind, you create an environment in which they can learn. Only *they* can break through their own resistance; *your* job is to *help* them [Ury, 1993, pp. 10–11].

This strikes me as rather apt and succinct supervision, as does the following excerpt from a Kettering Foundation Manual for facilitators (moderators) of the prenegotiation process they all call "sustained dialogue" with representatives of antagonistic social groups:

Perhaps the most important thought to keep in mind is this: Treasure
the participants' resistance to moving forward because you will learn
much from it [see also Freud, 1914; Bromberg, 1995]. It is not a nui-
sance or a hindrance but a concentrated opportunity for unlocking
another door to further progress.

Resistance is an almost inevitable response to the possibility of
change at every stage. People are often reluctant to change for good
reason. The most productive approach is not to try to persuade participants to give up their reluctance: "Trust me. It will be OK. You are
safe in this group." The most productive approach is to say and to
demonstrate that you understand that reasons for resistance are real
for the participant [Saunders and Slim, n. d., p. 5].

Saunders and Slim emphasize that their intervention of "sustained dialogue" is a *prenegotiation* because "people in deep-
rooted human conflict have little to negotiate—at least initially
—because identity, historic grievances, fears, stereotypes, are not
negotiable" (p. 7). Like the analyst who faces the nonnegotiable
when a patient is without hope for the potential in a relational
engagement of need, affect, or desire, the would-be negotiator (or
facilitator) cannot engage a process of negotiation as long as the
parties remain exclusively in conflict. Parties negotiate not
because they are in conflict, but because they are in a condition
of *both* conflict *and* interdependence. I think of this as *the paradox of conflict*. Whether the parties in question are landlord and
tenant, father and son, husband and wife, Israel and Egypt, or
Division 39 and the American Psychoanalytic Association, negotiation of their conflictual self-interests will begin only when each
party recognizes (tacitly or explicitly) some significant area of
overlapping interests. This paradox of the interdependence of conflicting parties—and the search for the area of overlap that coex-
ists with opposition—is the common point of departure for most
negotiation theorists, as they variously give it articulation. Fisher
and Ury (1981) assert that "each side has multiple interests," and
that, "you will be simultaneously pursuing both your independent
and your shared interests" (p. 47). Ury (1991) broadly defines
negotiation as "the process of back-and-forth communication
aimed at reaching agreement with others when some of your interests are shared and some are opposed" (p. 4). Janos Nyerges
(1991), former Special Representative of the Hungarian Govern-
ment at international economic negotiations, put it this way:

"Negotiators are in a contradictory situation: Each wants the problem resolved in a self-interested way. This separates them. On the other hand, each of them has to resolve the same problem, and this unites them" (p. 191).

And Nyerges advises, "Put yourself in the shoes of your opponent, but do not remain there too long" (p. 191). Rubin and Rubin (1991) have argued that the critical element for effective conflict settlement may be termed "enlightened self-interest." Citing Deutsch's belief that "the key to conflict resolution is movement from competitive behavior to cooperation" (p. 162)—and its attendant emergence of some measure of reciprocal trust and "liking"— Rubin and Rubin indicate that contemporary negotiation theory deemphasizes "cooperation" and accentuates each side's motivation to do as well for itself as possible, a more "individualistic orientation." From this perspective, "one's objective is not to cooperate with, trust, or be generous toward the other disputant— only to behave in ways that leave the door open to the other person finding an agreement that is attractive. One's objective is neither to help nor hinder the other person, only to be enlightened about the existence of agreements that work well for both sides" (pp. 162–163). Thus, each person's goal is to arrive at an arrangement that "keeps you from getting in my way." Rubin (1988) has further elaborated this perspective:

> Notice that what I am describing here is neither pure individualism (where one side does nor care at all how the other is doing) nor pure cooperation (where each side cares deeply about helping the other to do well, likes and values the other side, etc.)—but an amalgam of the two.
>
> Trivial though this distinction may seem, it has made it possible in recent years for work to develop that, paradoxically, creates a pattern of *inter*dependence out of the assumption of *in*dependence. Earlier work, focusing as it did on the perils of competition and the virtues of cooperation, made an important contribution to the field of conflict studies; but in so doing, this effort also shifted attention away from the pathway of individualism—a pathway that is likely to provide a way out of stalemate and toward a settlement of differences. I don't have to like or trust you in order to negotiate wisely with you as a partner. Nor do I have to be driven by the passion of a competitive desire to beat you. All that is necessary is for me to find some way of getting what I want—perhaps even *more* than I considered possible— by leaving the door open for you too to do well [p. 6].

Rubin's argument stresses that competent negotiation is based on "the understanding of what the other person may want or need." As I see it, such "enlightened self-interest" straddles the paradox of ruthlessness and concern, in the Winnicottian sense, because the other must be recognized in terms of his or her (or their) separate, distinct subjective sense of need, vulnerability, vital interest, value, or constraint. Once such elements of dialogue are engaged, then self-interest can be pursued through the competent application of (at least rudimentary) intersubjectivity. I believe this paradox forms the basis for "Principled Negotiation," the process popularized by Fisher and Ury (1981) wherein opponents turn from declaring their "positions" toward inquiring into the "interests" underlying each other's (and their own) positions. Rubin (1988) illustrates "positional" negotiation, and its costs, with the anecdote of the two sisters who argue over the division of an orange:

> Each would like the entire orange, and only reluctantly do the sisters move from extreme demands to a 50/50 split. While such a solution is eminently fair, it is not necessarily wise: One sister proceeds to peel the orange, discard the peel, and eat her half of the fruit; the other peels the orange, discards the fruit, and uses her 50% of the peel to bake a cake! If only the two sisters had understood what each wanted the orange for—not each side's "position," but rather each's underlying "interest"—an agreement would have been possible that would have allowed each to get everything that she wanted [pp. 6–7].

Rubin's "optimal solution" suggests to me the opening of a potential space in which destruction and creativity, separateness and interrelatedness intersect, and inquiring dialogues that permit "cross-identifications" (Winnicott, 1969) sponsor the "use" of objects, even against an ongoing back-drop of destructiveness. As Rubin (1988) puts it:

> The lesson for international relations is instructive. For the United States and the Soviet Union, Israel and its Arab neighbors, Iran and Iraq, the Soviet Union and Afghanistan, the United States and Nicaragua to do well, neither cooperation nor competition is required, but rather an arrangement that acknowledges the possibility of a more complex mixture of these two motivational states with enlightened individualism [p. 7].

Prior to the point of readiness to enter into "principled" negotiation and begin reciprocal communication of the "interests" underlying intractably oppositional "positions," adversarial parties must experience sufficient disillusionment or despair with the status quo, along with some hope that a negotiated solution would be better than continuing the present situation. Until they arrive at such a juncture, leaders may believe that by perpetuating their entrenched positions, using either power or delay, they are best serving their own interests. The psychoanalytic analogy, in the area of the nonnegotiable considered in Chapter 5, is the patient's unrelenting deployment of action defenses, compulsions, externalizations, and sadomasochistically controlling imperatives. In the realm of international diplomacy, Saunders (1991) observes that, "in analyzing why a party refuses to negotiate, we must determine why that party believes that perpetuating the present situation serves its interests" (p. 65). Fisher and Ury (1981) refer to such beliefs with the acronym BATNA (Best Alternative to a Negotiated Agreement), and regard each party's BATNA to hold the paradoxical potential to be both a short-sighted resistance and a selfish reassurance at the threshold of negotiation. Analyzing the "resistance" in "the Israeli-Palestinian Case," Saunders reflects that

> neither party has believed that the passage of time without negotiation would irretrievably hurt its cause. Israel under the Begin-Shamir leadership judged that negotiating would create a situation from which the only outcome could be some Israeli withdrawal from territories occupied in 1967. Israel's stated policy was to use time to establish its irreversible presence in territories that would otherwise be lost in negotiation. The Palestinians and other Arabs in the past seem to have judged that time was on their side—that over time they would accumulate the military power to force Israel to some kind of accommodation [p. 65].

On the other hand, analysis of resistance might yield eventual realizations about each side's overestimation of its BATNA: Does Israel want a 40% voting minority of Palestinians? Will Palestinians ever have a state if they demand all disputed territory? "Resistance analysis" brings into focus the self-defeating features of one's BATNA: positional repetitions don't work; one's "ideal" solutions are unattainable.

In the realm of psychotherapeutic analysis of resistance, Stark (1994) has outlined the patient's attachment to his BATNA and the clinical process of elucidating both the functions and the limitations of entrenched intrapsychic and object relational positions. And Bromberg (1995) described a patient who, the night before his first analytic session, dreamt that he was in a burning building and yet threw rocks down on the fireman climbing up a ladder to help rescue him. As Bromberg explains, this patient well knew that, in entering an analytic relationship, he faced an intersubjective negotiation that would inevitably require him to vacate familiar, and desperately held, inner territory; even as the flaming building indicated his awareness that his BATNA was a doomed structure.

In my own work with Everett, described in Chapter 5, his persistent enactment of nonnegotiable "positions" suggests to me that he could not yet (in Saunder's, 1991, terms) "judge whether a negotiated solution would be better than continuing the present situation." Instead of opening himself to a consideration of the "interests" underlying his position—his cumulative history of need, pain, violation, humiliation, mystification, and grievance—Everett positioned me where I found myself unable to convey my own "interests" in sustaining a therapeutic dialogue with him. I believe that Everett did not find it in himself to tolerate the existence of my own separate subjectivity—I could remain for him only an object to check on the game board, repudiated as a subject by his unremitting *disidentification*. Faced with Everett's inability to sustain recognition of me as, in Benjamin's (1995) terms, a "like subject," I experienced an erosion of my own ability to "like" him, to identify empathically with his subjectivity, to inquire into the "interests" underlying the positions he imposed on me, to cultivate "a meeting of minds" (Aron, 1996). Struggling as I was for the survival of my own subjectivity in our relationship, I slipped over the pitfalls that Ury (1991) warned of in negotiations with difficult adversaries: I began to argue, reject, and push. I defaulted to my own "positional" negotiation when, faced with Everett's scheme to embezzle funds, I declared, "Don't do it!" In retrospect, one way to understand Everett's aborted treatment is to consider my own positional statement to have been a bad negotiation technique, foreclosing inquiry into why Everett was "peeling the orange" as he was. Reduced to our complementary

positions—of "doer and done to" (Benjamin, 1995)—our therapeutic negotiation stalemated. I wonder how—and whether—
Everett's therapist may have sustained a "peace process" and
transformed the win–lose positional scenario (power facing power)
into a mutual focus on "interests." On the other hand, I also wonder if my own best alternative in the face of Everett's relentlessly
mounting malevolent positioning may have been the deployment
of a more forceful positional statement, such as, "Everett, if you
violate my limits, I will not continue to work with you."

While Fisher and Ury (1981) do not believe that shifts from
"positional" to "principled" negotiation are always possible, or
even advisable, they offer an inspiring example of an impasse
resolved at an international level:

> The Egyptian–Israeli peace treaty blocked out at Camp David in 1978
> demonstrates the usefulness of looking behind positions. Israel had
> occupied the Egyptian Sinai Peninsula since the Six Day War of 1967.
> When Egypt and Israel sat down together in 1978 to negotiate a peace,
> their positions were incompatible. Israel insisted on keeping some of
> the Sinai. Egypt, on the other hand, insisted that every inch of the
> Sinai be returned to Egyptian sovereignty. Time and again, people
> drew maps showing possible boundary lines that would divide Sinai
> between Egypt and Israel. Compromising in this way was wholly unac-
> ceptable to Egypt. To go back to the situation as it was in 1967 was
> equally unacceptable to Israel.
>
> Looking into their interests instead of their positions made it pos-
> sible to develop a solution. Israel's interest lay in security; they did
> not want Egyptian tanks poised on their border ready to roll across at
> any time. Egypt's interest lay in sovereignty; the Sinai had been part
> of Egypt since the time of the Pharaohs. After centuries of domina-
> tion by Greeks, Romans, Turks, French, and British, Egypt had only
> recently regained full sovereignty and was not about to cede territory
> to another foreign conqueror.
>
> At Camp David, President Sadat of Egypt and Prime Minister Begin
> of Israel agreed to a plan that would return the Sinai to complete
> Egyptian sovereignty and, by demilitarizing large areas, would still
> assure Israeli security. The Egyptian flag would fly everywhere, but
> Egyptian tanks would be nowhere near Israel.
>
> Reconciling interests rather than positions works for two reasons.
> First, for every interest there usually exist several possible positions
> that could satisfy it. All too often people simply adopt the most obvi-
> ous position, as Israel did, for example, in announcing that they
> intended to keep part of the Sinai. When you look behind opposed

positions for the motivating interests, you can often find an alternative position which meets not only your interests but theirs as well.
In the Sinai, demilitarization was one such alternative.

Reconciling interests rather than compromising between positions
also works because behind opposed positions lie many more interests
than conflicting ones.

Behind opposed positions lie shared and compatible interests, as
well as conflicting ones [pp. 41–42].

Here again is the paradox of conflict. When parties in conflict
can bridge between their areas of divergence and their areas of
overlap, straddling individualistic and mutualistic perspectives, a
potential space may open in which mutual needs, mutual goals, and
mutual gains are recognized or invented (Fisher and Ury, 1981).
We might say, "Where imperatives were, there shall options be."

Some overlapping interests (e.g., global warming, the nuclear
threat) are so clearly superordinate that enemies like the United
States and the former U.S.S.R. pursued limited cooperation with
the very parties they sought to eliminate. Some smaller scale problems introduce an opportunity for adversaries to discern the
"enlightened self-interest" in joint problem solving. In one such
case, the Jordanians and the Israelis were each spraying to get rid
of an infestation of mosquitoes in the Gulf of Aqaba, which bor-
ders both countries. As each country sprayed, the problem was
simply sent back and forth across the Gulf, until Israel and Jordan
addressed the mosquitoes together. (In a similar spirit, Division
39, the American Psychoanalytic Association, the American
Academy of Psychoanalysis, and the National Membership Committee on Psychoanalysis in Clinical Social Work formed a
Consortium to address such issues as managed care and the efforts
of the NAAP to gain recognition as the exclusive accrediting body
in psychoanalysis.) While Rubin and Rubin (1991) argue that such
coordinated enactments of "enlightened self-interest" need not
entail trust, altruism, or mutual "liking," I believe that such ongoing conversations, exchanges, and efforts among opposed parties
carry the hope of eventual steps toward mutual recognition, trust,
and healing. The pursuit of mutual self-interests tends to foster
relationship-building; maximizing the small "yeses" around the
persisting "nos" may work, through accretion toward reciprocal
perceptual and attitude shifts (like the working through of transferences, the surrendering of negative projections). The very

practice of listening to one's opponent in a process of joint problem solving can be a step among steps away from the paranoid-
schizoid position of demonizing, essentializing, and objectifying
the opposition—as a more multifaceted, contradictory, and
humanized representation comes into focus. As Fisher, Kopelman,
and Schneider (1996) suggest, "Demonstrating that we understand
their point of view may allow them to move beyond defending it"
(p. 29)—an observation indeed consistent with psychoanalytic
experience, as Slavin and Kriegman (1992) note: "*Unfulfilled
needs can only be relinquished and mourned once their validity
is recognized*" (p. 257). Indeed, I believe that one significant
source of resistance to joint problem solving, or "sustained dialogue," among adversaries is their dread of the destablizing effect
of cross-identifications (accompanied by an internal shift toward
the depressive position); the strain of absorbing the separate subjectivity of the opposed object, of tolerating the resultant relational
(and internal) space for multiplicity, contradiction, and ambiguity—the strain of negotiating paradox.

The challenge of sustaining a paradoxical potential space for
ongoing negotiation and the pull toward foreclosure, splitting, and
dichotomous categorization, are illustrated by an observation of
Kelman's (1997) in his report on years of facilitating "group
process" workshops in the service of resolving international conflicts, particularly between Israelis and Palestinians. Kelman's project entailed the identification and recruitment of influential
representatives of both sides—community leaders, academicians,
policy advisors, journalists—who were sufficiently "moderate" to
agree to sit down with their enemy counterparts in a "joint problem-solving workshop." The purpose of these workshops, as conceived by Kelman and his colleagues, was to use "group dynamics"
techniques to promote "changes in the workshop participants
themselves—changes in the form of more differentiated images of
the enemy. . . , a better understanding of the other's perspective
and of their own priorities, greater insight into the dynamics of the
conflict, and new ideas for resolving the conflict and for overcom-
ing the barriers to a negotiated solution" (p. 214). Kelman's hope
was that these individuals, affected by the group process to shift
toward a more mutually empathic perspective, would carry their
new understanding and sensitivity back into their own communi-
ties, where they might conduct themselves in their influential

positions in such a way as to translate personal changes into policy changes. In essence, Kelman sought to create coalitions across conflict groups. Kelman describes the painstaking work through which group members communicated, entangled, and ultimately transcended their historical hurts, fears, suspicions, and hostilities and approached relationship based more on elements of mutual recognition. Kelman's groups did form coalitions across conflict lines, uneasy as they were, "insofar as coalition members are bona fide representatives of their national groups" (p. 218). Kelman asserts that this reality constitutes "barriers to coalition work," and then he makes the astonishing statement that "it is not only difficult to overcome these barriers, it may in fact be counterproductive to overcome them entirely" (p. 219). Kelman further suggests that it is "important for the coalition to remain uneasy to enhance the value of what participants learn in the course of workshops," and he supports this contention by citing research that

> suggests that direct contact between members of conflicting groups may have a paradoxical effect on intergroup stereotypes. If it becomes apparent, in the course of interaction with representatives of the other group, that they do not fit one's stereotype of the group, there is a tendency to differentiate these particular individuals from the group: to perceive them as nonmembers. Since they are excluded from the category, the sterotype about the group itself can remain intact. This process of differentiating and excluding individual members of the other group from their category could well take place in workshops in which a high degree of trust develops between the parties. Therefore, it is essential for the participants to reconfirm their belongingness to their national categories—thus keeping the coalition uneasy—if they are to demonstrate the possibility of peace not just between exceptional individuals from the two sides but between the two enemy camps [p. 219].

I believe that Kelman is describing not "a high degree of trust," but a group defense against preserving the paradox that group members remain enemies while becoming "friends." By recommending an "uneasy" coalition, I think Kelman is seeking to retain the tension among coalition members of recognizing their likenesses and differences (Benjamin, 1995) at the same time, of straddling the paradoxical coexistence of irreducibly divisive and mutualistic interests. Kelman's findings seem to me consistent with the human tendency to regress from "both/and" thinking to "either/or" thinking. Perhaps Kelman's workshops would benefit from the inclusion of some focus on (or training in?) a recognition, and tolerance, of paradox.

NEGOTIATION THEORY AND RELATIONAL PSYCHOANALYSIS

My review of negotiation theory leads me to a further reflection: on the aptness of a relational approach to psychoanalytic technique. Immediately, the reader may be wondering (may, indeed, have wondered earlier throughout this chapter) what the principles of negotiation in adversarial relationships could possibly have to do with our models of the psychoanalytic relationship. After all, where else in human experience, other than parenting, do we find one person so consistently, concertedly, even devotedly focused on attending to, understanding, accepting, empathically reaching, and ultimately serving deeply the life interests of another person? Yet we have only to remind ourselves of Freud's (1912, 1914) military metaphors for the forces of transference resistance facing the "conquistador" analyst, or the dream of Bromberg's patient described earlier in this chapter, to orient ourselves to the ubiquitous presence of oppositions, conflicts, destructive gestures, "crunches," and clashes of interest—even threats to identity—in the analytic dyad (as in my work with Everett). And, as Slavin and Kriegman (1992, 1998) have emphasized, the analyst whose (spoken or unspoken) claim is, "I'm only trying to help," is engaging in deception, self-deception, or both. Bromberg (1996) claims that a full analytic result will not have been achieved if he has not repeatedly gone "head to head" with his patient—a butting of heads cofunctions with a meeting of minds. In this context, I juxtapose here ideas about the negotiation process with ideas about the analytic process.

As we have seen, the common basic threads running throughout negotiation theories are their emphasis on a movement from enacted "positions" toward articulated "interests"; a practice of listening and acknowledging the credibility even of that which is opposed; a cultivation of mutualistic attitudes; a reduction of power imbalances; a joint approach to problem solving; and a recognition of interdependence concurrent with separateness. I will elaborate just a few of these points, noting their application to the analytic process, to gather my argument about a relational technique (including constructivist, perspectivist, interpersonal, or "intersubjective" emphases).

Ury (1991) notes, "Every human being, no matter how impossible, has a deep need for recognition. . . . Ackowledging the other person's point does *not* mean that you agree with it. It means that you accept it as one valid point of view among others. It sends a message 'I can see how you see things'" (p. 58). How well this outlook squares with Gill's (1982) recognition of the plausibility of each patient's transference construction of the analyst (see also Bollas, 1989; Benjamin, 1995; Aron, 1996; Myerson, 1990).

Saunders (1991), exploring the many factors underlying resistance or reluctance to negotiate, observes that "one side may be ready to negotiate but refuse to do so because it does not want the humiliation of offering to negotiate with an adversary who does not take the process seriously" (p. 67). I believe it is not a stretch to relate this statement to the issues that inhere to analytic anonymity, opaqueness, and authority. The traditional psychoanalytic setup of a nondisclosing analyst, who arrogates to himself the nonnegotiable position of arbiter of reality and sits as a neutral observer outside the one-person dynamic system, is inherently *humiliating* to the patient and may well iatrogenically embed resistances to negotiating a change process. Thus, I agree with Boesky's (1990) recognition that an "interactional experience" lies at the heart of any analysis, even while preserving an intrapsychic focus, and that resistances are always negotiated in each analytic dyad. I particularly agree with Boesky when he asserts, "If the analyst does not get emotionally involved sooner or later in a manner that he had not intended, the analysis will not proceed to a successful conclusion" (p. 573). Slavin and Kriegman (1998) similarly recognize this issue in the very title of their paper, "Why the Analyst Needs to Change: Toward a Theory of Conflict, Negotiation, and Mutual Influence in the Therapeutic Process." And Renik (1995) has argued that the "ideal of the anonymous analyst," who seeks assiduously to avoid enactments or disclosure of analytic subjectivity, preserves an unnecessary and obstructive, as well as narcissistically self-serving, power imbalance in the treatment relationship. Renik instead advocates the analyst's sharing what he is making of what he hears, how he arrives at his interpretations, and where he understands himself to be heading with his patient.

Commenting on the balance of power in international relations, Saunders (1991) notes, "The Arabs have normally seen Israeli military power as precluding a fair negotiation. Syria's President Assad is quite open in saying that the Arabs cannot negotiate a settlement of their conflict with Israel until they are Israel's military equal" (p. 68). Saunders goes on to say that one of Anwar Sadat's motives for Egypt to go to war with Israel in 1967 was to demonstrate that "limited Arab military power" had the "capacity at least to inflict on Israel a serious psychological shock and significant war losses" (p. 68). We might ask to what extent a patient, regardless of particular formative history or psychopathology, may be incited by the experienced power disparity of the analytic set-up to shake up the unilateral locus of power and establish that he or she can inflict harm. While I agree with Aron (1996) and Hoffman (1994, 1996) that an irreducible, inescapable—and, in some ways, essential—asymmetry structures the relationship between analyst and patient, I suggest we take into account how power asymmetry in the therapeutic relationship delivers its own problematics, perturbing the negotiation of a healing process. On one hand, as Hoffman (1994) asserts, "those of us who are interested in developing more mutual and egalitarian relationships with our patients should not deny or forget the extent to which we are drawing upon the ritualized *asymmetry* of the analytic situation to give that mutuality its power" (p. 200). On the other hand, as McLaughlin (1995) has reported, the more the analyst assumes a remote, autocratic, and inscrutable perch, the more the analysand manifests regressive enactments. Or, as Balint (1968) declared,

> The more the analyst's technique and behaviour are suggestive of omniscience and omnipotence, the greater is the danger of a malignant form of regression. . . . The more the analyst can reduce the inequality between his patient and himself, and the more unobtrusive and ordinary he can remain in his patient's eyes, the better are the chances of a benign form of regression [p. 273].

I do not mean to suggest (nor does Balint) that the analyst should strive to remain "unobtrusive" at all times. Such a categorical position, which denies the analyst's true and essential power, would be naive. In any analysis, there are moments for quiet, unobtrusive holding of a patient's solitary reverie and other moments for conspicuous asymmetry and influence (Mitchell, 1997) made manifest in confrontation, challenge, or inquiry. Indeed, the multiple "interests" of the patient that emerge in a variety of affective states, states of consciousness, or relational "positions" will require the contemporary analyst to move continually along the asymmetry axis (Aron, 1996), guided by empathy, countertransference responsiveness, and the analyst's own multiple "interests" or personal limits. I would emphasize the analyst's need to maintain a paradoxical position—a multiple and contradictory, and hence flexible and versatile position—toward asymmetry: to exercise a necessary analytic power, which is the application of personal discipline and professional competence in the service of clinical responsibility to the patient, while remaining mindful of how that very asymmetry of relationship may at any time be verging on an unnecessary derogation and provocation of the patient, or an analytically unproductive, defensively non-negotiable preservation of the analyst's "position." While classical analysts have argued that traditional technique is particularly well suited for the analysis of aggression and negative transferences, it may well be that the maximized power asymmetry of the classical (patriarchal, patronizing) analytic position, in its very structure, actually *incites* aggression by dichotomizing power in ways that inherently humiliate the patient with its a priori terms for negotiating the treatment. Hoffman (1994) quotes Searles (writing in 1949!), who seems to have been commenting on a form of treatment relationship that Aron (1996) might describe as highly asymmetrical and minimally mutual:

> The analyst who attempts to adhere to the classical behavior of unvarying "dispassionate interest" toward his patients regularly finds the patients to be irritated by such behavior which, after all, they have to cope with in everyday life only in so far as they may deal with schizoid other persons. . . . For the analyst to reveal, always in a controlled way, his own feelings toward the patient would thus do away with what is often the source of our patients' strongest resistance: the need to force the analyst to admit that the patient is having an emotional effect on him [Searles, quoted in Hoffman, 1994, p. 191].

Clearly, the analytic relationship is a far cry from the concrete actualities of Sadat's relationship to Israel in 1967, where mutuality and healing had no part in the equation. Yet I believe that we can usefully metaphorize Sadat's position (his need to demonstrate a capacity for impact) to capture schematically what Sadat had in common with "our patients' strongest resistance": the failure of any relationship to negotiate sufficiently asymmetries of power stirs a pressing need to demonstrate force. Thus, in analysis, aggressive resistance on the part of the patient may not be an "enemy of the treatment" but a signal of the need for power asymmetries to be renegotiated in the analytic relationship (if only the analyst would read the signal).

Resistance, as it is defined and redefined by different psychoanalytic schools, neatly epitomizes the ways in which analysts vary in their positions toward the place of negotiation in the analytic relationship. Aron (1996) deftly summarizes the evolution of the concept of resistance in contemporary psychoanalysis:

> Contemporary analysts have approached the concept of resistance quite differently from the way in which it has been treated by classical analysts. Classical analysis views resistance as *opposition to* the analytic work. In early Freudian thinking, resistance was viewed as opposition to remembering traumatic events. Later, its connotation shifted to opposition to the uncovering of repressed infantile wishes [p. 184].

From this perspective, classical psychoanalysis takes the "position" that resistance represents the patient's adversarial "position," a force opposing the analyst's efforts to lift repression. Aron notes that relational trends in analytic thinking have reconsidered both whether resistance is located *in the patient* and whether resistance *opposes* the treatment process (p. 184). Thus, relational psychoanalytic perspectives tend to locate resistance in the interactive field between two persons, patient and analyst, and approach resistance more affirmatively as an intrinsic component of the unfolding analytic work; in short, resistances come to be viewed as stations along the way of analytic negotiations. Along with outlining the contributions of Ferenczi, Rank, Fairbairn, Guntrip, and Kohut, Aron particularly notes Schafer's advocacy of a more affirmative reconceptualization of resistance, one that appreciates the positive functions served by a patient's resistances rather than indicting them as opposition. As Aron writes, "Schafer suggests that the classical tradition encourages an adversarial conception of resistance that leads away from an analytic attitude and potentially represents a significant interference with the analyst's empathy" (p. 185).

Schafer (1983) lists the various self-stabilizing "strategies" deployed by patients who are resisting in the analytic process. While these patterns of resisting do consolidate a patient's "closed world," which excludes new experiences or mutative analytic influences (defining what I would term the particularly "nonnegotiable" in each analysis), and while these resistances may well tax the analyst's empathic capacity and faith in the analytic enterprise, nonetheless Schafer asserts that at "one time or another, the analyst must empathize with each of these facets of resistant activity and not rush the analysand into confronting any of them consciously, not to say giving them up prematurely" (p. 72). Thus, Schafer urges the analyst to consider the "interests" that underlie a patient's resistant "position" and, by maintaining an analytic attitude, avoid degenerating into a "counterpositional" autocratic stance that hectors the patient into giving up the fight against the analysis. Schafer affirms, "Analysis of resisting now seems coterminous with the analysis as a whole" (p. 72). And, once resistance is no longer viewed simply in oppositional terms, "one sees it as taking in virtually all of the analysand's psychical reality. The analyst's understanding that, as a focus for analysis, resisting transcends mere opposition makes much clear that otherwise would remain baffling" (p. 73). Resistance now defines all that the analytic process may seek to negotiate on behalf of a patient's release from the positional status quo of a neurotically "closed world"; that is, where imperatives were, there shall options be. However, Schafer also declares, "It is all too easy for the analyst to lose sight of this broad and no longer purely oppositional conception of resisting and the importance of resisting to the analysand. The analyst's narcissistically needing to get 'results' plays a big part in developing this blind spot" (p. 73).

The analyst who is vexed with an analysand's resistances and is alienated by the analysand's "closed world" may shift in attitude away from empathy and toward attacking the resistance. In its extreme, the analyst "may end up insisting narcissistically that the analysand be another kind of analysand" (p. 73). I believe this argument of Schafer's cogently depicts the "positional" approach to analytic negotiation, wherein the analyst appears to regard resistance as *lesé majéste*, an insult to the analyst's just and entitled authority. This is what I have defined as bad negotiation technique, inherently humiliating and provocative of a patient's raw aggressive transference positions (or, alternatively, compliant, masochistic submission to the tyrannical power of entrenched and nonnegotiable analytic "authority").

Bromberg (1995) offers a particularly empathic and appreciative view of resistance, one that recognizes the inherent place of resistance in the dialectics of clinical psychoanalysis. As he postulates, "The human personality possesses the extraordinary capacity to negotiate stability and change simultaneously, and it will do so under the right relational circumstances—conditions that preserve every patient's necessary illusion that 'he can stay the same while changing'" (pp. 176–177). Thus, Bromberg views resistance as the "enacted communication" of a patient's struggle to straddle the paradoxes of self-continuity and change in the analytic process. Resistance intensifies as the patient experiences the analyst's unilateral efforts at understanding to be insufficiently negotiable. Resistance, then, is the patient's reaction to the analyst's "positional" negotiation of meaning. Much as I stated, in Chapter 1, how the patient may at times declare, "No, you can't make this of me. But you can make that of me," Bromberg recognizes the patient's need, at times, to proclaim, "This is *not* who I am!" (p. 176). Bromberg aptly observes that the analyst's unilateral interpretive perspective may itself stand in opposition to the patient's need "to preserve the continuity of self-experience in the process of growth," and thereby threaten the patient with potential retraumatization (p. 174). In this way, Bromberg locates resistance distinctly *between* patient and analyst as part of the "dialectic between preservation and change."

Sensitive to the multiple and contradictory nature of the self, however, Bromberg also does locate resistance *within* the patient, in a unique way: as the voice of "opposing realities *within* the patient's inner world that are being enacted in the intersubjective and interpersonal field between analyst and patient" (p. 174, italics added). Thus the dialectic of self-continuity and change in clinical psychoanalysis may be conceived as an *intrasubjective* negotiation among subselves, or nonlinear self-states, that bear multiple and contradictory "interests" in the inner world of each patient. And resistance, at times, may entail the nonlinear emergence into the therapeutic dialectic of one of a patient's inner voices, insisting that its particular "interests" be taken into account. Just as Schafer (1983) encourages the analyst to assume an empathically appreciative attitude toward each of the analysand's modes of "resisting," Bromberg (1991) urges the analyst to seek to know the patient inside out; that is, to communicate empathically (and, at times, emphatically) with each of the patient's various (and perhaps dissociated) subselves as they engage in the complex intersubjective and intrasubjective dialectics of the treatment relationship. In this light, resistance may be recognized as the patient's use of some aspect of the analyst's person to connect with a dimension of self-experience that must be included in the analytic relationship, even if it presents manifestly as obstructiveness, disdain, mistrust, confusion, fragmentation, withdrawal, disconnection, or some other relational mode that could register in the mind of the analyst (who is thereby feeling objectified) as "resistance." Bromberg (1995) asserts:

> From this vantage point, the task for any analyst is to be able to live with paradox (Ghent, 1992; Pizer, 1992). He must not on his own either reject or accept the status of "object," but must learn from his patient how to be a "usable" object for that patient—a complex relational negotiation that depends upon remaining alive and related as a person in his own right [p. 178].

When the analyst sustains such an affirmatively interested relationship to the patient's ways of resisting (in Ury's, 1991, terms, "I can see how you see things"), rather than taking a dismissive or scolding "position" in counterreaction (counterresistance) to the perturbations, discomforts, and impediments thus introduced into the analyst's own countertransference experience, then subtleties of "interest" within the patient may be given recognition as they are enacted via the resistant "positions" adopted by the patient in the unfolding process of therapeutic negotiation. Russell (unpublished) has argued that resistance is always the analyst's resistance to feeling whatever it is that the patient needs him to feel in the treatment relationship. Far from being an opposition to the analysis, then, resistance can be considered, according to Bromberg (1995), "as a way of noting or marking the existence of a dissociated aspect of self with its own reality that has to be accessed and 'consulted,' rather than simply a defense against taking responsibility for one's own actions" (p. 184). Once "consulted" in the analytic exchange, such aspects of self may begin to join in the intricacies of internal and relational negotiations and, over time, may find it tenable to relinquish more jarringly categorical, or dissociatively disconnected, enactments of resistant "positions." A relational analyst, whose perspective guides him to meet the gesture that arises from multiple remote trajectories within the patient, makes available a relational dialogue that may promote increasingly competent internal dialogue within the patient, transforming dissociatively solipsistic voices of "resistance" into the dialectics of internal conflict and the potential straddling of internal contradiction and paradox. As one patient put it, "I believe we're both together in this battle. Except, I'm on *both* sides, and you're only on one side!"

In my clinical work, I have been amazed at how many times, and how readily, patients have made use of a particular metaphor[1] when I have introduced it. I invite the patient to consider that "inside you there is a kind of internal executive committee sitting around a conference table. Everyone around the table is an aspect of you. The committee operates by consensus. And woe unto you if anyone at the table does not get a hearing or a vote—because, somehow, they'll be sure to make their interests known!" Several patients (none of them multiple personalities!) have found it easy to identify with the imagery of this metaphor and to use it as a way of grasping the presence of continual, ongoing internal and relational negotiations that represent multifarious interests (affects, intentions, moods, desires, fears, identifications, needs) housed within their singular selves. One patient, while embracing the metaphor, declared, "Mine's not a conference table. Mine's more like a large Italian family around the dinner table: all ages, everyone's talking at once, and no one's listening very well!"

In summary, negotiation theory supports more mutualistic (Aron, 1996), intersubjective (Benjamin, 1995), approaches to the analytic process, in which the analyst shares countertransference experience (Bollas, 1987; Ehrenberg, 1992), discloses aspects of

---

[1] I am grateful to Barbara Pizer for sharing with me her own use of this metaphor in her clinical work.

her own subjectivity (B. Pizer, 1997), monitors the irritating or humiliating potential in the necessarily asymmetrical analytic relationship, and accommodates "resistances" in more affirmative rather than oppositional terms, seeking the articulation and inclusion of those multiple "interests" served by a patient's presentation of various resisting stances in the analytic potential space. Classical technique—based as it is on adherence to ideals of neutrality, anonymity, authority, and abstinence from enactment—is a "positional" approach to negotiation with the patient (who is then implicitly humiliated by being invited unilaterally to express her "interests"). The principles of negotiation support the principles of a relational psychoanalysis.

Epilogue
"The Scent of a Spring Day"

Throughout this book I have emphasized that the process, experience, and practice of negotiation lie at the heart of therapeutic action in clinical psychoanalysis. In each therapeutic partnership, two persons negotiate, from their respective positions of outlook, resistance, and intention, the possibilities and limitations that determine the shape, the course, and the therapeutic outcomes of their work together. As they join at this particular moment in the intersection of their two lives, analyst and patient will negotiate the boundaries, the purposes, the affective range, the linguistic tools, and the tonalities that will characterize their particular relationship. Over time, they negotiate the therapeutic work that can be done together in the time they have, the work that cannot be done by this particular pair (at this time in their lives), and how they each may understand their shared experiences. Analyst and patient negotiate who they may (or may not) be to each other, how they will each tolerate the givens and constraints and excitements of their relationship, and what can be the scope of their therapeutic mission.

As they negotiate their convergent and divergent interests, their conflicts of purpose and passion, their loves and hates, values and rigidities, both parties will face challenges that perplex and perturb their senses of who they are and who they each might be. They negotiate what is to be their potential space, their area of play, wherein their imaginations and anxieties, their phantoms and fallacies, their memorial and inventive repertoires exert mutual and reciprocal influences and set in motion a creative and developmental process that will destabilize and change both of their lives. Ultimately, analyst and patient negotiate a good-bye to their paradoxically intimate relationship. Postanalytically, both persons will carry impressions of each other and of their shared experiences and negotiated meanings that may remain fixed or continue to evolve. They will, at times, wonder about each other, noticing subjectively both an absence and a presence in their lives. The analysand will likely need to negotiate, in life and relationships outside of analysis, the uses and implications of analytically revised defenses and perspectives on self and other and will discover which aspects of the analysis will be held on to or let go. One way the analyst may find himself holding on to and letting go of the analysand may be by writing about the work.

As I close this book, I want to revisit the analysis of Donald, who figured so prominently in Chapters 1 and 2, and further describe particular developments in our therapeutic negotiations. I return to Donald because of his significant place in the birth of this book.

Toward the end of his analysis, Donald began to read Asian philosophy. Nearing termination, he shared with me the Japanese term *Sasumisan*, which (he explained) refers to the attitude of honor and respect between strangers who encounter each other without yet knowing their relative positions in a formal social hierarchy of honor and status. A chance encounter, such as asking for directions in the street, is governed by the mutual attitude and greeting language of *Sasumisan*, which translates literally as "connectedness never ends; indebtedness is forever." As Donald told me, "I picture how we met each other as strangers who could not know each other's status. And then we influenced each other." Having felt walled in to a profoundly lonely existence, Donald had come to "sense that people are there," to believe that "there will always be someone there." I too feel a connectedness that never ends and an indebtedness forever to Donald for the therapeutic experiences that we could negotiate together. I want to present here some highlights of the complex process of negotiation that reflected and crystalized our ultimate mutual indebtedness.

It is perhaps both ironic and apt that I have written so extensively about the treatment of a patient whose early requests for me to provide helpful readings I had initially refused. In Chapters 1 and 2, I related the passage of our earliest negotiations regarding what I could or could not provide for Donald, who I could or could not be for him—and, particularly, how my failure to fill the shoes of his lost father could eventually serve as the paradoxical presence of an absence that could be addressed, challenged, grieved, and metaphorically fulfilled. But the story of Donald's analytic negotiations is not as neat and simple as I narrated earlier in this book. While true indeed, my narration is necessarily and inescapably selective, a story that is smaller than the large reality it seeks to represent. I especially wish to emphasize that analytic negotiation is not a matter of a simple deal, a focal conflict resolution, a singular accretion of self-structure. Rather, analytic negotiation, like the development of a healthy self, is a matter of multiple, concurrent, convergent, and contradictory strands of dialogue, adjustment, and mutual influences, and also a matter of cascading shifts in understanding, affect, and structured states of consciousness in both participants.

In Donald's analysis, the establishment of a potential space in which metaphorized dimensions of fathering and "holding" became usable components of our relationship and helped Donald to feel increasingly companioned, mentored, and held together (and to grieve for a missing father) was not the whole story. Subsequent to these analytic developments, Donald's sessions fell into prolonged doldrums, in which Donald perseverated on his frustrating (and eventually untenable) relationship with his girlfriend and spent months repeating complaints about getting nowhere either in that relationship or in his treatment relationship with me. He felt mired and motionless (to himself and to me) and bemoaned the absence of progress toward the treatment goals he had defined at our very start together: to learn how to live a richer life and how to conduct a successful relationship.

This entrenched "position" of Donald's began to yield when we were able to identify together some of the vital "interests" behind a stubbornly "resistant" stuckness that held us both, at times, in a state of frustration, boredom, or discouragement. Our opening came when Donald began to venture some conjectures about my character and subjectivity, and I met his speculations with interest and acknowledged their plausibility. Donald then experienced a wave of distrust that he recognized as a transference signal. He imagined that I was disingenuously accepting his thoughts about myself in order to artificially bolster his self-esteem, that I was patronizing him with a phony "respect." He drew the analogy of the mother of an untalented child who tries to "pump up" her son by saying he's "all kinds of wonderful things that he isn't really." Donald then took the step of saying, "Anyway, what I think . . . I don't dare to say it—well, yes, I *do* dare to say it. I feel like it's being . . . seductive. Like you're being seductive . . . for your own ego. Like, if I ever do something well, you can feel '*I* made you this. *I* did this for you!'"

Donald immediately accessed a set of associations about his relationship with his mother: "That's really how my mother was, making a big deal out of what I could do in school . . . to boost *her* ego really. She didn't really see me. She didn't know who I was inside. But she talked me up to be all these great things because she was depressed, and it boosted *her* ego." "So," I responded, "if Mother Stuart is gonna take pride in what *you're* proud of—and even write about it—you'll be damned if you'll offer *that* satisfaction." "Right!" replied Donald; "I won't give you that." I went on, "If my ego could be feeding off of what you build for yourself, you'll hold yourself back to spite me." "Yes!" declared Donald. I then suggested, "How dangerous for you: to win by losing because you'd lose by winning." Donald answered, "Yes, I can see that. Maybe that's why I haven't brought in positive things about myself. I won't show you that I'm changing. Like . . . I won't inflate myself in front of you." Donald and I then were able to explore the multiple unconscious meanings embedded in the densely resonant word "inflate": a dread that mother would fill her emptiness with anything (phallic or otherwise) that Donald might inflate in front of her; a fear of competitive or envious feelings between us; a fear of expansive, enthusiastic, or loving feelings in our relationship. Donald then accessed his recurrent feelings of inequality and unworthiness in relationship to me, his dependent longings and his envy of my perceived "position" in life. He could now recognize his unconscious intention to defeat me and withhold from me possible feelings of success as his analyst.

Soon thereafter, Donald turned his attention to a sustained exploration of his own depression, negativity, and anger. This analytic work culminated in a dream: Donald found himself on a college campus, pursued by a vast and mysterious dark hulk that was out to kill him. It stalked him all the way to his apartment, where, to Donald's amazement, he found himself accompanied by many friends who supported him to stand firm and boldly square off against this glowering hulk. Finding within himself a surprising tone of humor and competence, Donald addressed the monster in his doorway, saying, "So, what's your problem?"

While my presentation of a clinical narrative in this highlighted form implies an illusory focus and linearity of process and development, like a stone skipping in a track along the surface of deep and roiling waters, I do want to share at least a sense of where Donald's analytic negotiations led him. Following his dream of the angry hulk, Donald again wondered why he had for so long been unable to feel that my responses to him were useful. On one hand, he had wanted from me signs that I cared about him and believed in him; on the other hand, he had disbelieved my feelings for him or just had not registered my subjectivity as I participated in our therapeutic dialogue. "Besides," he emphasized, "the goal-directed side of me didn't want an echo or a mirror; what I wanted was answers and explanations and the rules for living." Donald went on to say that he now noticed two states in himself: one "active, ambitious, goal-directed, and also agitated"; and the other "more relaxed, like lying in a hammock, more calm and receptive and reflective." He wondered, "Can I ever bring them together? Can I be active, but more calmly? Can I be receptive and reflective, while also being active?" Reflecting now on his awareness of internal multiplicity, Donald said, "I feel that I've changed. I feel like I'm in a transition." This particular session occurred just before another Christmas holiday, and Donald remarked, "I think of Scrooge. I don't feel identified with him so much anymore. I guess everyone has to hear the echoes of the past and wake up to the present."

In the session that followed, Donald said to me, "I can see now that when I started here with you I really didn't want a relationship. I wanted information!" Donald continued, "It's connected to the active part of me—that's aggressive. But it's not just active and aggressive. It's like something that comes out in me whenever I'm supposed to comply. I think of how Winnicott wrote that play and compliance are sort of opposites. And I think I get this way when I think I'm expected to comply." I commented, "That reminds me of how you mobilized aggressive activity to propel you from home, where you were expected to comply." "Yes," said Donald, "where I grew up there was really no 'not-me object' that I could connect with. There was no person outside myself to really connect to. That's what I needed with you. I had to get interested in who other people were. And that's why I like what you're writing about negotiating in therapy. You have to give up some of your own restraints as a therapist to be another person for the patient. But, still, I wonder why I couldn't use your echoing then like I can now. I feel like I'm in a transition. From one land . . . but my foot is not squarely on the other one yet. I'm sort of in between . . . I feel like . . . I can understand things you've said all along—well, I always could *understand* it . . . but now it feels like a different *sensation* of understanding."

Donald said he wanted to "rag" psychoanalysis and renamed the talking cure "the silent treatment." But, in the week following this Christmas holiday, he experienced a new potential in silence. Donald lay on the couch and began a session with 25 minutes of total silence. Then he said, "I can believe why therapists write that they can sit for months with a silent patient and believe that something is happening. I don't *understand* it, but I *believe* that something is happening right now! I've needed all along to integrate thought and feeling. It's like I have a split in the brain that needs resolving. Can it be done? I can see how I cognitize . . . and talk . . . and don't have feelings about it. I've been split for so long. Can that change now?" For the next several weeks, sessions in which Donald would ramble or complain about disappointing relationships were interspersed with sessions in which Donald would lie in prolonged silence, during which I felt tenderly close to him.

After one long silence, Donald said, "I'm thinking that I can accept myself more. Partly it's—this is a funny thought—but I think, *we're* not so different after all. Then there's this voice in me that steps in and says 'Come on, Donald. Don't be so presumptuous.'" And, at this, Donald cracked up laughing. After another lengthy silence on the couch, Donald said, "You know those two states. I'm feeling more relaxed lately . . . and I am now. But I also go way inside, really withdrawn . . . and it's a kind of squinting concentration. I was getting in that state, and then I thought of you sitting back there with me silent for so long. And when I thought that you were probably *thinking*, I immediately began to feel more relaxed again. I thought, you may be trying to figure out what's happening with me right now. Or, you may be thinking of your grocery list for all I know [laughs]. But . . . it doesn't matter. Maybe you're just waiting . . . whatever. It's just the thought of you there that made me relax. I don't get it." I replied, "I don't believe I fully understand it either. But it seems like, whether I may be trying to figure out what's going on within you or I may be checking in and out of my grocery list, your sense that I'm alive, and that my mind is working, gives you something. You have a sense of my separate mind, my own separate state, while I am *with you*."

Donald and I now entered a termination phase that lasted another year. He reported feeling "both calm and restless." At one point, he remarked, "I think of what you said about the people sitting around the table . . . the congeries of people inside oneself. When I started here, I thought I needed one thing, and I got another." Again Donald mused about his initial therapeutic goals—information, insight, and explanations—and how, as we negotiated a process between us over time, his awareness had awakened to the importance of involvement in relationship, experience of affect, and attention to inner states. He marveled at how he could now sense what it was to be himself with another person and to sense feeling in the other person as well. Donald made the following remarkable statement to me: "I thought I'd come here to fix my life. The only way I could think was in a kind of linear, logical, problem-solving way. Now, it's like my mind works differently, at least sometimes. Now my mind is more like the scent of a spring day." This man, whose first negotiation with me was over the use of deodorant to allow us to sit together, now conjured such a resonant and transformative olfactory image to indicate the gathering together of previously dissociated, nonlinear dimensions of self within him, and a metaphorical competence for communicating his own subjective experience and touching the heart of another. As Aron (1996) has written:

> If we negotiate who we will be for . . . patients, and who they will be for us, we also negotiate how we view the *goals* of each analysis. The patient presents one set of problems, and we hear a different set of problems. We hope that over the course of the analysis, the patient will come to see the problems more as we do. And yet, as the analysis progresses, we may also let go of some [of] our preconceptions and recognize that there was more in the patient's perspective than we at first could see. . . . Since this interpersonal process is mutual and

reciprocal, the patient continually influenced by the analyst and vice versa, one can legitimately claim that the very essence of who the patient and analyst are with each other is negotiated [p. 95].

During the spring of Donald's termination year, he joined a cooperative gardening group in a country town. One Monday he came to our session eager to tell me of an experience from his weekend at the garden. He had been traversing the path into the garden, "grown over like a meadow with purple flowers," when he encountered a huge swarm of bees and was stung. "Well,' he said, "the stings are really nothing. The *big* thing was suddenly seeing all those bees in the air over the path. It was . . . like . . . right there in focus, and yet beyond comprehension." And, with enthusiasm, Donald continued, "And that's the way I feel about my life now in general. It's a whole different sense of being alive. Like an intuition . . . or just an outlook . . . but beyond comprehension. I don't know if I can explain it clearly . . . although, I may be easy to understand now. But, when I started here, I think I was certainly not a person that could be easily understood. And . . . that's the paradox! I don't really understand myself now. I don't even think I ever *could* really understand myself . . . where I came from, how I got here, what this process has been. Like all those bees in the air—it's *there*, but beyond comprehension. But now I *feel* more understandable. Like the meadow full of bees . . . sometimes the thing to do is not to intellectualize, but just to step back and observe and enjoy the beauty of it." "Donald," I said, "today you are my teacher." Donald added, "And that's how I carry inside all those experiences with you over the years. And I think the most healing moments have not been interpretations or understandings. I think of your references to analysis as a duet, experiences of being together." I risked a bad pun, "Not stinging interpretations, but many ways to be." I too felt quietly and contentedly together with Donald, in the swarm of feeling.

Again, within a week of his encounter with the bees in the meadow, Donald entered a session eager to share with me a moment of novel personal experience that had felt to him like the signal of a threshold. He was attending a workshop and driving to a restaurant during a lunch break when his car ran out of gas on the highway. He walked to the nearest exit and found a service station. Carrying a can of gas, as he walked along the shoulder of the highway back to his car, Donald had what he now happily called "an uninterpreted experience." Suddenly, Donald said, he found himself aware of the sloshing fluid inside the can, both the feeling and the sound, and the feeling of his own walking on the pavement beside the road. It was like a "click" inside him, an enjoyment of the freedom of experience. And he thought, "This moment is also a part of the workshop," and, instead of feeling anger, he felt alive. Then he thought, "I am a mess." Telling me his story, Donald said, "Mess was not bad. It felt rich. Complex. The emphasis was on *am*. The word *am*—me—being me. And then I thought, 'good,' and then my tears came freely." And so did mine.

Analyst and patient must both negotiate their acceptance of all that could—and all that could not—be done between them in the analytic process. Soon after Donald's walk along the highway, I had a dream in which Donald and I were walking together down a street near my office. We were walking in the road. And, although I was walking on the outside, I nonetheless was thinking that it was not good for me to walk in the road with Donald because, to the extent that he identified with me, after termination he might be more likely to walk in the road himself and thus be exposed to danger from passing cars. Perhaps our relationship had exposed Donald to an internalization of my own bad habits. I woke up from this dream wondering how much our work might have been misguided, how much my own personality, my own limitations as person and analyst, my own rigidities and risks might not have served Donald's particular needs and interests. In that day's session, Donald again made reference to his community garden, saying, "It's a long time since I've had fresh-grown tomatoes." He then reminisced about his grandfather's garden, where he had learned to grow tomatoes. Donald recalled to mind that his mother also had gardened for a time, when he was eight or ten years old, but had found it to be too much to maintain. "Actually," Donald added, "she planted corn last year, but the raccoons ate nearly all of it. I looked it up in a book, and it has a special section on corn and raccoons—they go together. You can hardly keep the raccoons out." Donald's thoughts moved on to his imminent termination. He said, "I'm looking back and feeling like we've finished." Probably influenced by the residue of my dream, I asked Donald, "I wonder, as you look back and sense that our work is done, is your feeling one of satisfaction, or disappointment, or both?" "Both," Donald readily replied; "a lot has changed. A whole lot. And I know that no one ever finishes a completely stable person or fully developed." "So," I pursued, "how much corn have we harvested, and how much have the raccoons gotten?" After a long silence, Donald said with deliberateness, "That's what I have to accept. What the raccoons have gotten is theirs. And what I've gotten is enough. There's no need to do like my mother or grandmother . . . sit and stare at the husks and complain about what's been lost to life and nature. Let the raccoons have what they got!"

And so Donald's analysis ended, with a sense of connection and a mutual indebtedness that never ends. As it happens, two years after our last session, and just one month before my writing this Epilogue, I bumped into Donald. It was another Christmas season, and we met, of course, in a bookstore. On a Saturday afternoon, as I made my harried way through my list of holiday shopping errands, in a state of inner compression (and outer haggardness), I encountered Donald looking fresh, buoyant, at ease in his body, and taller than I'd remembered. We were both grayer. I commented on how well he looked, and Donald said, "Of course, I just came from a morning of Tai Chi." Donald reported that he had recently joined in the start-up of a small and successful company and that he was having lots of fun. I told him I was soon to write again about our work together, and he expressed a sponsoring interest in my completing this book and reaffirmed his willingness to review what I wrote about our analytic negotiations. In our moment of conversation, I felt Donald's independence, his well being, and his warmth, along with my own deep connection to him, my love, and my gratitude.

I believe that, as therapists or analysts, while we do not—and must not—present our own raw life needs to be processed or provided for in the therapeutic relationship, we are engaged in an intimate negotiation in which, just as much as in any other vitally intimate personal relationship in our lives, we are totally on the line, confronting the competence and value of our own particular ways of loving and working. I believe in the necessarily steady asymmetry of the analyst's and the patient's different roles in the treatment relationship and clinical process—the distinct responsibilities and exposures that both must bring to their respective jobs in the joint task. Yet, I would radically state the mutuality, and spirit, of analytic negotiation in these terms: we depend on each other.

References

Abraham, R. H. (1995), Erodynamics and the dischaotic personality. In: F. D. Abraham & A. Gilgen (eds.), *Chaos Theory in Psychology*. Westport, CT: Praeger, pp. 157–167.

Adler, G. (1989), Transitional phenomena, projective identification, and the essential ambiguity of the psychoanalytic situation. *Psychoanal. Quart.*, 58:81–104.

Altman, N. (1995), *The Analyst in the Inner City*. Hillsdale, NJ: The Analytic Press.

Aron, L. (1996), *A Meeting of Minds: Mutuality in Psychoanalysis*. Hillsdale, NJ: The Analytic Press.

Bales, R. F. (1970), *Personality and Interpersonal Behavior*. New York: Holt, Rinehart Winston.

Balint, M. (1968), *The Basic Fault*. London: Tavistock Publications.

Beebe, B., Jaffe, J. & Lachmann, F. (1992), A dyadic systems view of communication. In: N. J. Skolnick & S. C. Warshaw (eds.), *Relational Perspectives in Psychoanalysis*. Hillsdale, NJ: The Analytic Press, pp. 61–81.

———— & Lachmann, F. (1992), The contribution of mother–infant mutual influence to the origin of self- and object representations. In N. J. Skolnick & S. C. Warshaw (eds.), *Relational Perspectives in Psychoanalysis*. Hillsdale, NJ: The Analytic Press, pp. 83–117.

Benjamin, J. (1988), *The Bonds of Love*. New York: Pantheon Books.

———— (1995), *Like Subjects, Love Objects*. New Haven, CT: Yale University Press.

———— (1996), In defense of gender ambiguity. *Gender and Psychoanalysis*, 1:27–43.

Bloom, A. (1981), *The Linguistic Shaping of Thought: A Study in the Impact of Language on Thinking in China and the West*. Hillsdale, NJ: Laurence Erlbaum Associates.

Boesky, D. (1990), The psychoanalytic process and its components. *Psychoanal. Quart.*, 59:550–584.

208 ◆ References

Bollas, C. (1987), *The Shadow of the Object*. New York: Columbia University Press.
—— (1989), *Forces of Destiny*. London: Free Association Books.
—— (1995), *Cracking Up*. New York: Hill & Wang.
Bromberg, P. M. (1991), On knowing one's patient inside out: The aesthetics of unconscious communication. *Psychoanal. Dial.* 1:399–422.
—— (1993), Shadow and substance: A relational perspective on clinical process. *Psychoanal. Psychol.*, 10:147–168.
—— (1994), "Speak! that I may see you": Some reflections on dissociation, reality and psychoanalytic listening. *Psychoanal. Dial.*, 4:517–547.
—— (1995), Resistance, object-usage, and human relatedness. *Contemp. Psychoanal.*, 31:173–191.
—— (1996), Standing in the spaces: The multiplicity of self and the psychoanalytic relationship. *Contemp. Psychoanal.*, 32:509–535.
Bruner, J. (1990), *Acts of Meaning*. Cambridge, MA: Harvard University Press.
Butler, J. (1990), *Gender Trouble*. New York: Routledge.
Davies, J. M. (1996), Linking the "pre-analytic" with the postclassical: Integration, dissociation, and the multiplicity of unconscious process. *Contemp. Psychoanal.*, 32:553–576.
—— & Frawley, M. G. (1994), *Treating the Adult Survivor of Childhood Sexual Abuse: A Psychoanalytic Perspective*. New York: Basic Books.
Dimen, M. (1991), Deconstructing difference: Gender, splitting, and transitional space. *Psychoanal. Dial.*, 1:335–352.
Edelman, G. M. (1987), *Neural Darwinism*. New York: Basic Books.
—— (1989), *The Remembered Present*. New York: Basic Books.
—— (1992), *Bright Air, Brilliant Fire*. New York: Basic Books.
Ehrenberg, D. B. (1992), *The Intimate Edge*. New York: Norton.
Elkind, S. N. (1992), *Resolving Impasses in Therapeutic Relationships*. New York: Guilford.
Erikson, E. H. (1968), *Identity: Youth and Crisis*. New York: Norton.
Fairbairn, W. R. D. (1944), Endopsychic structure considered in terms of object-relationships. In: *An Object-Relations Theory of the Personality*. New York: Basic Books, 1952, pp. 82–132.
Fast, I. (1984), *Gender Identity*. Hillsdale, NJ: The Analytic Press.
Ferenczi, S. (1928), The elasticity of psychoanalytic technique. In: *Final Contributions to the Problems and Methods of Psycho-Analysis*, ed. M. Balint (trans. E. Mossbacher). London: Karnac Books, 1980, pp. 87–101.
Fisher, R. & Ury, W. (1981), *Getting to Yes: Negotiating Agreement Without Giving In*. New York: Penguin Books, 1983.
—— Kopelman, E. & Schneider, A. K. (1996), *Beyond Machiavelli: Tools for Coping with Conflict*. New York: Penguin Books.
Flax, J. (1990), *Thinking Fragments: Psychoanalysis, Feminism, and Post-Modernism in the Contemporary West*. Los Angeles: University of California Press.
—— (1996), Taking multiplicity seriously: Some consequences for psychoanalytic theorizing and practice. *Contemp. Psychoanal.*, 32:577–593.

Foucault, M. (1980), *Power/Knowledge*, ed. C. Gordon. New York: Pantheon Books.

Freud, S. (1900), *The Interpretation of Dreams. Standard Edition*, 4 & 5. London: Hogarth Press, 1953.

——— (1905), Fragment of an analysis of a case of hysteria. *Standard Edition*, 7:1–122. London: Hogarth Press, 1953.

——— (1912), The dynamics of transference. *Standard Edition,* 12:99–108. London: Hogarth Press, 1958.

——— (1914), Remembering, repeating, and working-through. *Standard Edition*, 12:145–156. London: Hogarth Press, 1958.

——— (1915a), Observations on transference-love. *Standard Edition*, 12:157–171. London: Hogarth Press, 1958.

——— (1915b), The unconscious. *Standard Edition*, 14:159–215. London: Hogarth Press, 1957.

——— (1917), Mourning and melancholia. *Standard Edition,* 14:237–258. London: Hogarth Press, 1957.

——— (1921), *Group Psychology and the Analysis of the Ego. Standard Edition*, 18:65–143. London: Hogarth Press, 1955.

——— (1923), *The Ego and the Id. Standard Edition*, 19:1–66. London: Hogarth Press, 1961.

Ghent, E. (1992), Paradox and process. *Psychoanal. Dial.* 2:135–159.

Gill, M. M. (1982), *Analysis of Transference, Vol. 1*. New York: International Universities Press.

Goldberg, A. (1987), Psychoanalysis and negotiation. *Psychoanal. Quart.*, 56:109–129.

Goldner, V. (1991), Toward a critical relational theory of gender. *Psychoanal. Dial.*, 1:249–272.

Greenberg, J. (1986), Theoretical models and the analyst's neutrality. *Contemp. Psychoanal.*, 22:87–106.

Harris, A. (1991), Gender as contradiction. *Psychoanal. Dial.*, 1:197–224.

——— (1992), Dialogues as transitional space: A rapprochement of psychoanalysis and developmental psycholinguistics. In: N. J. Skolnick & S. C. Warshaw (eds.), *Relational Perspectives in Psychoanalysis*. Hillsdale, NJ: The Analytic Press, pp. 119–145.

——— (1996), The conceptual power of multiplicity. *Contemp. Psychoanal.*, 32:537–552.

Hoffman, I. Z. (1991), Discussion: Toward a social-constructivist view of the psychoanalytic situation. *Psychoanal. Dial.*, 1:74–105.

——— (1994), Dialectical thinking and therapeutic action in the psychoanalytic process. *Psychoanal. Quart.*, 63:187–218.

——— (1996), The intimate and ironic authority of the psychoanalyst's presence. *Psychoanal. Quart.*, 65:102–136.

James, W. (1890), *The Principles of Psychology, Vol. 1*. New York: Holt.

Kelman, H. C. (1997), Group processes in the resolution of international conflicts: Experiences from the Israeli-Palestinian case. *Amer. Psychol.*, 52:212–220.

Kingston, M. H. (1976), *The Woman Warrior*. New York: Vintage International.

Kuhn, T. (1962), *The Structure of Scientific Revolutions*. Chicago: University of Chicago Press.

Kumin, I. M. (1978), Developmental aspects of opposites and paradox. *Internat. Rev. Psychoanal.*, 5:477–484.

Lacan, J. (1953), The function and field of speed and language in psychoanalysis. In: *Jacques Lacan: Ecrits. A Selection*, trans. A. Sheridan. New York: Norton, 1977, pp. 30–113.

Laing, R. D. (1969), *Self and Others*, 2nd rev. ed. New York: Pantheon Books.

Laub, D. & Auerhahn, N. C. (1993), Knowing and not knowing massive psychic trauma: Forms of traumatic memory. *Internat. J. Psycho-Anal.*, 74:287–302.

Layton, L. (1998), *Who's That Girl? Who's That Boy? Clinical Practice Meets Postmodern Gender Theory*. Northvale, NJ: Aronson.

Loewald, H. (1960), On the therapeutic action of psychoanalysis. In: *Papers on Psychoanalysis*. New Haven, CT: Yale University Press, 1980, pp. 221–256.

——— (1974), Psychoanalysis as an art and the fantasy character of the psychoanalytic situation. In: *Papers on Psychoanalysis*. New Haven, CT: Yale University Press, 1980, pp. 352–371.

——— (1980), Some considerations on repetition and repetition compulsion. In: *Papers on Psychoanalysis*. New Haven, CT: Yale University Press, pp. 87–101.

Lucy, J. (1992), *Language Diversity and Thought*. Cambridge: Cambridge University Press.

McDougall, J. (1992), The "dis-affected" patient: Reflections on affect pathology. In: N. G. Hamilton (ed.), *From Inner Sources*. Northvale, NJ: Aronson, pp. 251–273.

McLaughlin, J. (1995), Touching limits in the analytic dyad. *Psychoanal. Quart.*, 64:433–465.

Meares, R. (1993), *The Metaphor of Play*. Northvale, NJ: Aronson.

Miller, A. (1981), *Prisoners of Childhood*. New York: Basic Books.

Mitchell, S. (1988), *Relational Concepts in Psychoanalysis*. Cambridge, MA: Harvard University Press.

——— (1993), *Hope and Dread in Psychoanalysis*. New York: Basic Books.

——— (1997), *Influence and Autonomy in Psychoanalysis*. Hillsdale, NJ: The Analytic Press.

Modell, A. (1989), The psychoanalytic setting as a container of multiple levels of reality: A perspective on the theory of psychoanalytic treatment. *Psychoanal. Inq.*, 9:67–87.

——— (1990), *Other Times, Other Realities*. Cambridge, MA: Harvard University Press.

——— (1991), The therapeutic relationship as a paradoxical experience. *Psychoanal. Dial.*, 1:13–28.

——— (1993), *The Private Self*. Cambridge, MA: Harvard University Press.

Moi, T. (1990), Representation of patriarchy: Sexuality and epistemology in Freud's Dora. In: C. Bernheimer & C. Kahane (eds.), *In Dora's Case*. New York: Columbia University Press, pp. 181–199.

Myers, G. E. (1986), *William James: His Life and Thought*. New Haven, CT: Yale University Press.

Myerson, P. G. (1990), *Childhood Dialogues and the Lifting of Repression*. New Haven, CT: Yale University Press.

Nyerges, J. (1991), Ten commandments for a negotiator: In: J. W. Breslin & J. Z. Rubin (eds.), *Negotiation Theory and Practice*, Cambridge, MA: Program on Negotiation Books, pp. 187–193.

Ogden, T. (1986), *The Matrix of the Mind*. Northvale, NJ: Aronson.

―――― (1988), Misrecognitions and the fear of not knowing. *Psychoanal. Quart.*, 57:643–666.

―――― (1994), *Subjects of Analysis*. Northvale, NJ: Aronson.

Phillips, A. (1988), *Winnicott*. Cambridge, MA: Harvard University Press.

Pizer, B. (1997), When the analyst is ill: Dimensions of self-disclosure. *Psychoanal. Quart.*, 66:450–469.

Pizer, S. A. (1992), The negotiation of paradox in the analytic process. *Psychoanal. Dial.*, 2:215–240.

―――― (1996a), Negotiating potential space: Illusion, play, metaphor, and the subjunctive. *Psychoanal. Dial.*, 6:689–712.

―――― (1996b), The distributed self. *Contemp. Psychoanal.*, 32:499–507.

Putnam, F. (1988), The switch process in multiple personality disorder and other state-change disorders. *Dissociation*, 1:24–32.

Racker, H. (1968), *Transference and Counter-Transference*. New York: International Universities Press.

Renik, O. (1995), The ideal of the anonymous analyst and the problem of self-disclosure. *Psychoanal. Quart.*, 64:466–495.

Rose, J. (1990), Dora: Fragment of an analysis. In: C. Bernheimer & C. Kahane (eds.), *In Dora's Case*. New York: Columbia University Press, pp. 128–148.

Rubin, J. Z. (1988), Some wise and mistaken assumptions about conflict and negotiation. Working Paper Series 88–4, Program on Negotiation, Harvard Law School.

―――― & Rubin, C. M. (1991), Conflict, negotiation, and change. In: R. C. Curtis & G. Stricker (eds.), *How People Change: Inside and Outside Therapy*. New York: Plenum Press, pp. 157–169.

Russell, P. (unpublished), Crises of emotional growth (a.k.a. the theory of the crunch).

Sacks, O. (1995), *An Anthropologist on Mars*. New York: Knopf.

Sainsbury, R. M. (1988), *Paradoxes*. Cambridge: Cambridge University Press.

Sander, L. W. (1983), Polarity, paradox, and the organizing process in development. In: J. D. Call, E. Galenson & R. L. Tyson (eds.), *Frontiers of Infant Psychiatry, No. 1*. New York: Basic Books.

Sandler, J. (1976), Countertransference and role-responsiveness. *Internat. Rev. Psycho-Anal.*, 3:43–47.

Sanville, J. (1991), *The Playground of Psychoanalytic Therapy*. Hillsdale, NJ: The Analytic Press.

Saunders, H. H. (1991), We need a larger theory of negotiation: The importance of pre-negotiating phases. In: J. W. Breslin & J. Z. Rubin (eds.),

Negotiation Theory and Practice. Cambridge, MA: Program on Negotiation Books.

———— & Slim, R. (n.d.), Sustained dialogue: A process for changing dysfunctional community relationships. *Organizer's and Moderator's Manual*. Dayton, OH: Kettering Foundation.

Schafer, R. (1983), *The Analytic Attitude*. New York: Basic Books.

Schwaber, E. (1992), Countertransference: The analyst's retreat from the patient's vantage point. *Internat. J. Psycho-Anal.*, 73:349–361.

Shabad, P. (1993), Resentment, indignation, entitlement: The transformation of unconscious wish into need. *Psychoanal. Dial.*, 3:481–494.

Slavin, M. (1990), The dual meaning of repression and the adaptive design of the human psyche. *J. Amer. Acad. Psychoanal.*, 18:307–341.

———— & Kriegman, D. (1990), Toward a new paradigm for psychoanalysis: An evolutionary biological perspective on the classical-relational dichotomy. *Psychoanal. Psychol.*, 7(suppl.):5–31.

———— & ———— (1992), *The Adaptive Design of the Human Psyche*. New York: Guilford.

———— & ———— (1998), Why the analyst needs to change: Toward a theory of conflict, negotiation, and mutual influence in the therapeutic process. *Psychoanal. Dial.* 8:247–284.

Stark, M. (1994), *Working with Resistance*. Northvale, NJ: Aronson.

Stern, D. (1985), *The Interpersonal World of the Infant*. New York: Basic Books.

Sullivan, H. S. (1953), *The Interpersonal Theory of Psychiatry*. New York: Norton.

Trevarthen, C. (1979), Communication and cooperation in early infancy. In: M. Bullowa (ed.), *Before Speech*. Cambridge: Cambridge University Press, pp. 321–347.

Trivers, R. L. (1974), Parent-offspring conflict. *Amer. Zoologist*, 14:249–264.

———— (1985), *Social Evolution*. Boston: Addison-Wesley.

Ury, W. (1991), *Getting Past No*. New York: Bantam Books.

Vygotsky, L. (1962), *Thought and Language*, ed. & trans. E. Hanfmann & G. Vakar. Cambridge, MA: MIT Press.

White, R. W. (1963), Ego and reality in psychoanalytic theory. *Psycholog. Issues*. Monogr. 11. New York: International Universities Press.

Winnicott, D. W. (1951), Transitional objects and transitional phenomena. In: *Playing and Reality*. New York: Basic Books, 1971, pp. 1–25.

———— (1956), On transference. *Internat. J. Psycho-Anal.*, 37:386–388.

———— (1958a), The capacity to be alone. In: *The Maturational Processes and the Facilitating Environment*. New York: International Universities Press, 1965, pp. 29–36.

———— (1958b), *Collected Papers: From Paediatrics to Psychoanalysis*. London: Tavistock.

———— (1960), Ego distortion in terms of true and false self. In: *The Maturational Processes and the Facilitating Environment*. New York: International Universities Press, 1965, pp. 140–152.

———— (1962a), Providing for the child in health and crisis. In: *The*

Maturational Processes and the Facilitating Environment. New York: International Universities Press, 1965, pp. 64–72.

———— (1962b), Ego integration in child development. In: *The Maturational Processes and the Facilitating Environment.* New York: International Universities Press, 1965, pp. 56–63.

———— (1963a), Communicating and not communicating leading to a study of certain opposites. In: *The Maturational Processes and the Facilitating Environment.* New York: International Universities Press, 1965, pp. 179–192.

———— (1963b), From dependence towards independence in the development of the individual. In: *The Maturational Processes and the Facilitating Environment.* New York: International Universities Press, 1965, pp. 83–92.

———— (1967), The location of cultural experience. In: *Playing and Reality.* New York: Basic Books, 1971, pp. 95–103.

———— (1968), Communication between infant and mother, and mother and infant, compared and contrasted. In: *Babies and Their Mothers.* Reading, MA: Addison-Wesley, 1987, pp. 89–103.

———— (1969), The use of an object and relating through identifications. In: *Playing and Reality.* New York: Basic Books, 1971, pp. 86–94.

———— (1971a), Playing: Creative activity and the search for the self. In: *Playing and Reality.* New York: Basic Books, pp. 53–64.

———— (1971b), Playing: A theoretical statement. In: *Playing and Reality.* New York: Basic Books, pp. 38–52.

———— (1971c), *Playing and Reality.* New York: Basic Books.

———— (1974), Fear of breakdown. In: *Psychoanalytic Explorations.* Cambridge, MA: Harvard University Press, 1989, pp. 87–95.

Index